[mutants_of_X]
[the_world__X]

**S.W.O.R.D. BY AL EWING VOL. 2.** Contains material originally published in magazine form as S.W.O.R.D. (2020) #7-11 and CABLE: RELOADED (2021) #1. First printing 2021. ISBN 978-1-302-93146-9. Published by MARVEL WORLDWIDE, INC., a subsidiary of MARVEL ENTERTAINMENT, LLC. OFFICE OF PUBLICATION: 1290 Avenue of the Americas, New York, NY 10104. © 2021 MARVEL No similarity between any of the names, characters, persons, and/or institutions in this book with those of any living or dead person or institution is intended, and any such similarity which may exist is purely coincidental. **Printed in Canada.** KEVIN FEIGE, Chief Creative Officer; DAN BUCKLEY, President, Marvel Entertainment; JOE QUESADA, EVP & Creative Director; DAVID BOGART, Associate Publisher & SVP of Talent Affairs; TOM BREVOORT, VP, Executive Editor; NICK LOWE, Executive Editor, VP of Content, Digital Publishing; DAVID GABRIEL, VP of Print & Digital Publishing; JEFF YOUNGQUIST, VP of Production & Special Projects; ALEX MORALES, Director of Publishing Operations; DAN EDINGTON, Managing Editor; RICKEY PURDIN, Director of Talent Relations; JENNIFER GRÜNWALD, Senior Editor, Special Projects; SUSAN CRESPI, Production Manager; STAN LEE, Chairman Emeritus. For information regarding advertising in Marvel Comics or on Marvel.com, please contact Vit DeBellis, Custom Solutions & Integrated Advertising Manager, at vdebellis@ marvel.com. For Marvel subscription inquiries, please call 888-511-5480. **Manufactured between 12/3/2021 and 1/4/2022 by SOLISCO PRINTERS, SCOTT, QC, CANADA.**

10 9 8 7 6 5 4 3 2 1

| | |
|---|---|
| **Writer:** | **Al Ewing** |
| **Artists:** | **Stefano Caselli** (#7), |
| | **Bob Quinn** (*Cable: Reloaded*), |
| | **Guiu Vilanova** (#8) **&** |
| | **Jacopo Camagni** (#9-11) |
| **Color Artists:** | **Protobunker's** |
| | **Fernando Sifuentes** (#7-11) **&** |
| | **Java Tartaglia** (*Cable: Reloaded*) |
| **Letterers:** | **VC's Ariana Maher** (#7-11) **&** |
| | **Joe Sabino** (*Cable: Reloaded*) |
| **Cover Art:** | **Valerio Schiti &** |
| | **Marte Gracia** (#7-8) **and** |
| | **Stefano Caselli with** |
| | **Israel Silva** (*Cable: Reloaded*)**,** |
| | **Federico Blee** (#9, #11) |
| | **& Java Tartaglia** (#10) |
| Special thanks: | Abigail Johnson |
| **Head of X:** | **Jonathan Hickman** |
| **Design:** | **Tom Muller** |
| **Assistant Editor:** | **Lauren Amaro** |
| **Associate Editor:** | **Annalise Bissa** |
| **Editor:** | **Jordan D. White** |

| | |
|---|---|
| **Collection Editor:** | **Jennifer Grünwald** |
| **Assistant Editor:** | **Daniel Kirchhoffer** |
| **Assistant Managing Editor:** | **Maia Loy** |
| **Assistant Managing Editor:** | **Lisa Montalbano** |
| **VP Production & Special Projects:** | **Jeff Youngquist** |
| **SVP Print, Sales & Marketing:** | **David Gabriel** |
| **Editor in Chief:** | **C.B. Cebulski** |

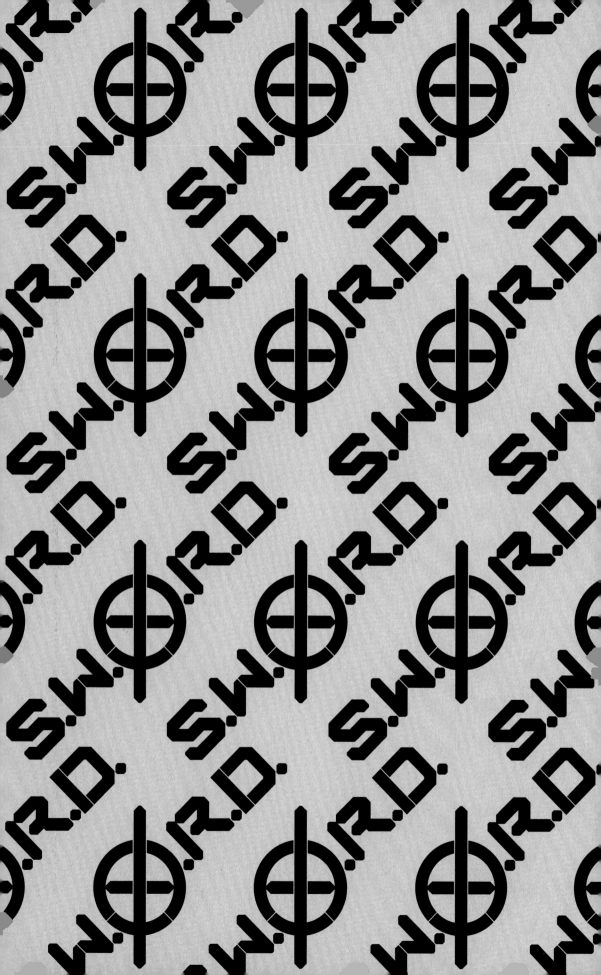

8X8X8X8X8X8X8X8

8X8 EMERGENCY
EXISTENTIAL THREAT TO LIFE
PLANETARY ATTACK
HALA/THRONEWORLD II
UNDER THREAT
EMPEROR HULKLING
RESPONDING
LAURI-ELL THE ACCUSER
RESPONDING
SKRULLOS
UNDER THREAT
PRINCE CONSORT WICCAN
RESPONDING
KNIGHTS OF THE INFINITE
RESPONDING
GUARDIANS NOTIFIED
GUARDIANS RESPONDING
GALACTIC COUNCIL NOTIFIED
GALACTIC COUNCIL RESPONDING
EARTH NOTIFIED
EARTH IS NOT RESPONDING
RESEND SIGNAL TO ALPHA FLIGHT:

# MINDLESS ONES DETECTED

8X8 EMERGENCY
8X8 EMERGENCY
8X8 EMERGENCY
8X8 EMERGENCY

EMERGENCY

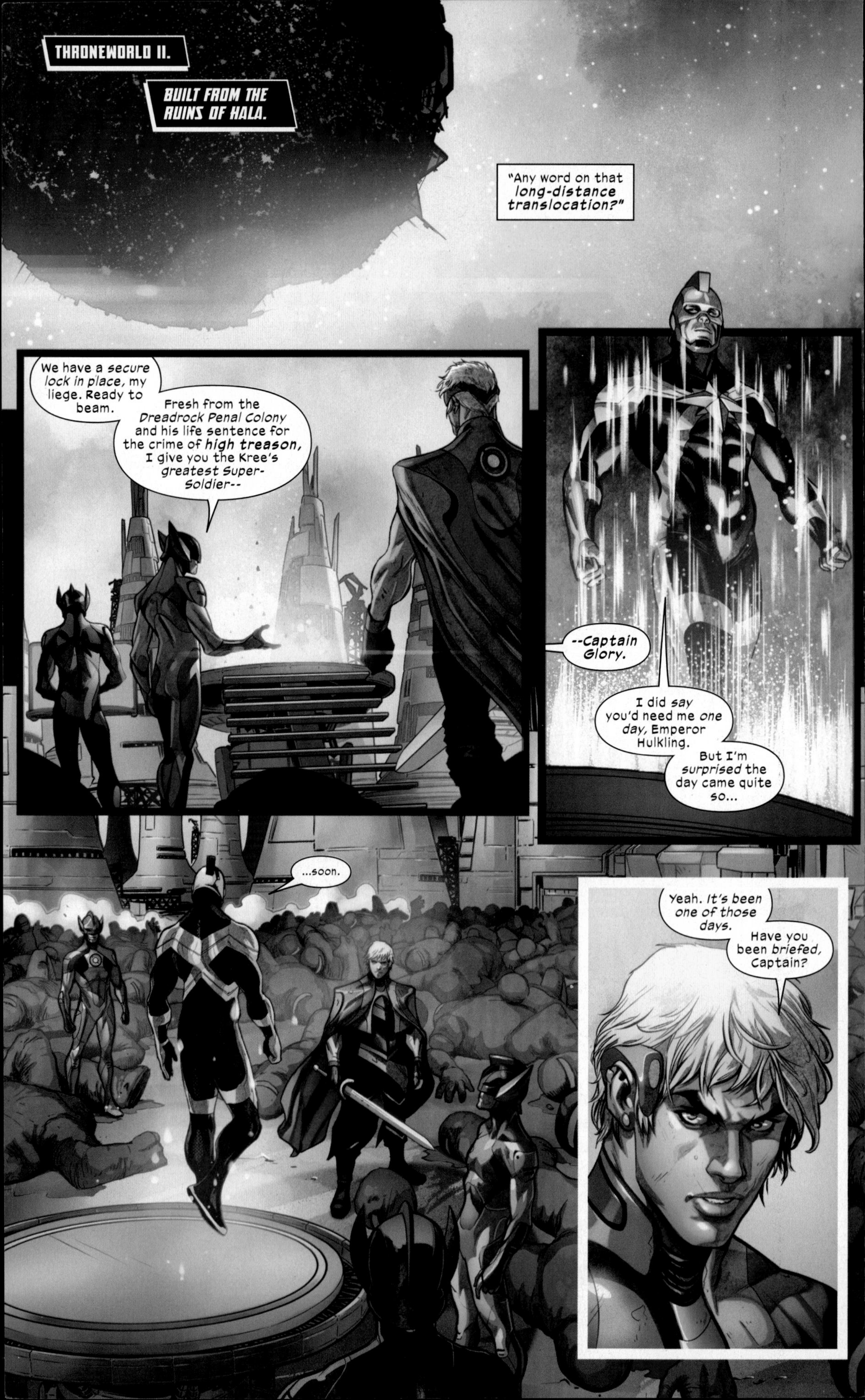
THRONEWORLD II.
BUILT FROM THE RUINS OF HALA.
"Any word on that long-distance translocation?"
We have a secure lock in place, my liege. Ready to beam.
Fresh from the Dreadrock Penal Colony and his life sentence for the crime of high treason, I give you the Kree's greatest Super-Soldier--
--Captain Glory.
I did say you'd need me one day, Emperor Hulkling.
But I'm surprised the day came quite so...
...soon.
Yeah. It's been one of those days.
Have you been briefed, Captain?

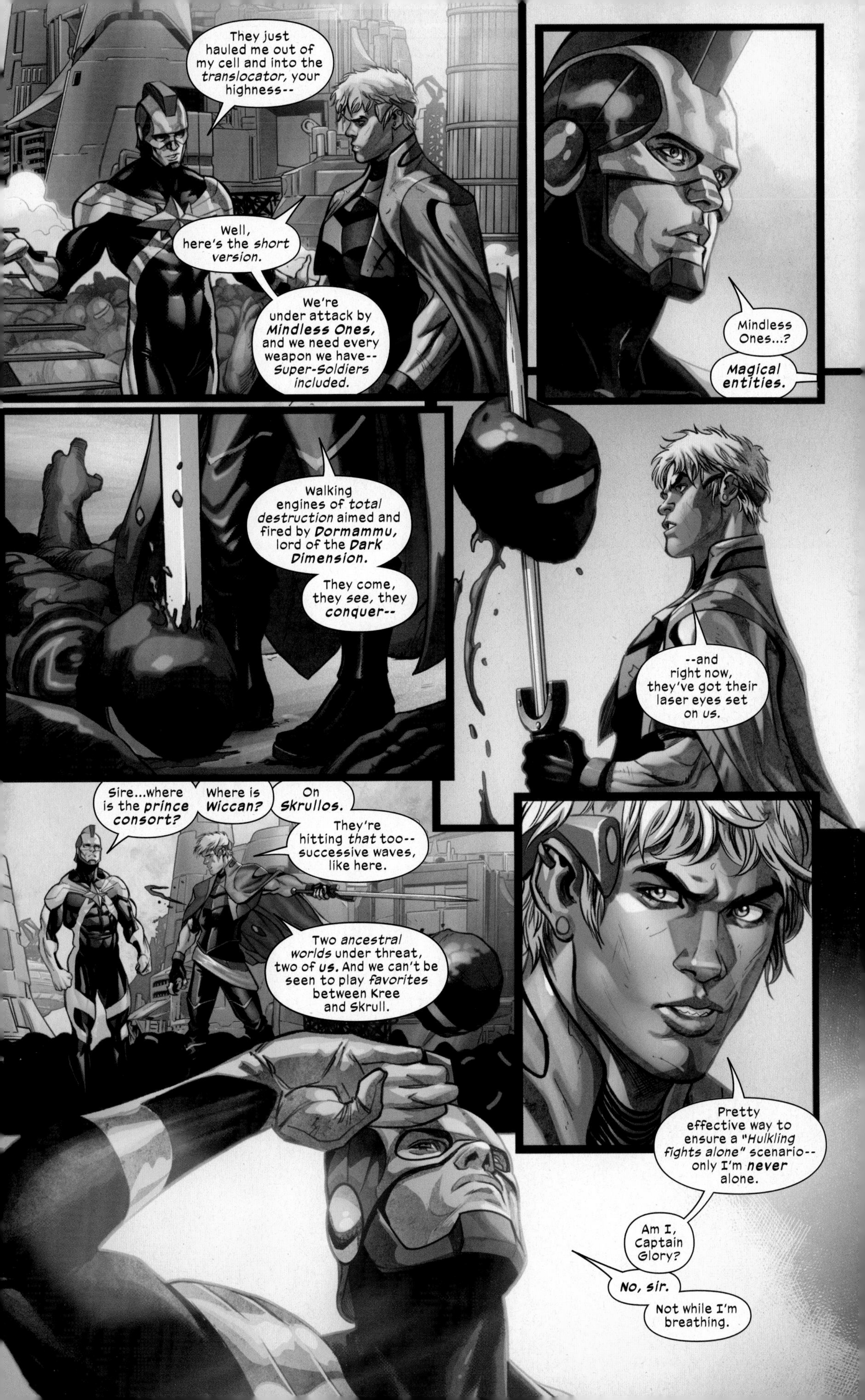
They just hauled me out of my cell and into the *translocator*, your highness--
Well, here's the *short* version.
We're under attack by ***Mindless Ones***, and we need every weapon we have-- *Super-Soldiers* included.
Mindless Ones...?
***Magical entities.***
Walking engines of *total destruction* aimed and fired by ***Dormammu***, lord of the ***Dark Dimension***.
They come, they *see*, they ***conquer***--
--and right now, they've got their laser eyes set on *us*.
Sire...where is the ***prince consort?***
Where is ***Wiccan?***
On ***Skrullos.***
They're hitting *that* too-- successive waves, like here.
Two *ancestral worlds* under threat, two of ***us***. And we can't be seen to play *favorites* between Kree and Skrull.
Pretty effective way to ensure a "*Hulkling fights alone*" scenario-- only I'm ***never*** alone.
Am I, Captain Glory?
*No, sir.*
Not while I'm breathing.

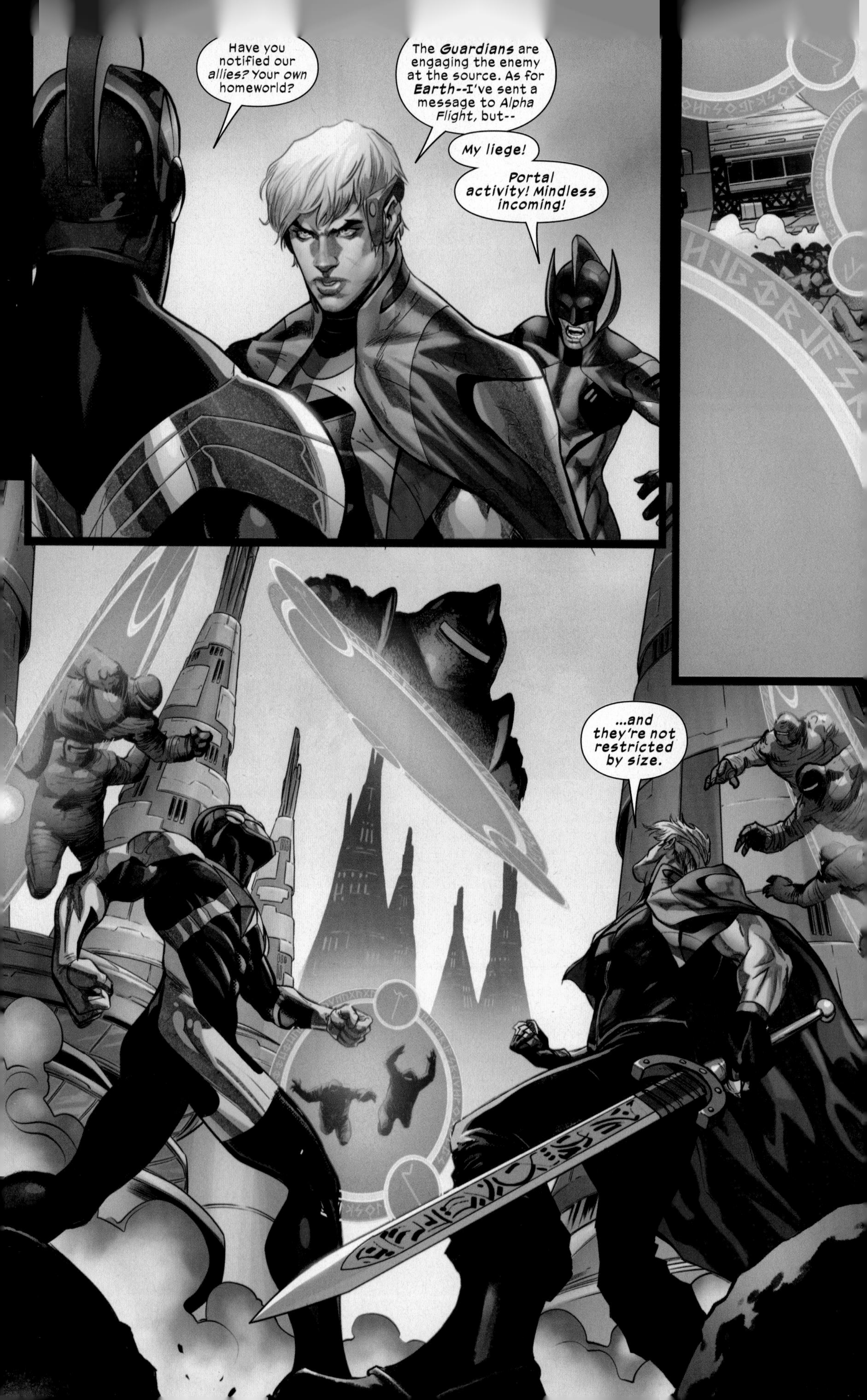
Have you notified our allies? Your own homeworld?
The Guardians are engaging the enemy at the source. As for Earth--I've sent a message to Alpha Flight, but--
My liege!
Portal activity! Mindless incoming!
...and they're not restricted by size.

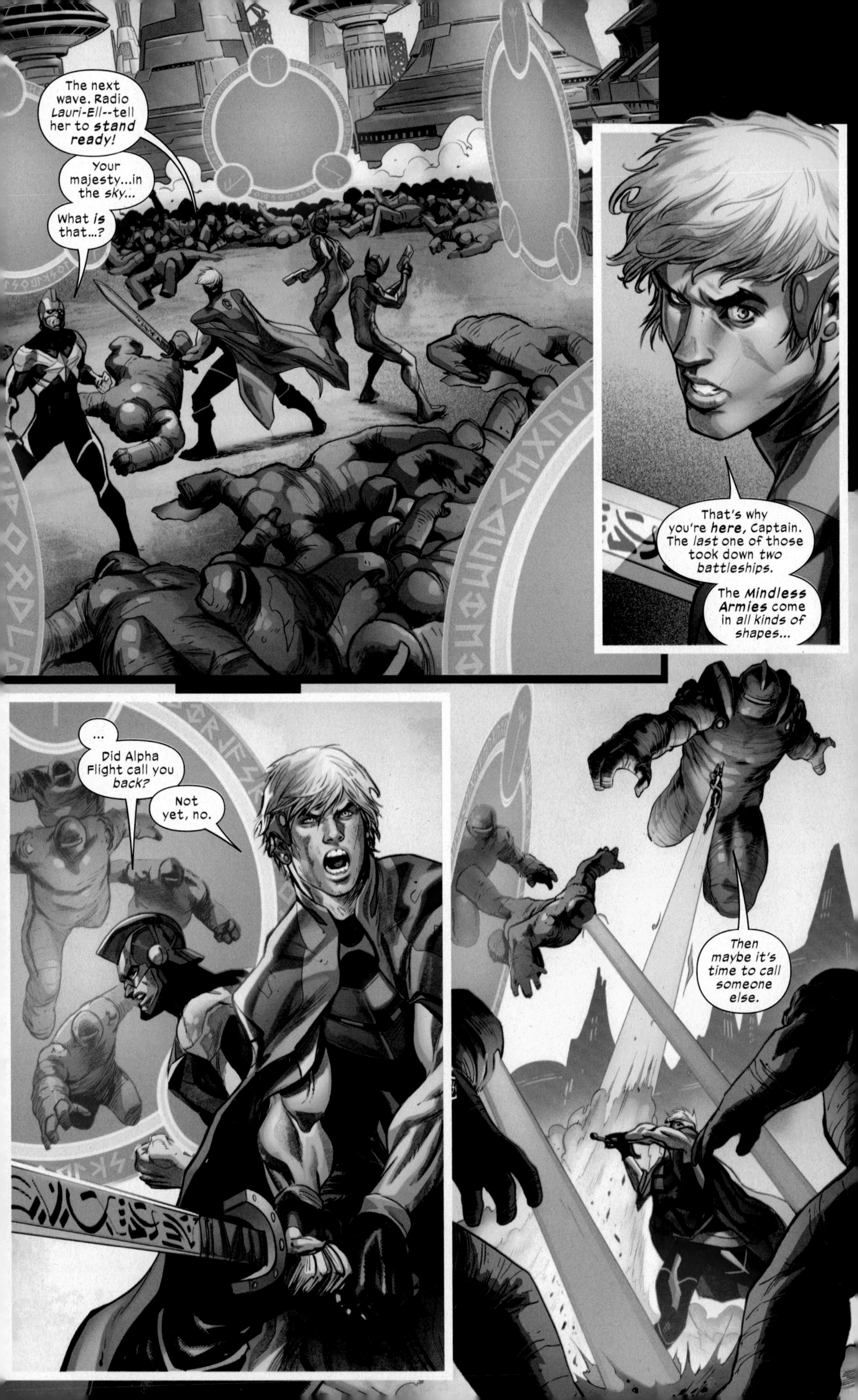

The next wave. Radio *Lauri-Ell*--tell her to ***stand ready!***
Your majesty...in the *sky...*
What *is* that...?
That's why you're ***here,*** Captain. The *last* one of those took down *two battleships.*
The ***Mindless Armies*** come in *all kinds of* shapes...
...
Did Alpha Flight call you *back?*
Not yet, no.
*Then maybe it's time to call someone else.*

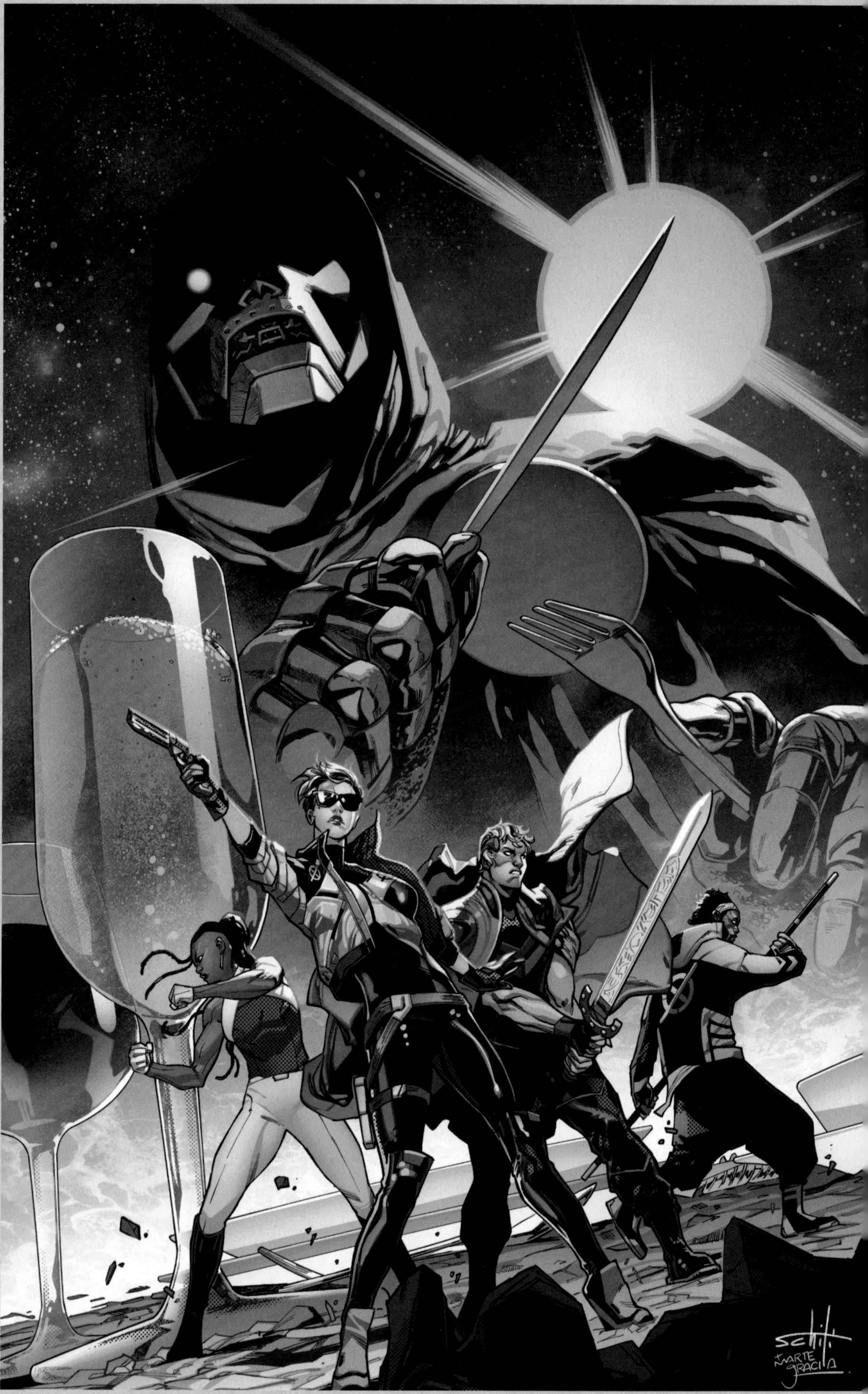

Full Spectrum Diplomacy

# THE LAST ANNIHILATION

Krakoa has terraformed and settled Mars with the mutants of the once-lost island of Arakko. Using the "miracle metal" mysterium, retrieved from higher space by the mutant circuit known as the Six, they have gained the favorable attention of the Galactic Council -- and bought full status and recognition for the Sol system, with the new Planet Arakko as its capital world. Storm, as Regent of Arakko and the Voice of Sol, is now our sun's representative in galactic affairs...

...and galactic affairs are heating up. The other-dimensional tyrant Dormammu has possessed Ego, the Living Planet, and is using him as the beachhead for a full assault on our reality -- starting with the Kree/Skrull Alliance.

Meanwhile, in the wake of the Hellfire Gala, certain guests have yet to return home...

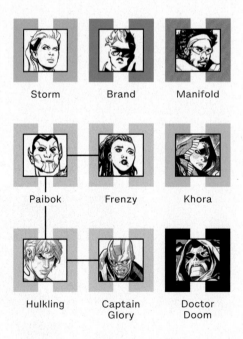

| Storm | Brand | Manifold |
| --- | --- | --- |
| Paibok | Frenzy | Khora |
| Hulkling | Captain Glory | Doctor Doom |

*Chapter 6 can be found in X-MEN: HELLFIRE GALA.

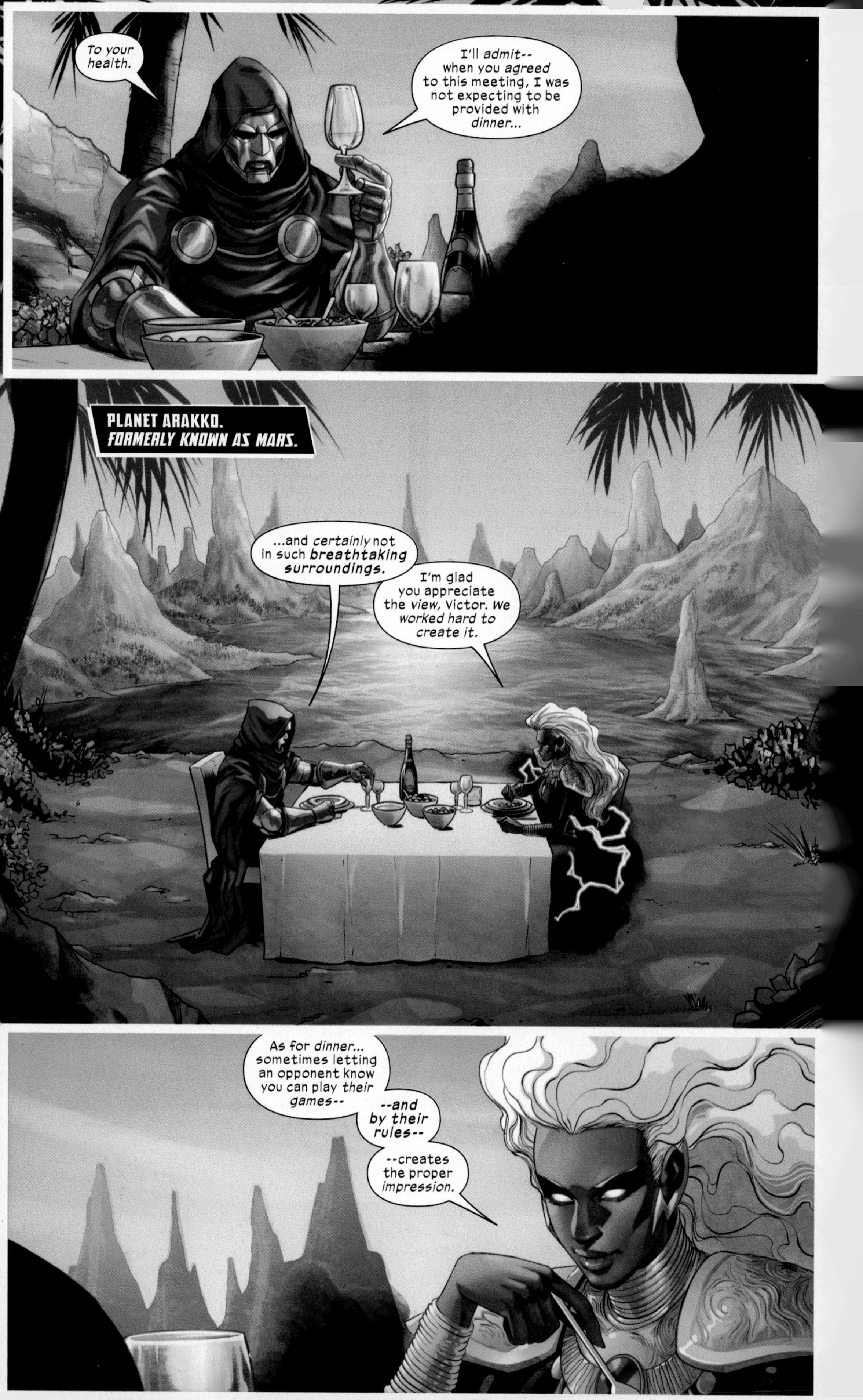

To your health.
I'll *admit*-- when you *agreed* to this meeting, I was not expecting to be provided with *dinner*...
PLANET ARAKKO. FORMERLY KNOWN AS MARS.
...and *certainly* not in such **breathtaking surroundings.**
I'm glad you appreciate the *view*, Victor. *We worked hard to create it.*
As for *dinner*... sometimes letting an opponent know you can play *their* games--
**--and by their rules--**
--creates the proper *impression*.

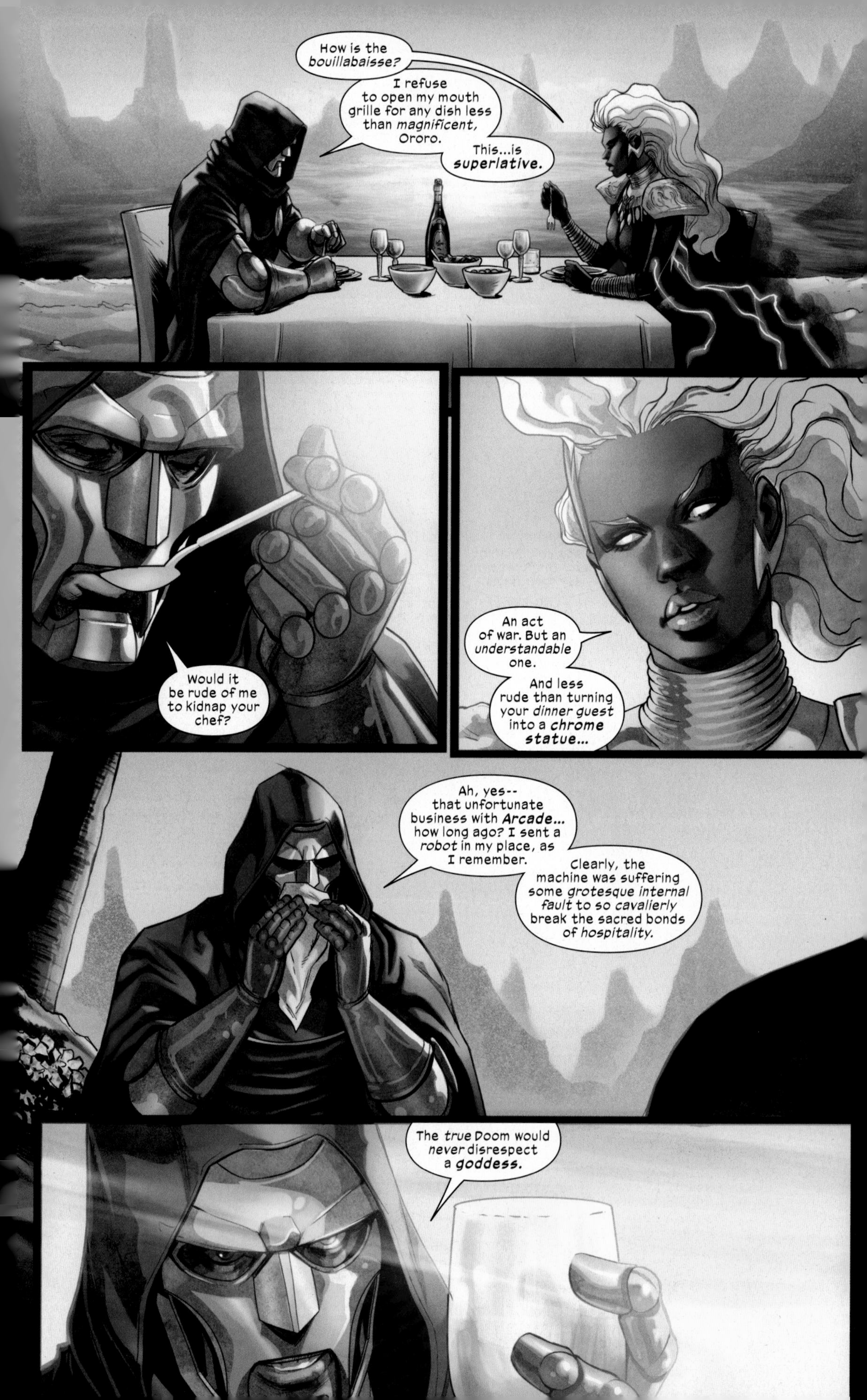
How is the bouillabaisse?
I refuse to open my mouth grille for any dish less than magnificent, Ororo.
This...is superlative.
Would it be rude of me to kidnap your chef?
An act of war. But an understandable one.
And less rude than turning your dinner guest into a chrome statue...
Ah, yes-- that unfortunate business with Arcade... how long ago? I sent a robot in my place, as I remember.
Clearly, the machine was suffering some grotesque internal fault to so cavalierly break the sacred bonds of hospitality.
The true Doom would never disrespect a goddess.

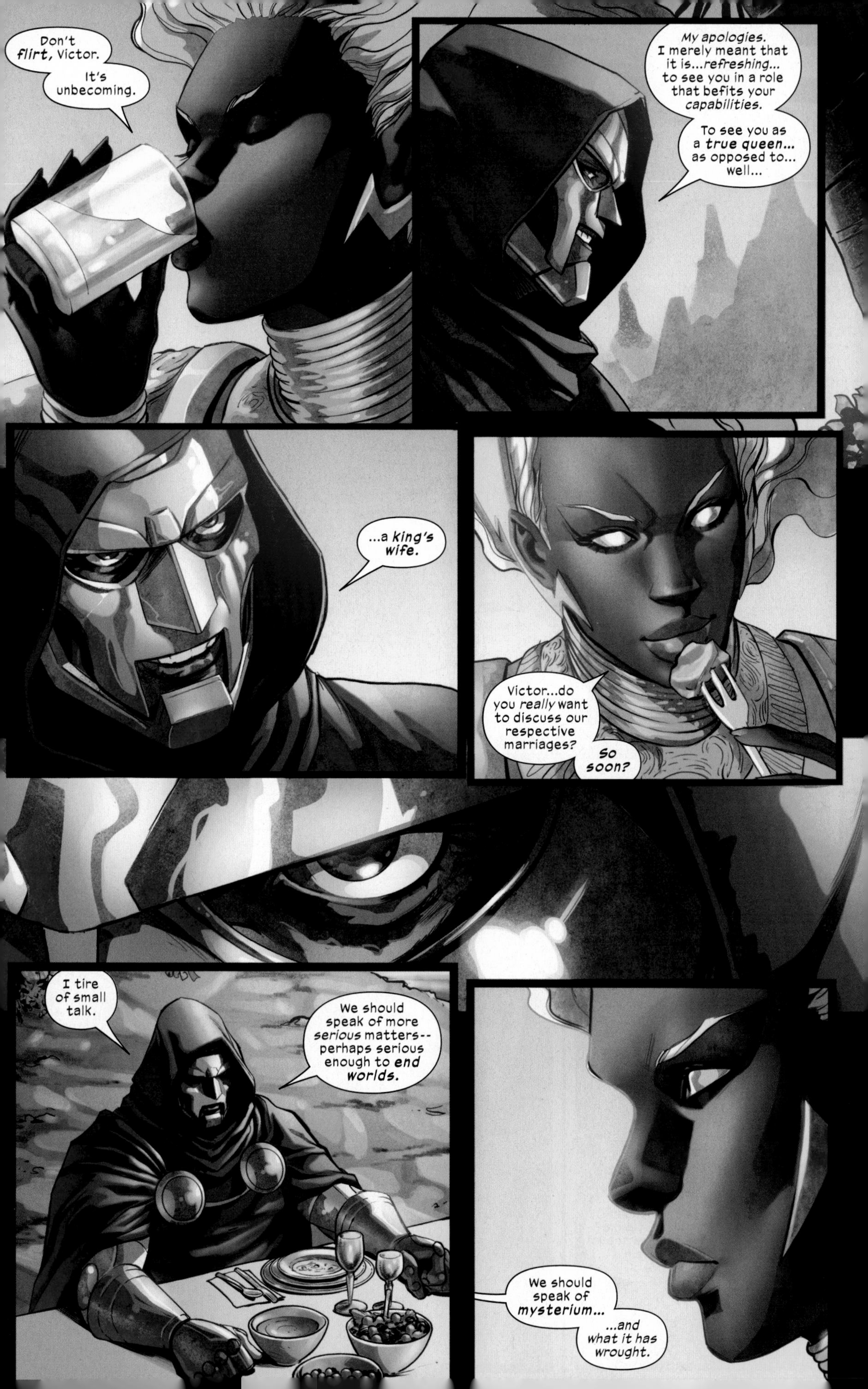
Don't flirt, Victor.
It's unbecoming.
My apologies. I merely meant that it is...refreshing... to see you in a role that befits your capabilities.
To see you as a true queen... as opposed to... well...
...a king's wife.
Victor...do you really want to discuss our respective marriages?
So soon?
I tire of small talk.
We should speak of more serious matters--perhaps serious enough to end worlds.
We should speak of mysterium...
...and what it has wrought.

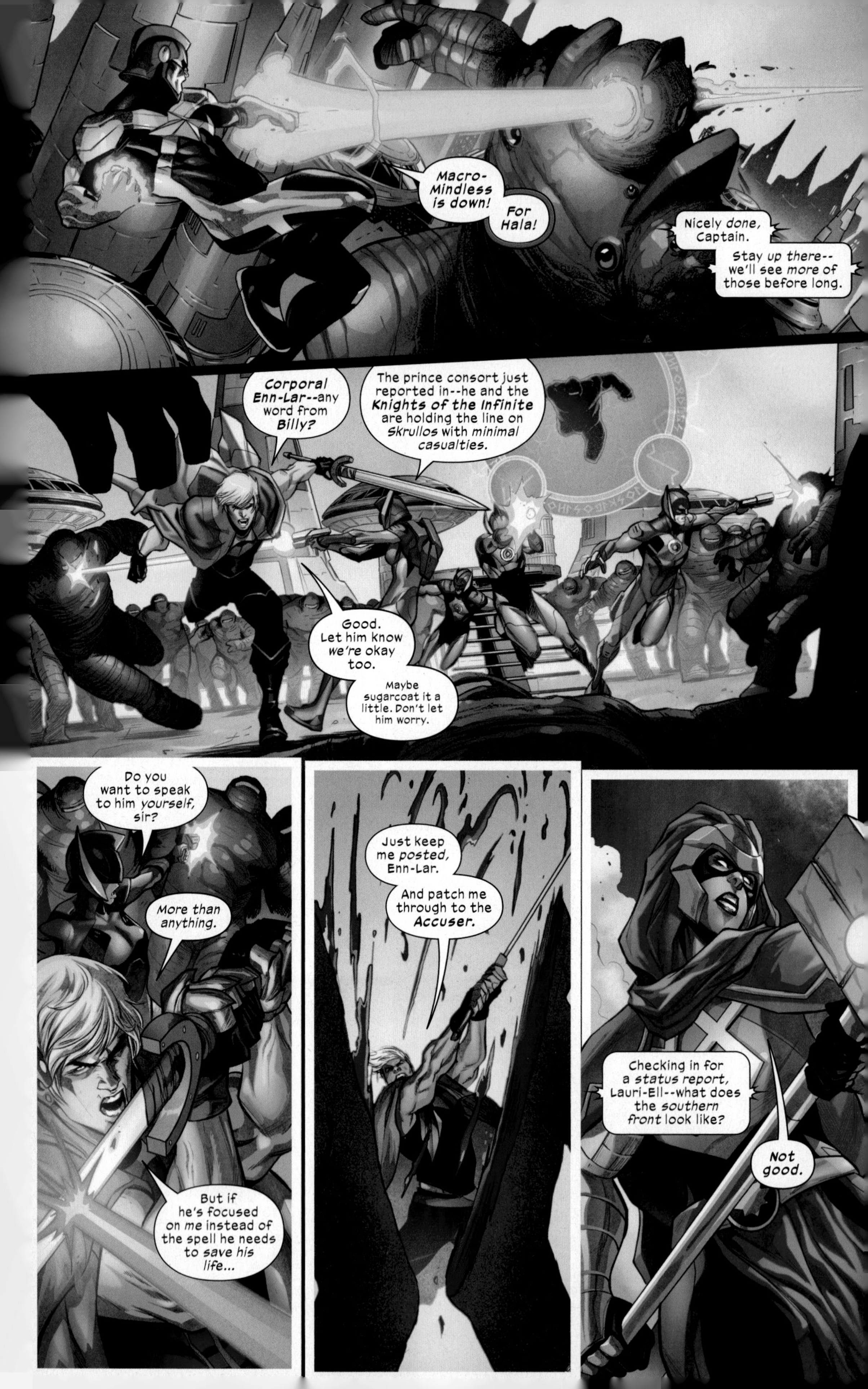
Macro-Mindless is down!
For Hala!
Nicely done, Captain.
Stay up there--we'll see more of those before long.
Corporal Enn-Lar--any word from Billy?
The prince consort just reported in--he and the Knights of the Infinite are holding the line on Skrullos with minimal casualties.
Good. Let him know we're okay too.
Maybe sugarcoat it a little. Don't let him worry.
Do you want to speak to him yourself, sir?
More than anything.
But if he's focused on me instead of the spell he needs to save his life...
Just keep me posted, Enn-Lar.
And patch me through to the Accuser.
Checking in for a status report, Lauri-Ell--what does the southern front look like?
Not good.

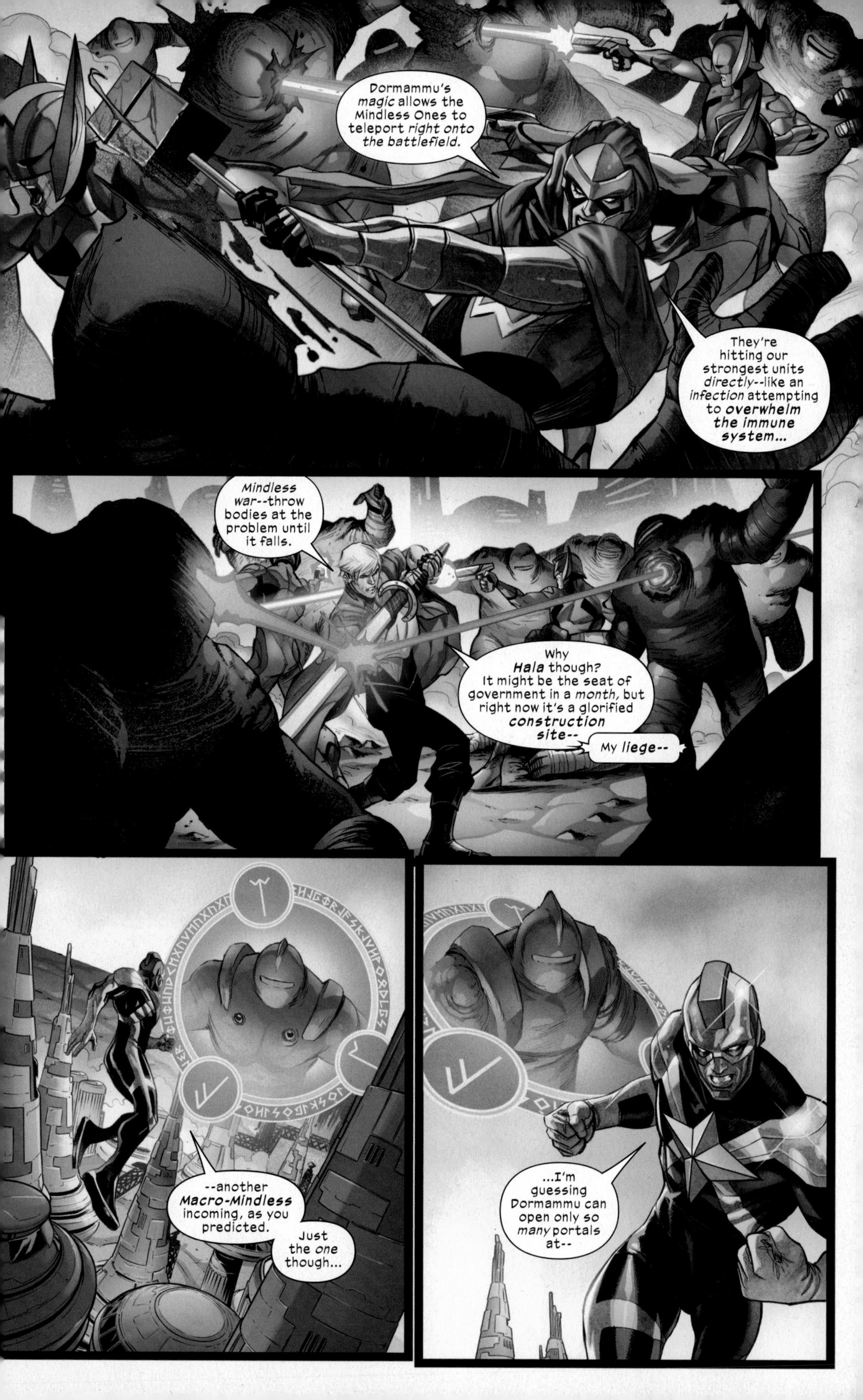
Dormammu's *magic* allows the Mindless Ones to teleport *right onto* the battlefield.
They're hitting our strongest units *directly*--like an *infection* attempting to ***overwhelm the immune system...***
*Mindless war*--throw bodies at the problem until it falls.
Why ***Hala*** though? It might be the seat of government in a *month*, but right now it's a glorified ***construction site--***
My ***liege--***
--another ***Macro-Mindless*** incoming, as you predicted.
Just the *one* though...
...I'm guessing Dormammu can open only so *many* portals at--

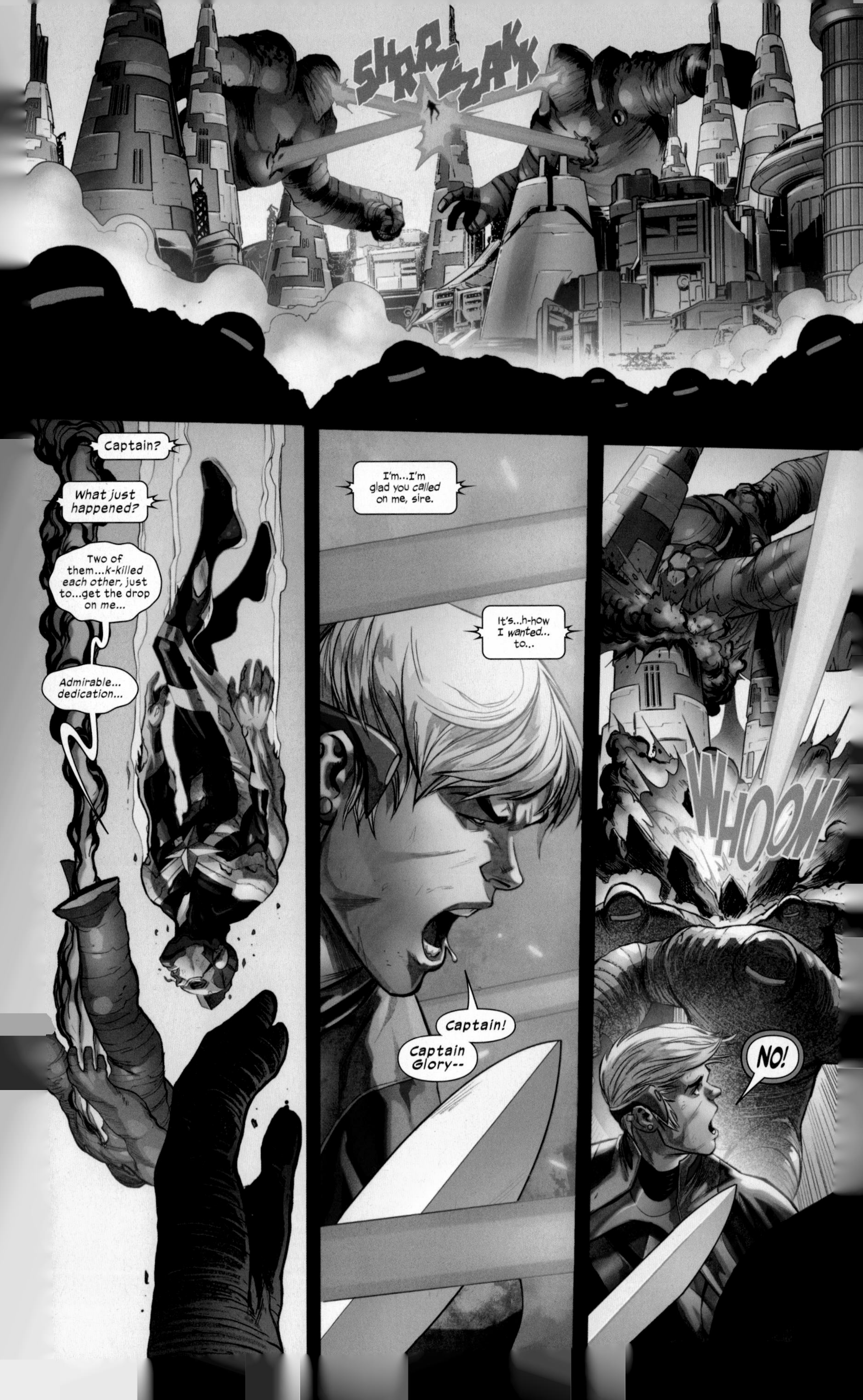
SHRZZZAKK
Captain?
What just happened?
Two of them...k-killed each other, just to...get the drop on me...
Admirable... dedication...
I'm...I'm glad you called on me, sire.
It's..h-how I wanted... to..
Captain!
Captain Glory--
WHOOM
NO!

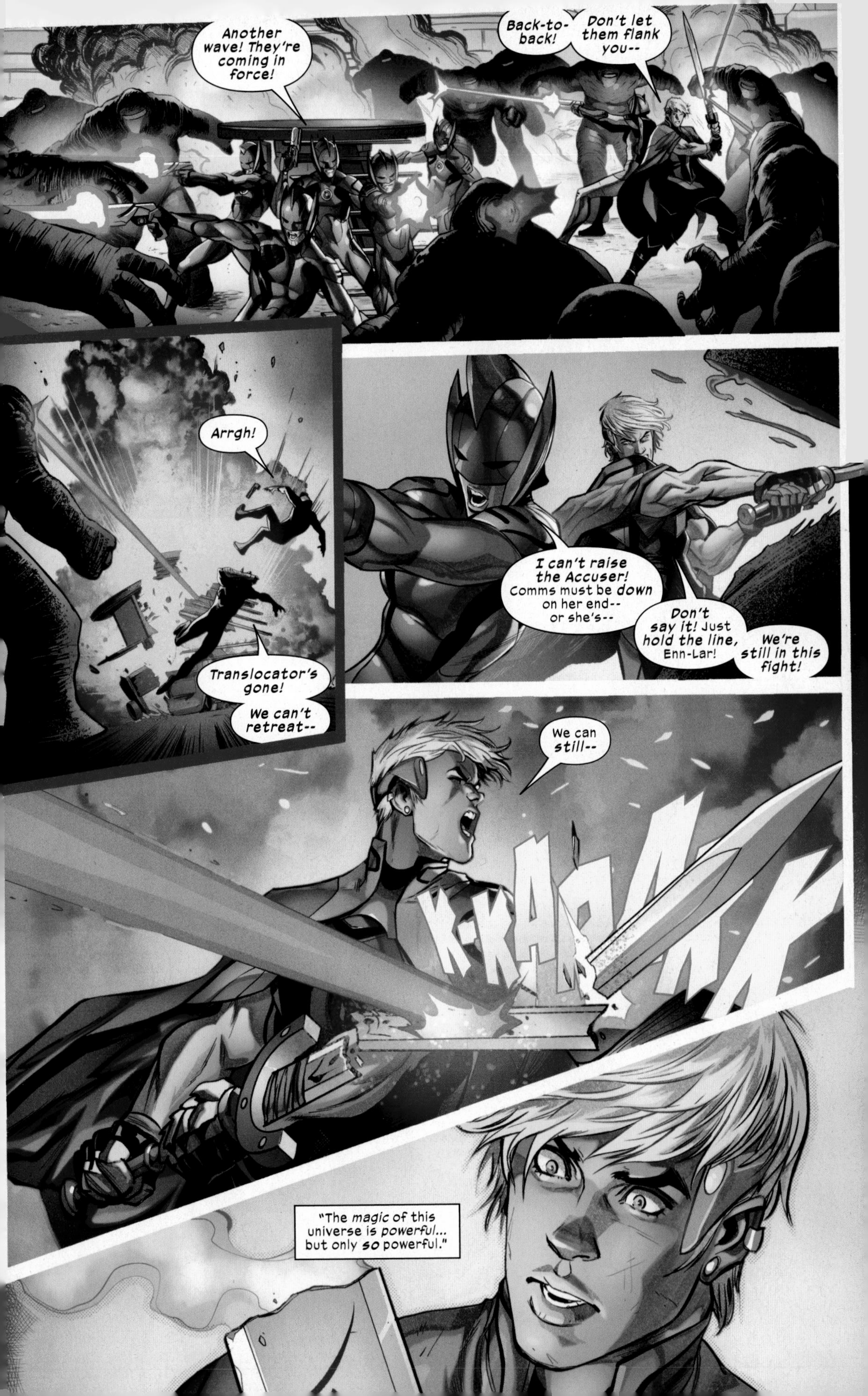
Another wave! They're coming in force!
Back-to-back!
Don't let them flank you--
Arrgh!
Translocator's gone!
We can't retreat--
I can't raise the Accuser! Comms must be down on her end-- or she's--
Don't say it! Just hold the line, Enn-Lar!
We're still in this fight!
We can still--
K-KA
"The magic of this universe is powerful... but only so powerful."

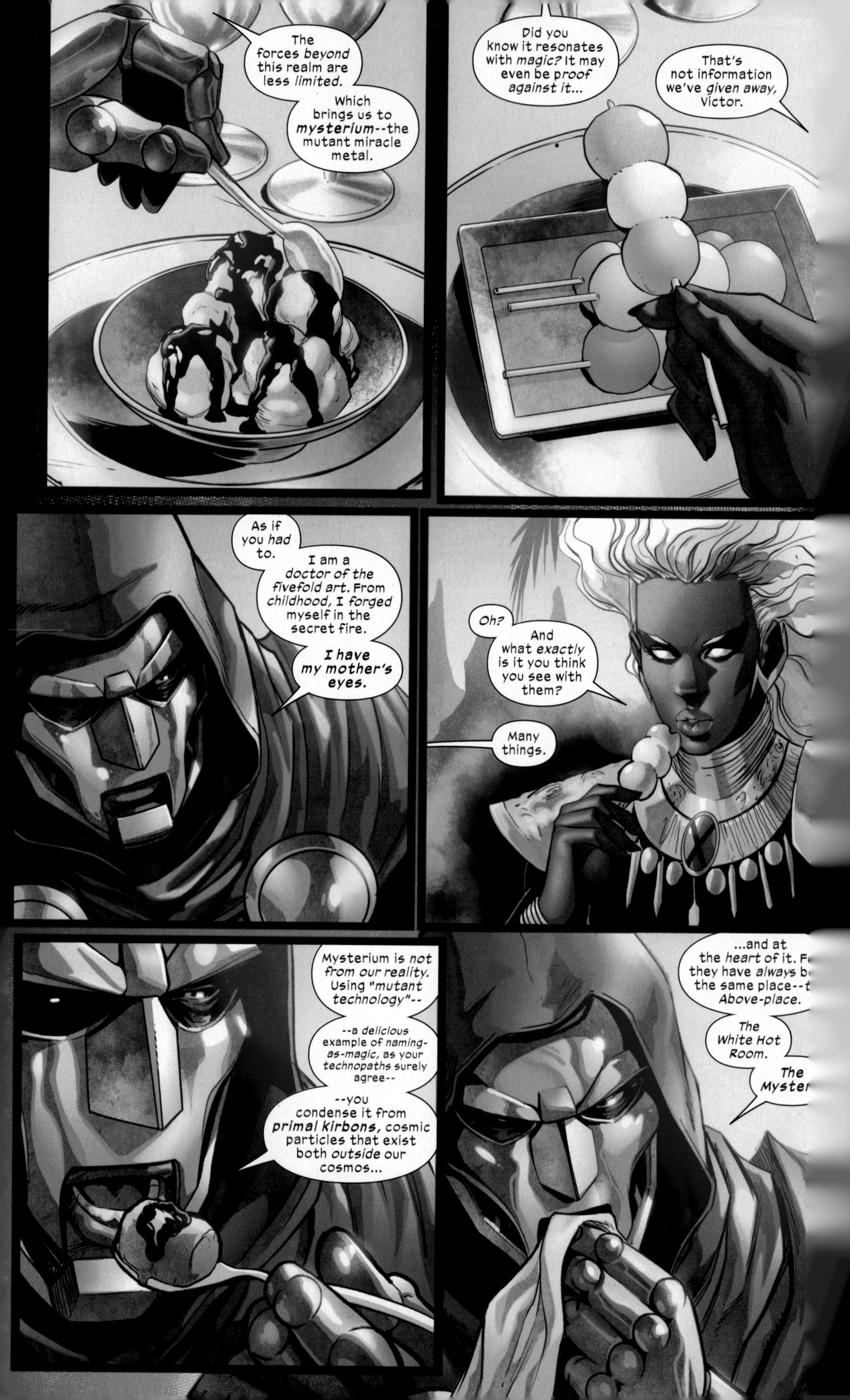

The forces *beyond* this realm are less *limited.*
Which brings us to ***mysterium***--the mutant miracle metal.
Did you know it resonates with *magic?* It may even be *proof against it...*
That's not information we've *given away,* Victor.
As if you *had* to.
I am a *doctor of the fivefold art.* From *childhood,* I forged myself in the secret fire.
***I have my mother's eyes.***
*Oh?*
And what *exactly* is it you think you see with them?
Many things.
Mysterium is *not from our reality.* Using *"mutant technology"*--
--a *delicious* example of *naming-as-magic,* as your *technopaths* surely agree--
--you condense it from ***primal kirbons,*** cosmic particles that exist both *outside* our cosmos...
...and at the *heart* of it.
*The White Hot Room.*

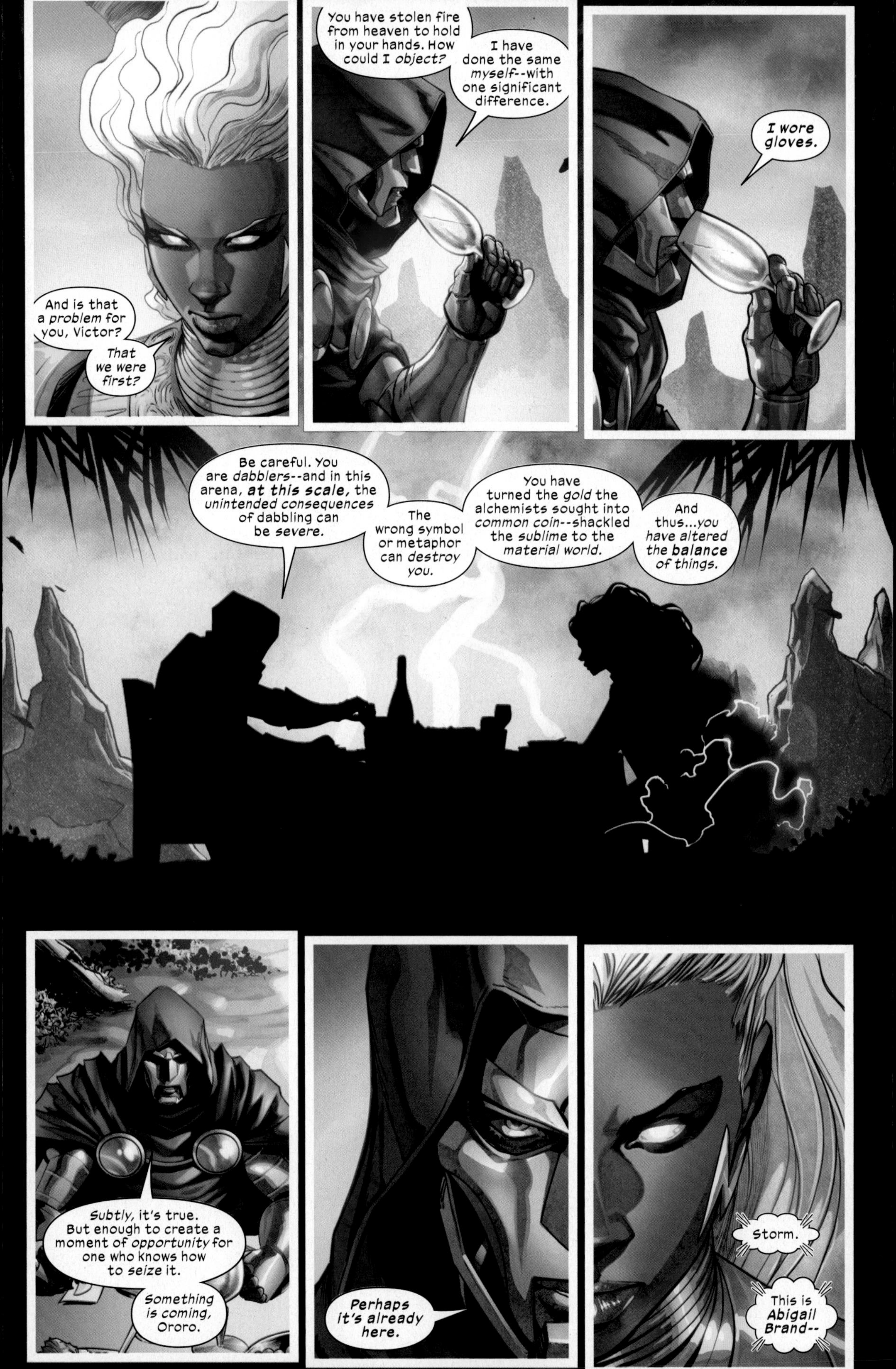

And is that a *problem* for you, Victor?
That we were *first?*
You have stolen fire from heaven to hold in your hands. How could I *object?*
I have done the same *myself*--with one significant difference.
*I wore gloves.*
Be careful. You are *dabblers*--and in this arena, **at this scale,** the *unintended consequences* of dabbling can be *severe.*
The wrong symbol or metaphor can *destroy you.*
You have turned the *gold* the alchemists sought into *common coin*--shackled the *sublime* to the *material world.*
And thus...*you have altered* the **balance** *of things.*
*Subtly,* it's true. But enough to create a moment of *opportunity* for one who knows how to *seize* it.
*Something is coming, Ororo.*
*Perhaps it's already here.*
Storm.
This is *Abigail Brand--*

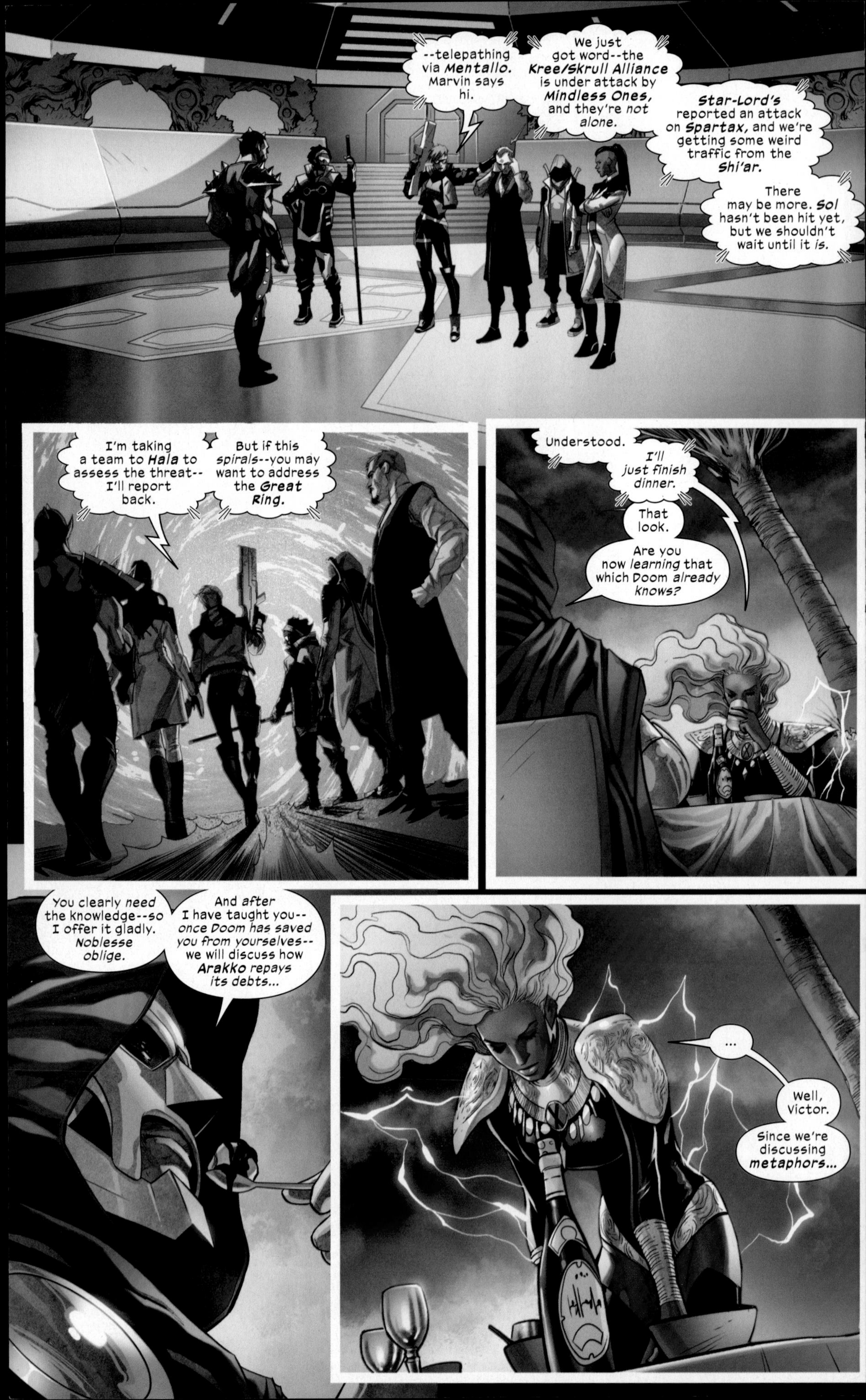
--telepathing via Mentallo. Marvin says hi.
We just got word--the Kree/Skrull Alliance is under attack by Mindless Ones, and they're not alone.
Star-Lord's reported an attack on Spartax, and we're getting some weird traffic from the Shi'ar.
There may be more. Sol hasn't been hit yet, but we shouldn't wait until it is.
I'm taking a team to Hala to assess the threat--I'll report back.
But if this spirals--you may want to address the Great Ring.
Understood.
I'll just finish dinner.
That look.
Are you now learning that which Doom already knows?
You clearly need the knowledge--so I offer it gladly. Noblesse oblige.
And after I have taught you--once Doom has saved you from yourselves--we will discuss how Arakko repays its debts...
...
Well, Victor.
Since we're discussing metaphors...

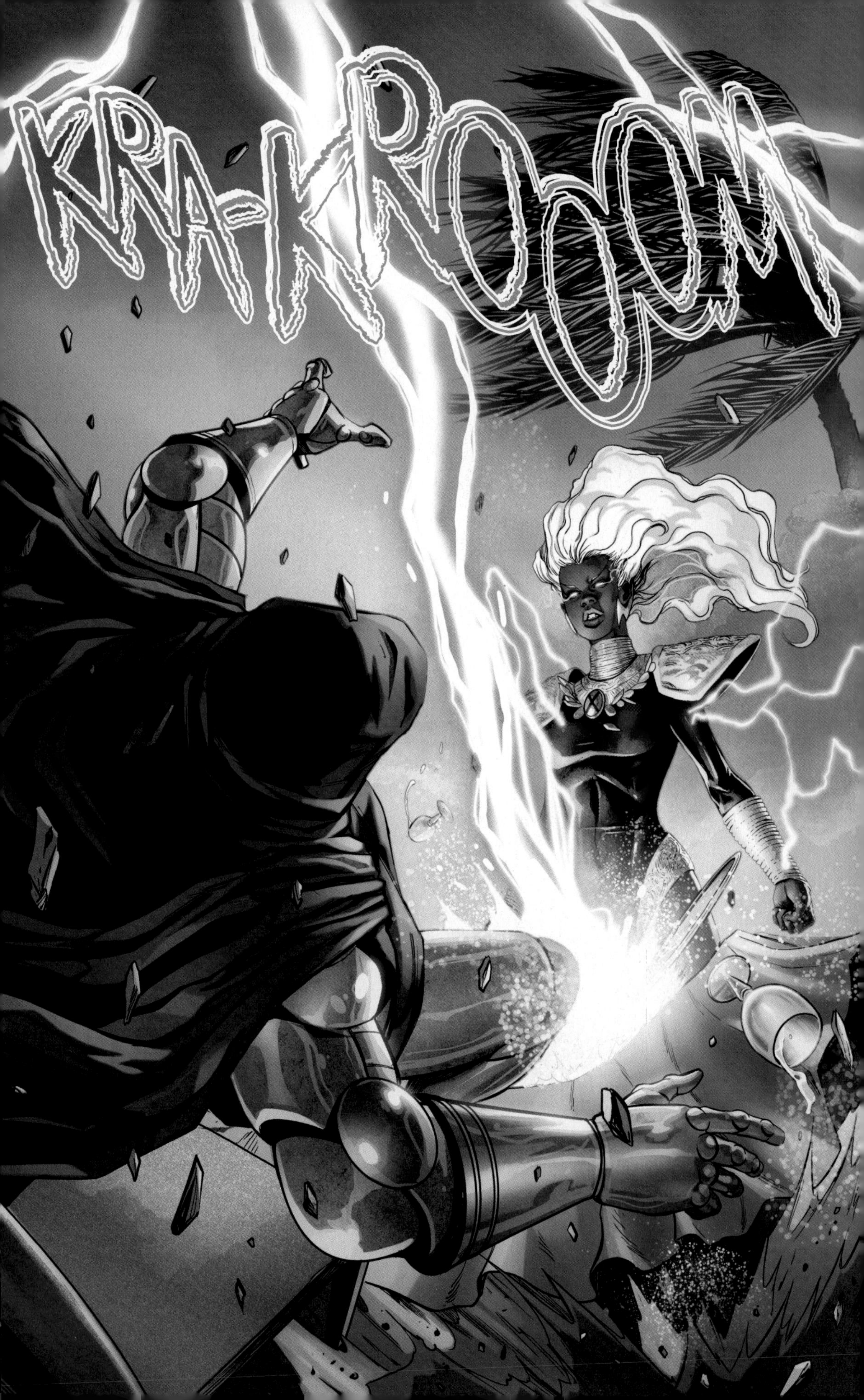
KRA-KROOOOM

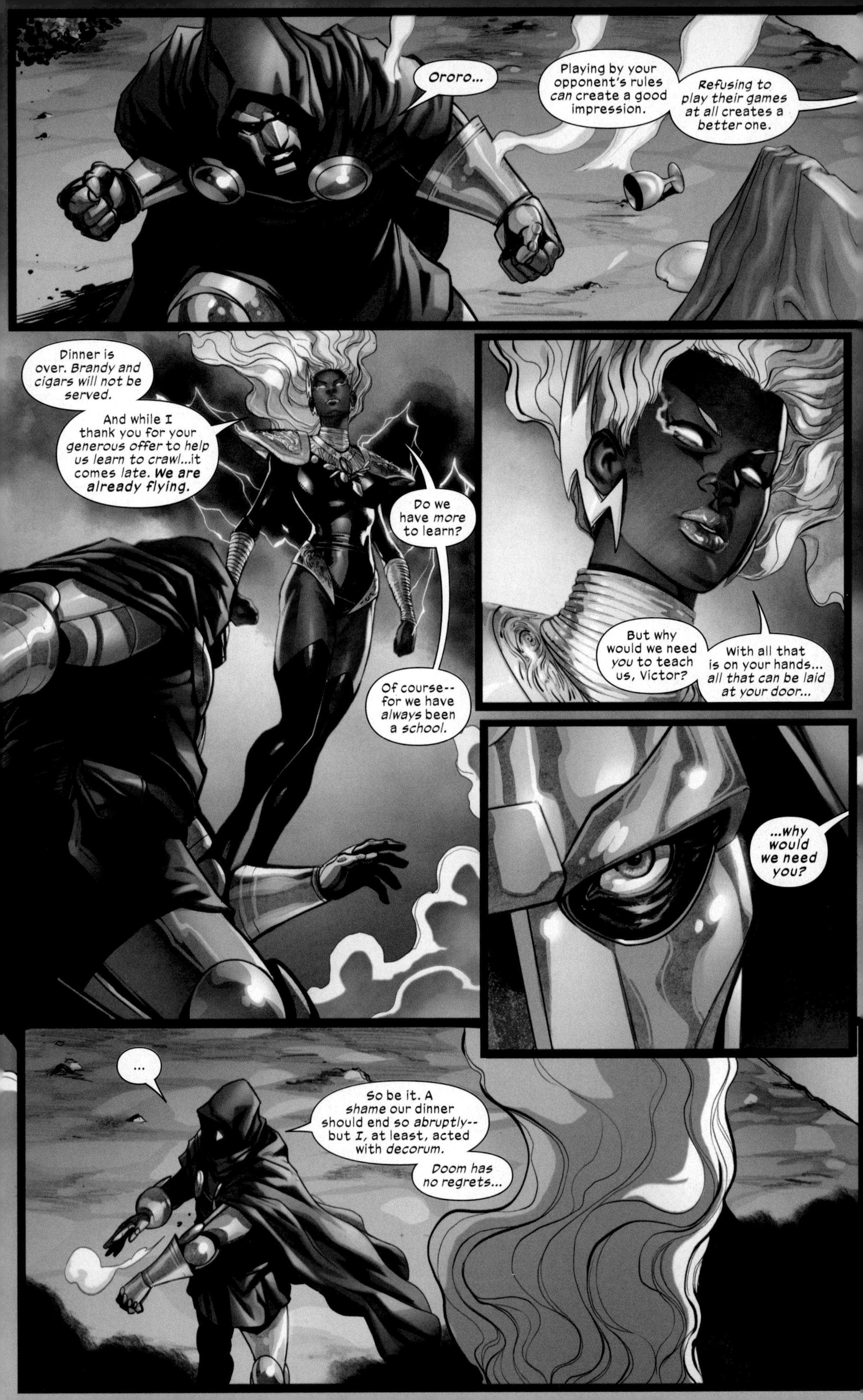
Ororo...
Playing by your opponent's rules can create a good impression.
Refusing to play their games at all creates a better one.
Dinner is over. Brandy and cigars will not be served.
And while I thank you for your generous offer to help us learn to crawl...it comes late. We are already flying.
Do we have more to learn?
Of course--for we have always been a school.
But why would we need you to teach us, Victor?
With all that is on your hands... all that can be laid at your door...
...why would we need you?
...
So be it. A shame our dinner should end so abruptly--but I, at least, acted with decorum.
Doom has no regrets...

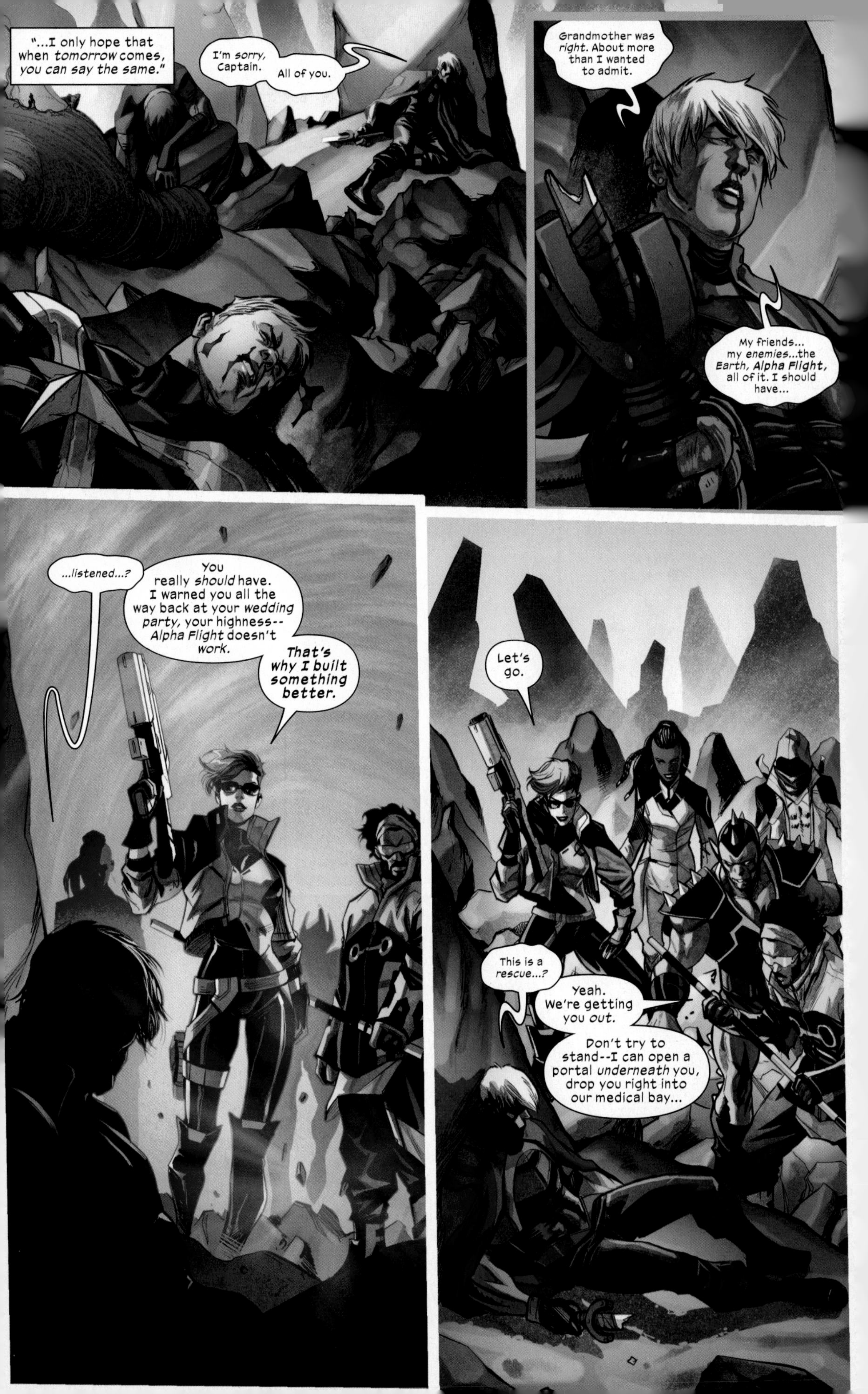

"...I only hope that when *tomorrow* comes, *you can say the same.*"
I'm *sorry*, Captain.
All of you.
Grandmother was *right*. About more than I wanted to admit.
My friends... my *enemies*...the *Earth, **Alpha Flight***, all of it. I should have...
*...listened...?*
You really *should* have. I warned you all the way back at your *wedding party*, your highness-- *Alpha Flight* doesn't *work*.
***That's why I built something better.***
Let's go.
This is a *rescue...?*
Yeah. We're getting you *out*.
Don't try to stand--I can open a portal *underneath* you, drop you right into our medical bay...

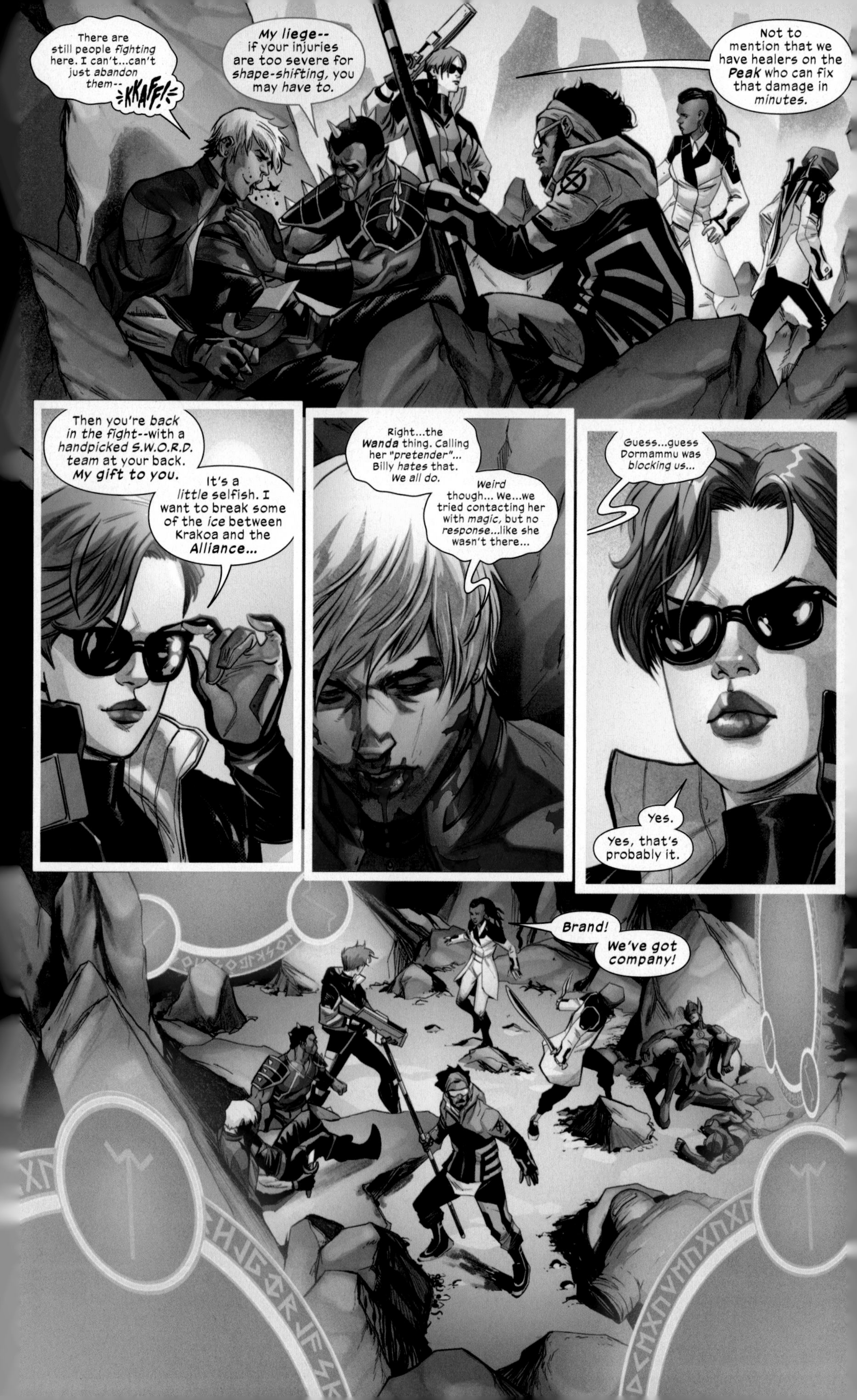

There are still people fighting here. I can't...can't just abandon them-- KKAFF!
My liege-- if your injuries are too severe for shape-shifting, you may have to.
Not to mention that we have healers on the Peak who can fix that damage in minutes.
Then you're back in the fight--with a handpicked S.W.O.R.D. team at your back. My gift to you.
It's a little selfish. I want to break some of the ice between Krakoa and the Alliance...
Right...the Wanda thing. Calling her "pretender"... Billy hates that. We all do.
Weird though... We...we tried contacting her with magic, but no response...like she wasn't there...
Guess...guess Dormammu was blocking us...
Yes.
Yes, that's probably it.
Brand!
We've got company!

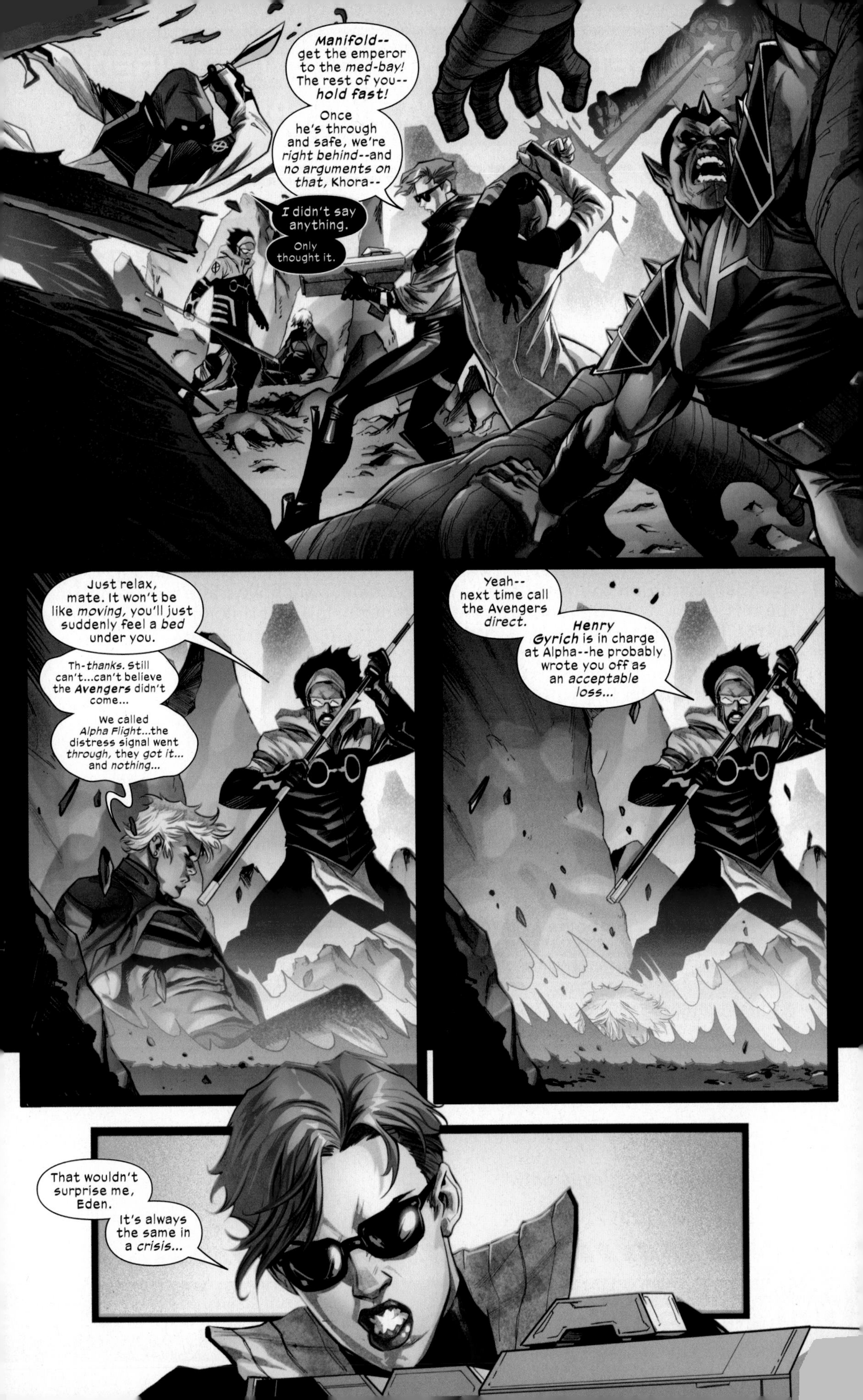
Manifold-- get the emperor to the med-bay! The rest of you-- hold fast!
Once he's through and safe, we're right behind--and no arguments on that, Khora--
I didn't say anything.
Only thought it.
Just relax, mate. It won't be like moving, you'll just suddenly feel a bed under you.
Th-thanks. Still can't...can't believe the Avengers didn't come...
We called Alpha Flight...the distress signal went through, they got it... and nothing...
Yeah-- next time call the Avengers direct.
Henry Gyrich is in charge at Alpha--he probably wrote you off as an acceptable loss...
That wouldn't surprise me, Eden.
It's always the same in a crisis...

# DEEP SECRET :: EYES ONLY :: DO NOT UNREDACT :: UTILIZE FULL TELEPATHIC SAFEGUARDS ::

[DE...[ep]__0X]
[SEC..[ret]_07]

# ABIGAIL BRAND :: PERSONAL LOG Z-1-12 21/6

*"Eyes only."* Never more than now. I'm only keeping this record in the event of post-resurrection memory loss -- it's important I know what I've done. And who I've done it to.

So, for the record -- when Emperor Hulkling sent that distress signal to Alpha Flight, there was every chance Gyrich would have passed it along to the Avengers. Hulkling's one of their own -- *their problem,* by his thinking. And, of course, they'd have all gone running to help.

*I just couldn't have that.*

It's not enough to have the Shi'ar and the Zn'rx in our corner. I need the Kree/Skrull Alliance as well if I want real pull with the Galactic Council. That means getting on the royal family's good side, which was already going to be difficult -- with the emperor's dead mother-in-law stinking up the after-party, it'll take a miracle.

So I intercepted the distress signal -- the way I can intercept all signals sent to the Alpha Flight Space Station.

And, of course, I blocked it.

Gyrich never even knew it existed -- neither will the Avengers. And S.W.O.R.D. gets to ride to the rescue. I've had nano-cameras on Throneworld since construction started, so I can pick the perfect moment to save the emperor's life. That way, even when he finds out about Maximoff and the crap really hits the fan -- *he'll owe me.* It's not perfect, but it'll let me start making the real moves.

Eventually, the goal is [redacted] Storm [redacted]

[redacted]

Needless to say, if the Quiet Council found out about *that*... Well.

That's why it's *"eyes only."*

[D_[en]Y........[0]
[EVE_r[yth]ING..[7]

S ONLY :: EYES ONLY :: EYES ONLY :: EYES ONLY :: EYES

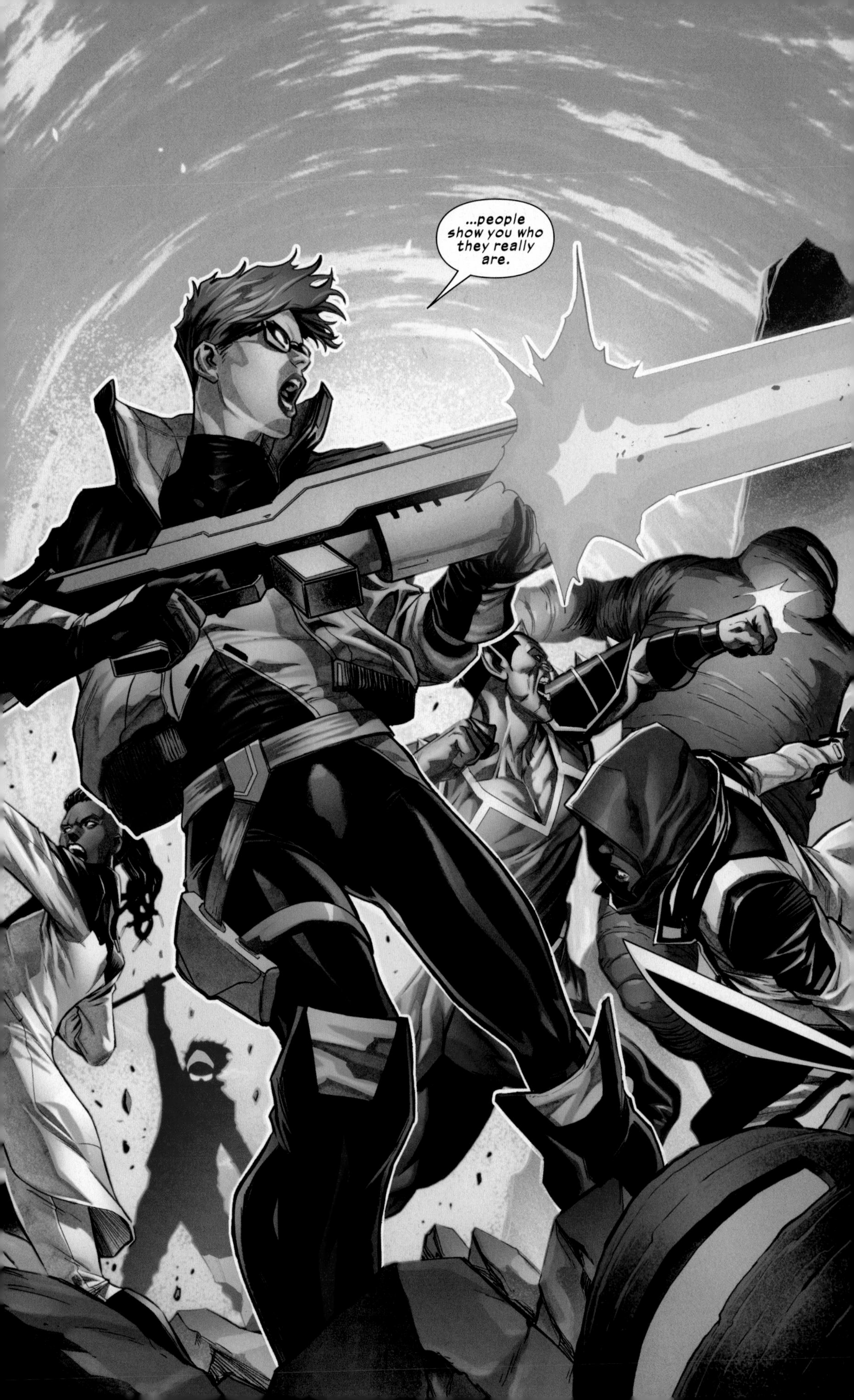
...people show you who they really are.

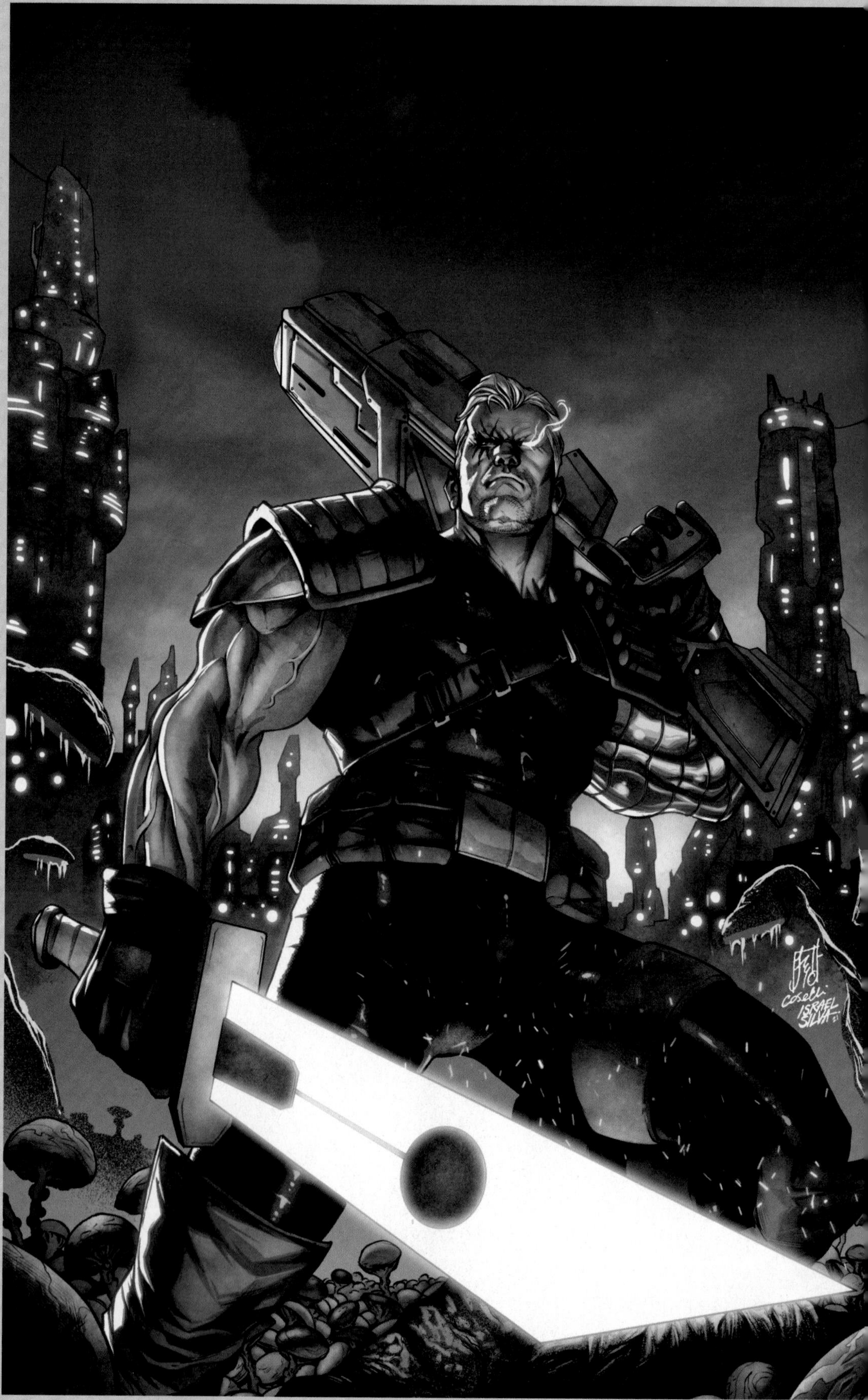

Call in the Big Gun

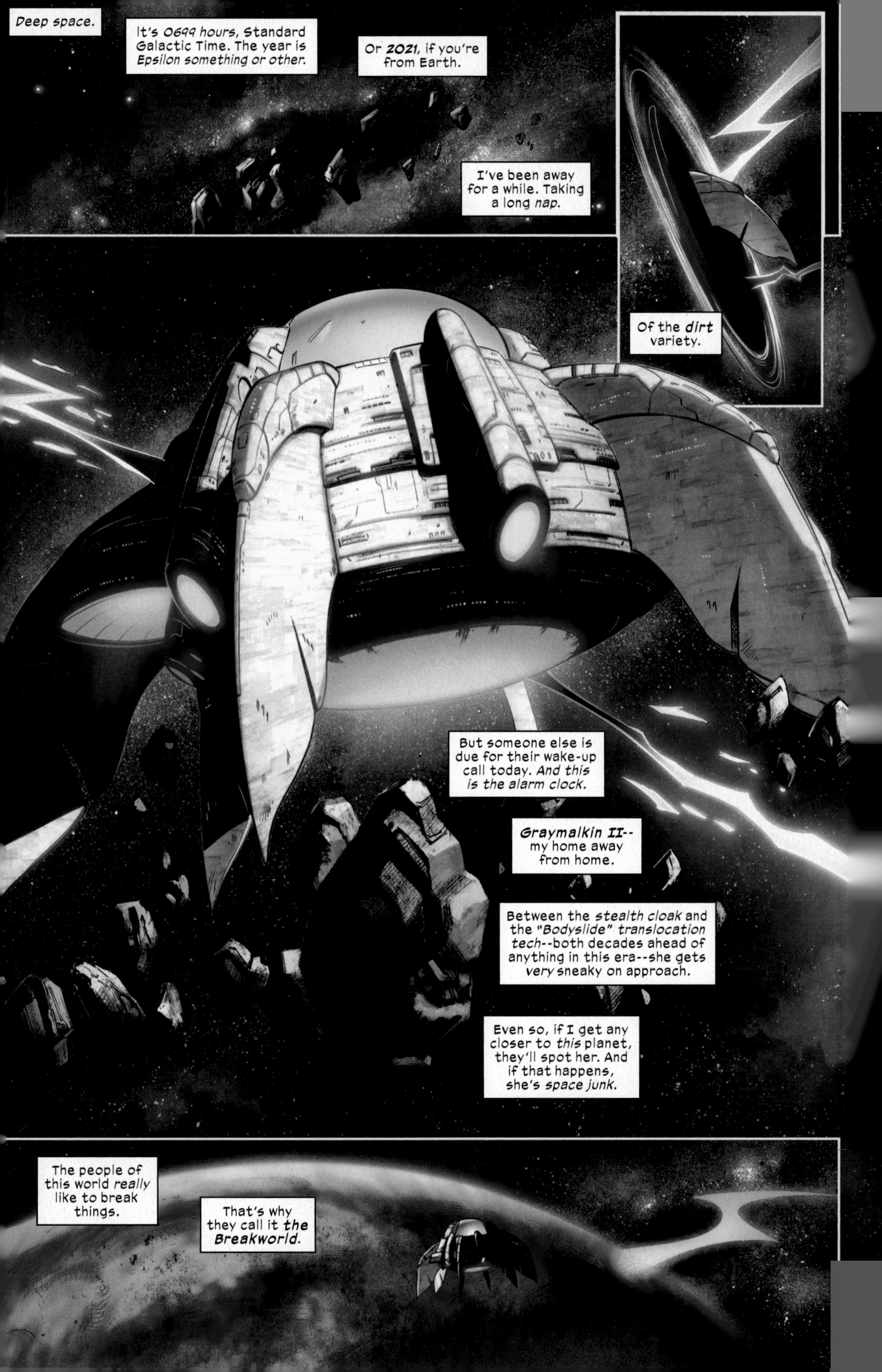
Deep space.
It's 0699 hours, Standard Galactic Time. The year is Epsilon something or other.
Or 2021, if you're from Earth.
I've been away for a while. Taking a long nap.
Of the dirt variety.
But someone else is due for their wake-up call today. And this is the alarm clock.
Graymalkin II-- my home away from home.
Between the stealth cloak and the "Bodyslide" translocation tech--both decades ahead of anything in this era--she gets very sneaky on approach.
Even so, if I get any closer to this planet, they'll spot her. And if that happens, she's space junk.
The people of this world really like to break things.
That's why they call it the Breakworld.

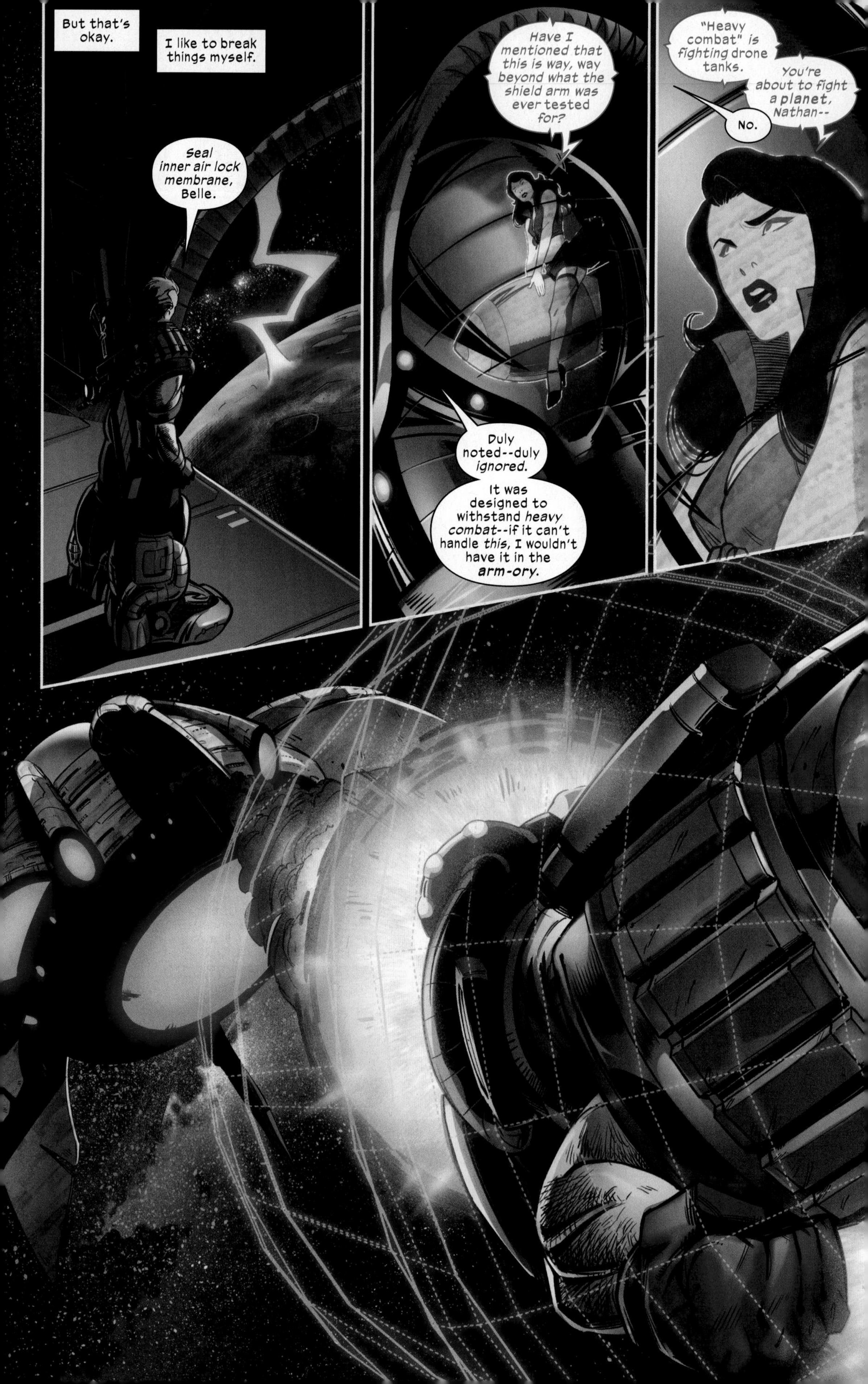
But that's okay.
I like to break things myself.
Seal inner air lock membrane, Belle.
Have I mentioned that this is way, way beyond what the shield arm was ever tested for?
Duly noted--duly ignored.
It was designed to withstand heavy combat--if it can't handle this, I wouldn't have it in the arm-ory.
"Heavy combat" is fighting drone tanks.
You're about to fight a planet, Nathan--
No.

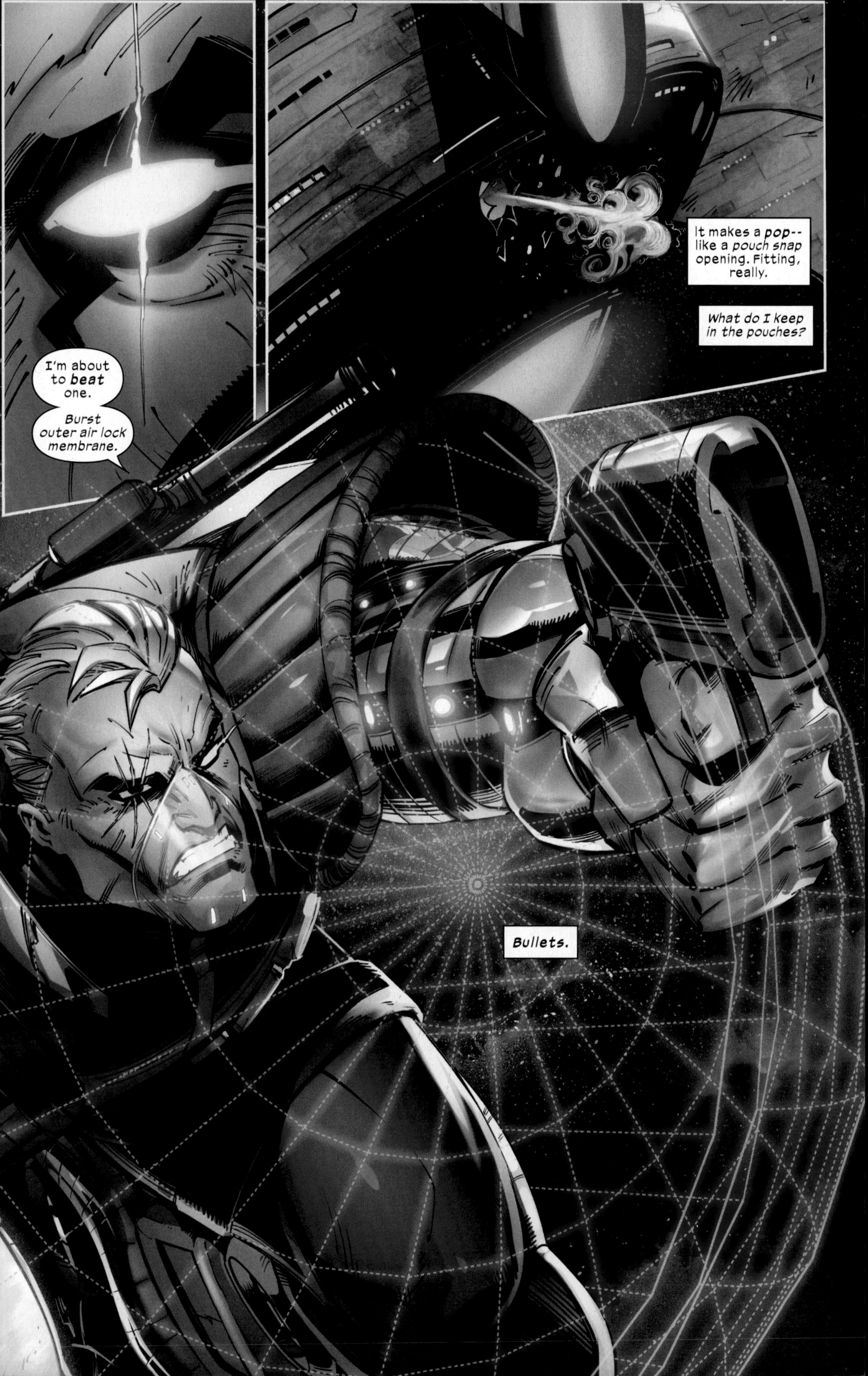
I'm about to **beat** one.
*Burst outer air lock membrane.*
It makes a ***pop***--like a *pouch snap* opening. Fitting, really.
*What do I keep in the pouches?*
*Bullets.*

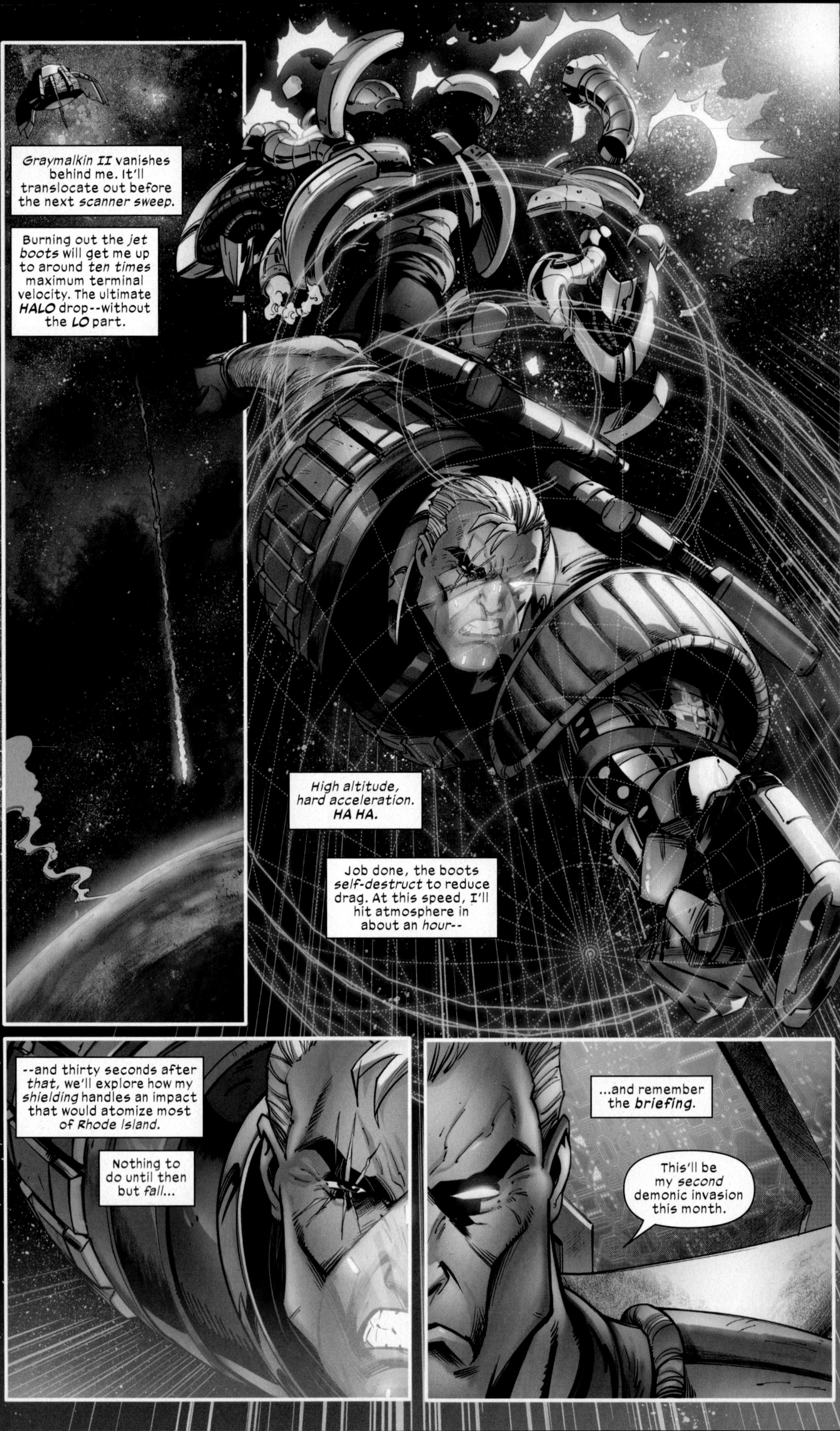

Graymalkin II vanishes behind me. It'll translocate out before the next scanner sweep.
Burning out the jet boots will get me up to around ten times maximum terminal velocity. The ultimate HALO drop--without the LO part.
High altitude, hard acceleration. HA HA.
Job done, the boots self-destruct to reduce drag. At this speed, I'll hit atmosphere in about an hour--
--and thirty seconds after that, we'll explore how my shielding handles an impact that would atomize most of Rhode Island.
Nothing to do until then but fall...
...and remember the briefing.
This'll be my second demonic invasion this month.

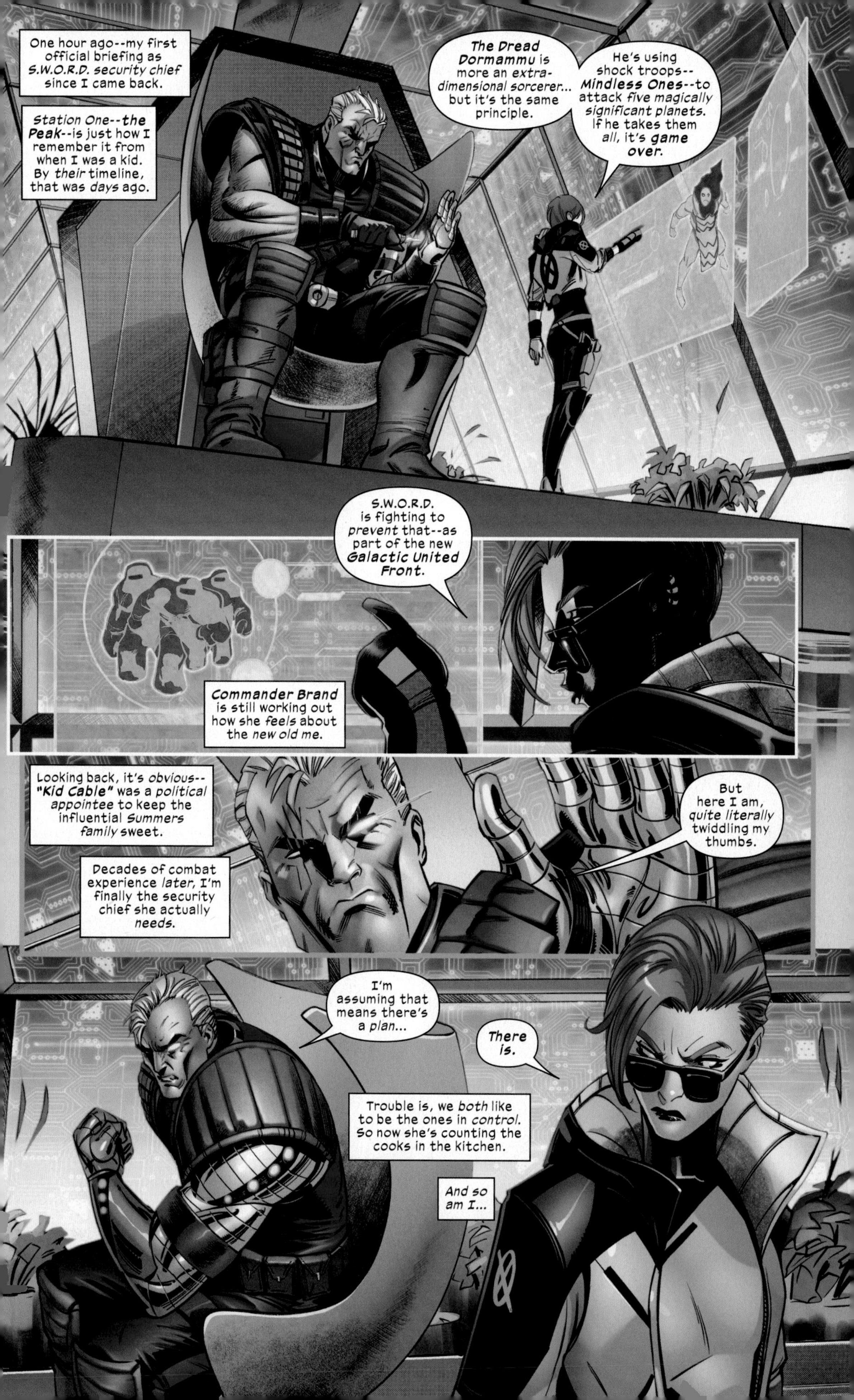
One hour ago--my first official briefing as S.W.O.R.D. security chief since I came back.
Station One--the Peak--is just how I remember it from when I was a kid. By their timeline, that was days ago.
The Dread Dormammu is more an extra-dimensional sorcerer... but it's the same principle.
He's using shock troops--Mindless Ones--to attack five magically significant planets. If he takes them all, it's game over.
S.W.O.R.D. is fighting to prevent that--as part of the new Galactic United Front.
Commander Brand is still working out how she feels about the new old me.
Looking back, it's obvious--"Kid Cable" was a political appointee to keep the influential Summers family sweet.
Decades of combat experience later, I'm finally the security chief she actually needs.
But here I am, quite literally twiddling my thumbs.
I'm assuming that means there's a plan...
There is.
Trouble is, we both like to be the ones in control. So now she's counting the cooks in the kitchen.
And so am I...

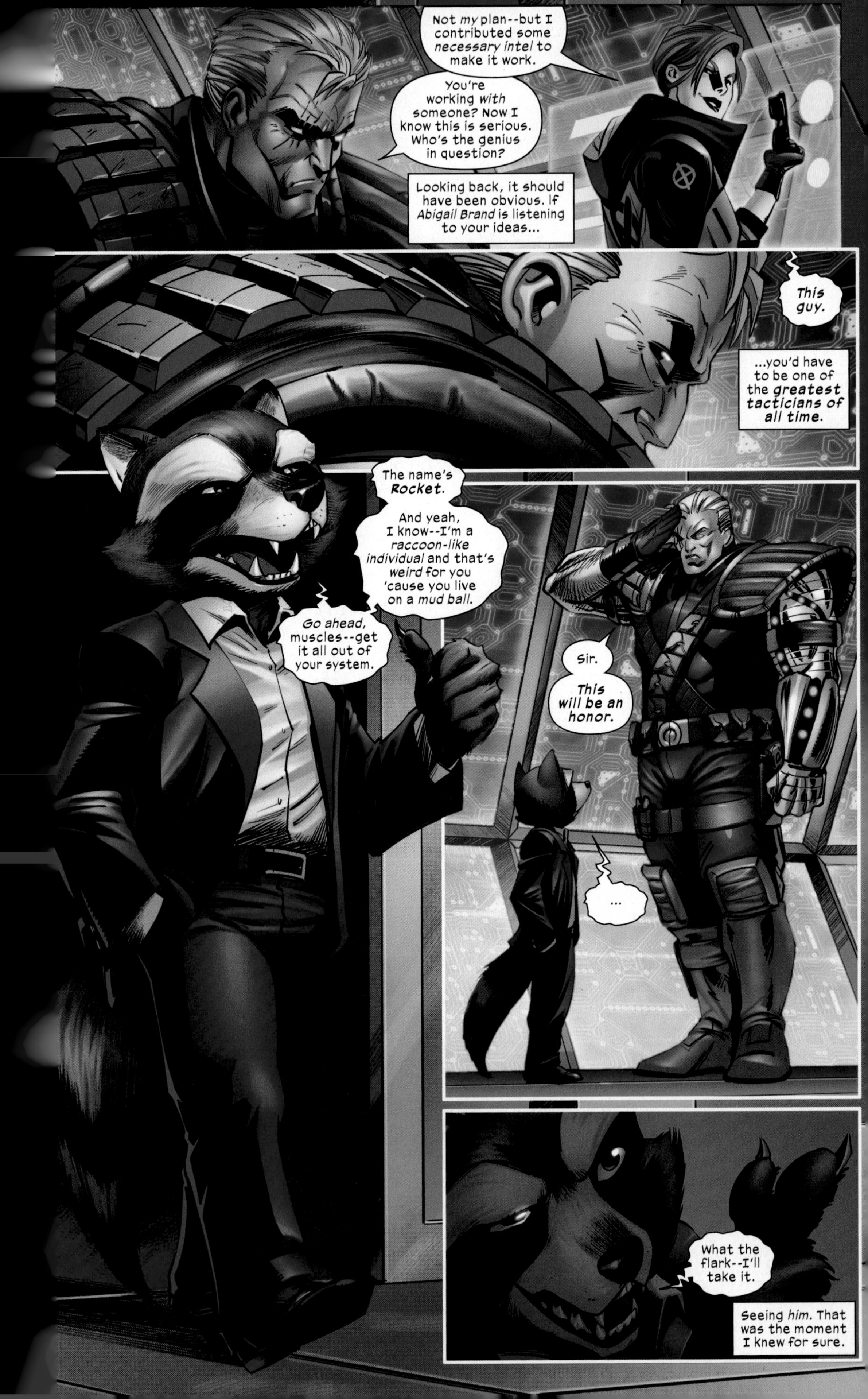
Not my plan--but I contributed some necessary intel to make it work.
You're working with someone? Now I know this is serious. Who's the genius in question?
Looking back, it should have been obvious. If Abigail Brand is listening to your ideas...
This guy.
...you'd have to be one of the greatest tacticians of all time.
The name's Rocket.
And yeah, I know--I'm a raccoon-like individual and that's weird for you 'cause you live on a mud ball.
Go ahead, muscles--get it all out of your system.
Sir.
This will be an honor.
...
What the flark--I'll take it.
Seeing him. That was the moment I knew for sure.

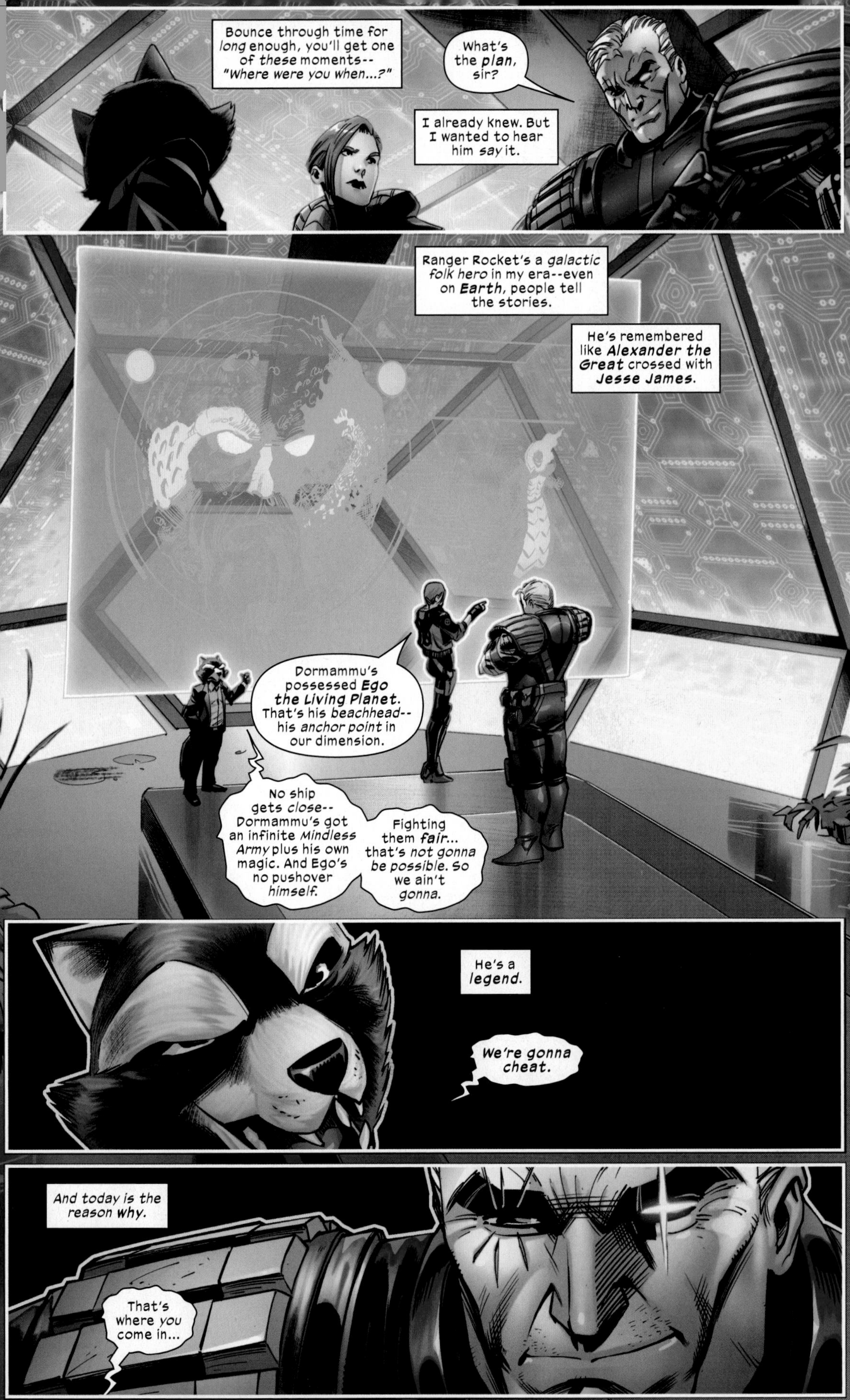

Bounce through time for long enough, you'll get one of these moments-- "Where were you when...?"
What's the plan, sir?
I already knew. But I wanted to hear him say it.
Ranger Rocket's a galactic folk hero in my era--even on Earth, people tell the stories.
He's remembered like Alexander the Great crossed with Jesse James.
Dormammu's possessed Ego the Living Planet. That's his beachhead-- his anchor point in our dimension.
No ship gets close-- Dormammu's got an infinite Mindless Army plus his own magic. And Ego's no pushover himself.
Fighting them fair... that's not gonna be possible. So we ain't gonna.
He's a legend.
We're gonna cheat.
And today is the reason why.
That's where you come in...

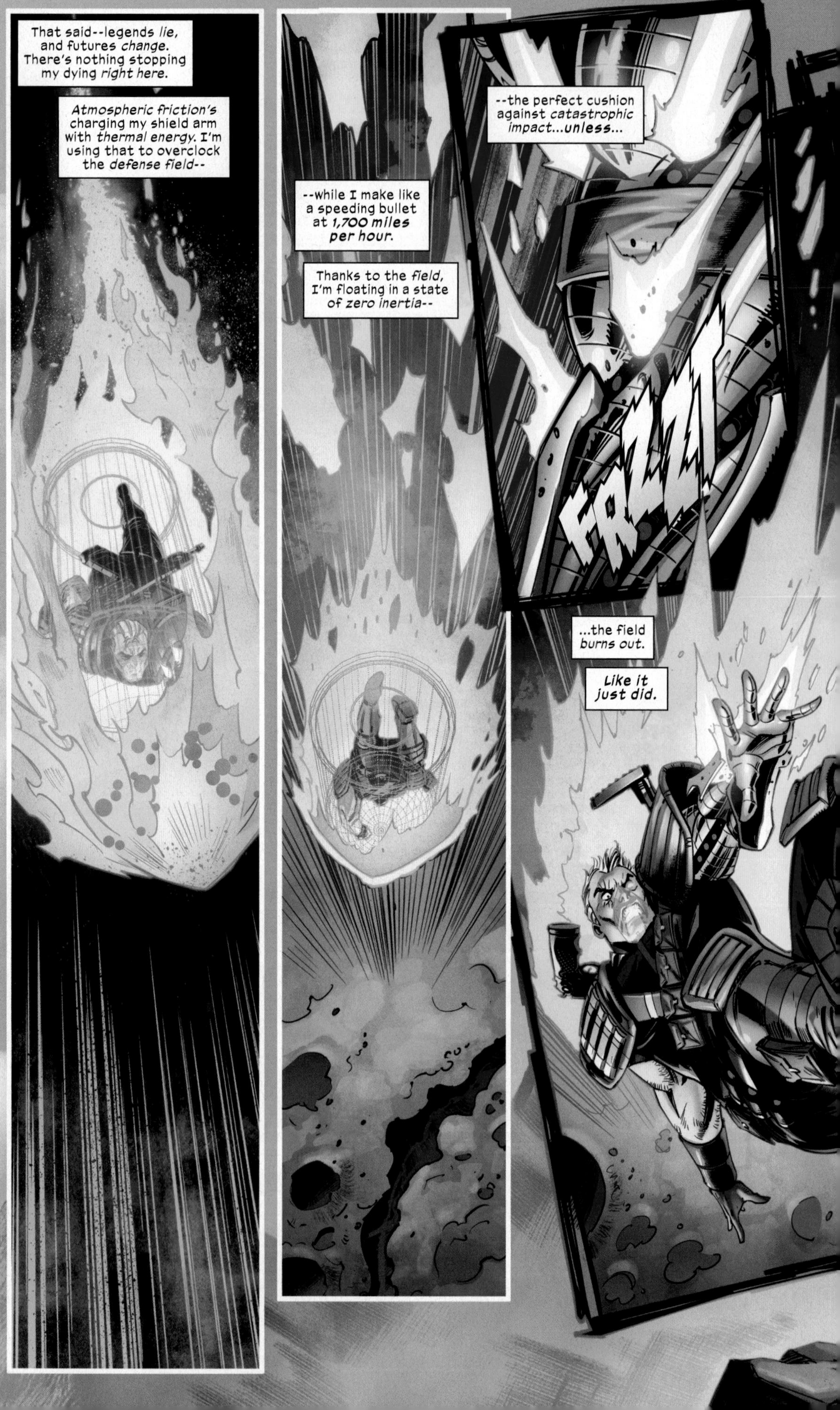
That said--legends lie, and futures change. There's nothing stopping my dying right here.
Atmospheric friction's charging my shield arm with thermal energy. I'm using that to overclock the defense field--
--while I make like a speeding bullet at 1,700 miles per hour.
Thanks to the field, I'm floating in a state of zero inertia--
--the perfect cushion against catastrophic impact...unless...
FRZZT
...the field burns out.
Like it just did.

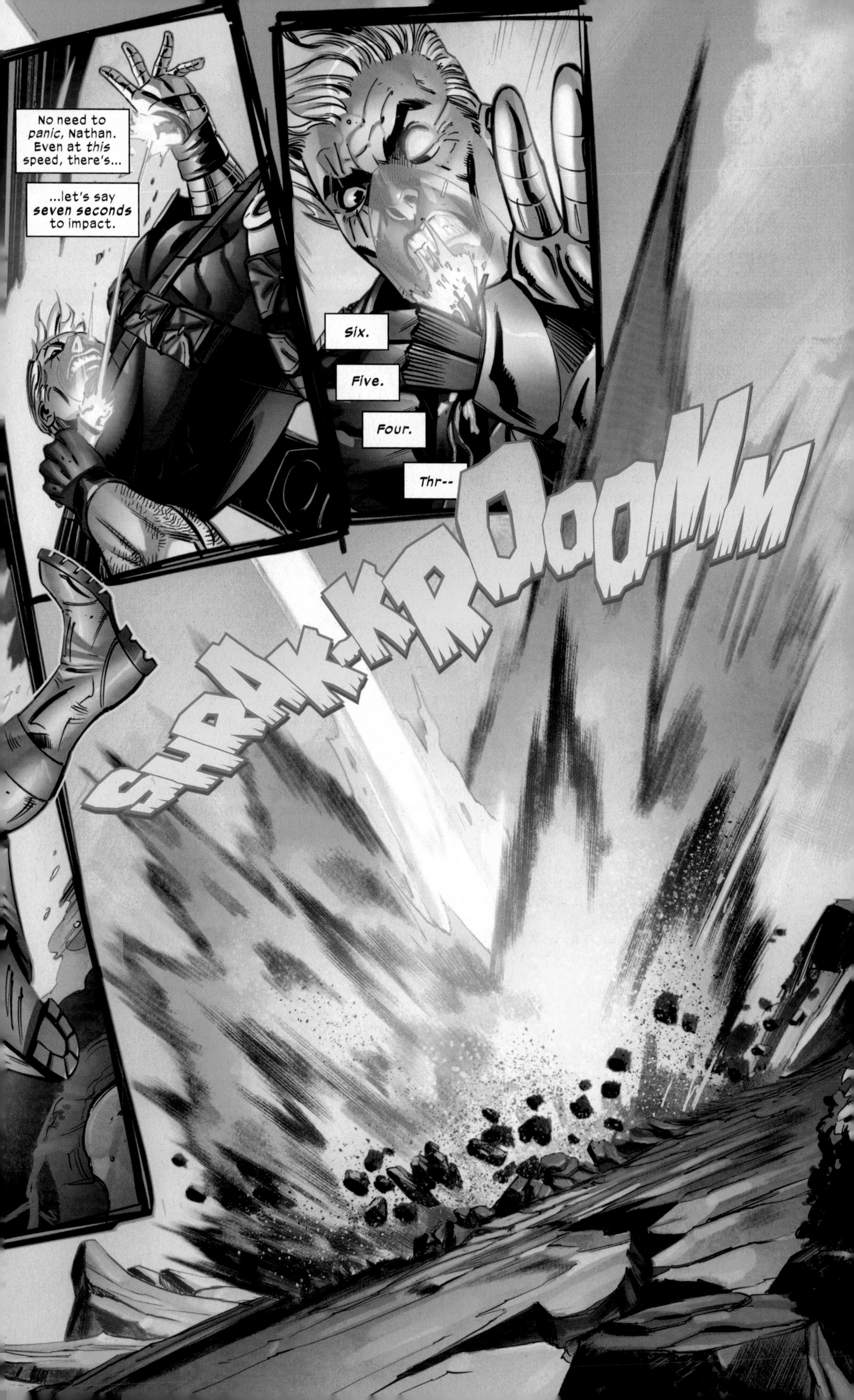

No need to *panic,* Nathan. Even at *this* speed, there's...
...let's say ***seven seconds*** to impact.
*Six.*
*Five.*
*Four.*
*Thr--*
SHRAK-KROOOOMM

# NATHANIEL D. A. SUMMERS::
# PERSONAL LOG Z-1-12 21/6::EYES ONLY

I wish I believed in history.

They say the past is another country. If so, I have a dual passport -- I've lived here for years. I have family here. Friends and loved ones.

And occasionally, as I wander through the country of the past, I'll come across a landmark I recognize.

Right now, I'm living -- again -- through the first Krakoan Age, when history says that mutants conquered Death. And for my sins, I get to live through what the alien civilizations of tomorrow will call the Last Annihilation. I get to be a single thread in the tapestry of a legendary hero.

But legends lie. Futures change. As a time-traveler, I can't afford to believe in history.

For example -- history says that mutants conquered Death.

Death is unconquered.

We've entered into a polite agreement with it, true. An arrangement. An armistice. Death has chosen, in the face of our great cleverness, to turn away from us.

That doesn't mean we won.

Dormammu is out there. While we were terraforming worlds and hosting galas, he was building his power and making his play -- possessing a living planet and turning it into a gateway for an infinite army.

Now those grim, gray, stony bastards are tearing apart Skrull warriors and Kree commandos, Shi'ar Superguardians and Spartoi astronomers. Even -- I am reliably informed by those who know -- the insectoid drones of the Chitauri.

Those people didn't get to sign the armistice. They're not part of the arrangement. They're Death's ace in the hole.

Because with every life lost, we come a little closer to Dormammu's victory.

When Death comes for us all, in a single moment...then we'll find out just how conquered it really is.

I should check the shield arm again. I wish I knew for a fact it wouldn't fail. I wish there were another way to get down there.

Lord, I wish I believed in history.

—

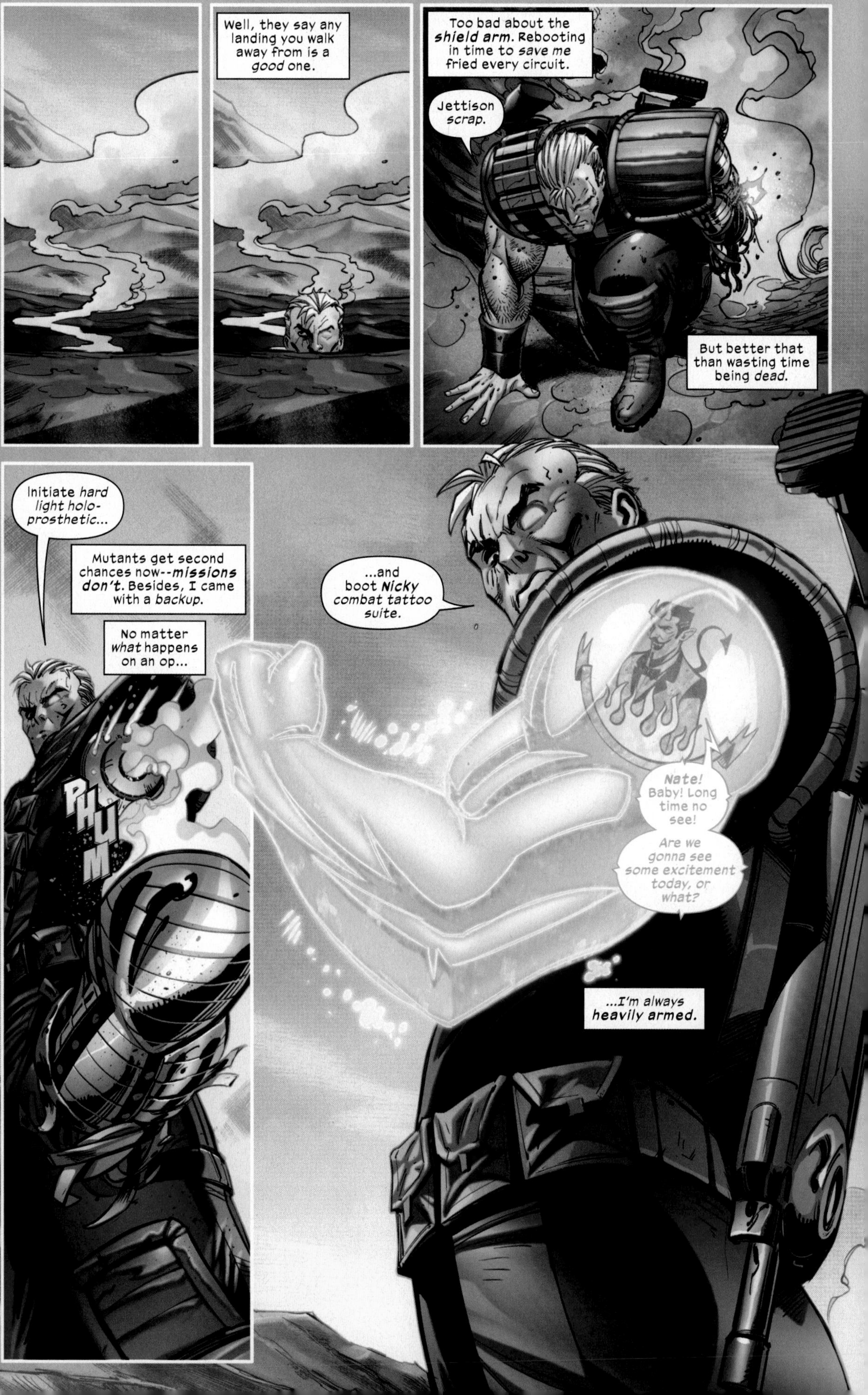

Well, they say any landing you walk away from is a *good* one.
Too bad about the ***shield arm.*** Rebooting in time to *save me* fried every circuit.
Jettison *scrap.*
But better that than wasting time being *dead.*
Initiate *hard light holo-prosthetic...*
Mutants get second chances now--***missions don't.*** Besides, I came with a *backup.*
No matter *what* happens on an op...
PHUM
...and boot ***Nicky*** *combat tattoo suite.*
***Nate!*** Baby! Long time no see!
*Are we gonna see some excitement today, or what?*
*...I'm always* ***heavily armed.***

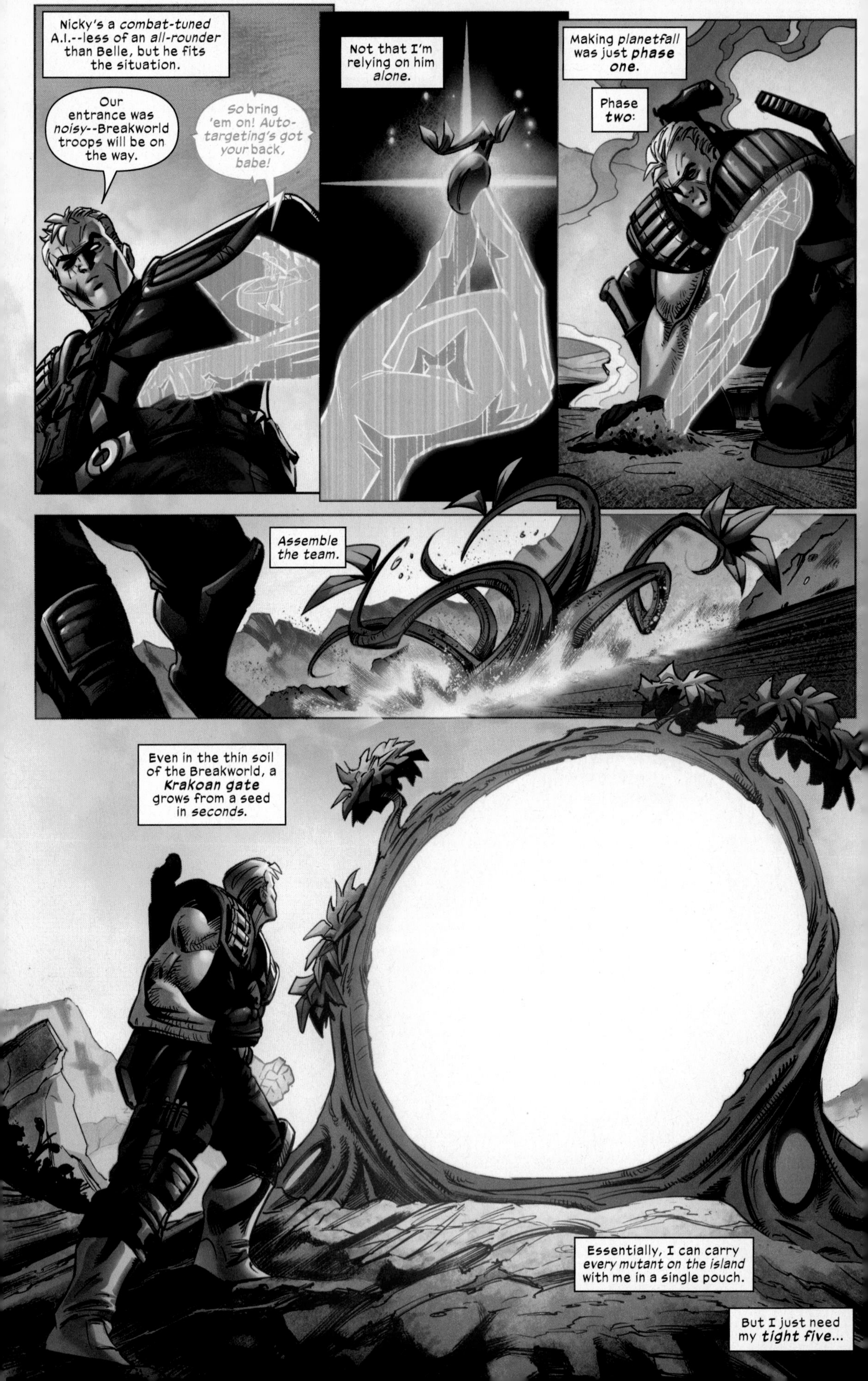
Nicky's a *combat-tuned* A.I.--less of an *all-rounder* than Belle, but he fits the situation.
Our entrance was *noisy*--Breakworld troops will be on the way.
So bring 'em on! Auto-targeting's got *your* back, babe!
Not that I'm relying on him *alone*.
Making *planetfall* was just ***phase one.***
Phase *two*:
Assemble the team.
Even in the thin soil of the Breakworld, a ***Krakoan gate*** grows from a seed in *seconds*.
Essentially, I can carry *every mutant on the island* with me in a single pouch.
But I just need my ***tight five...***

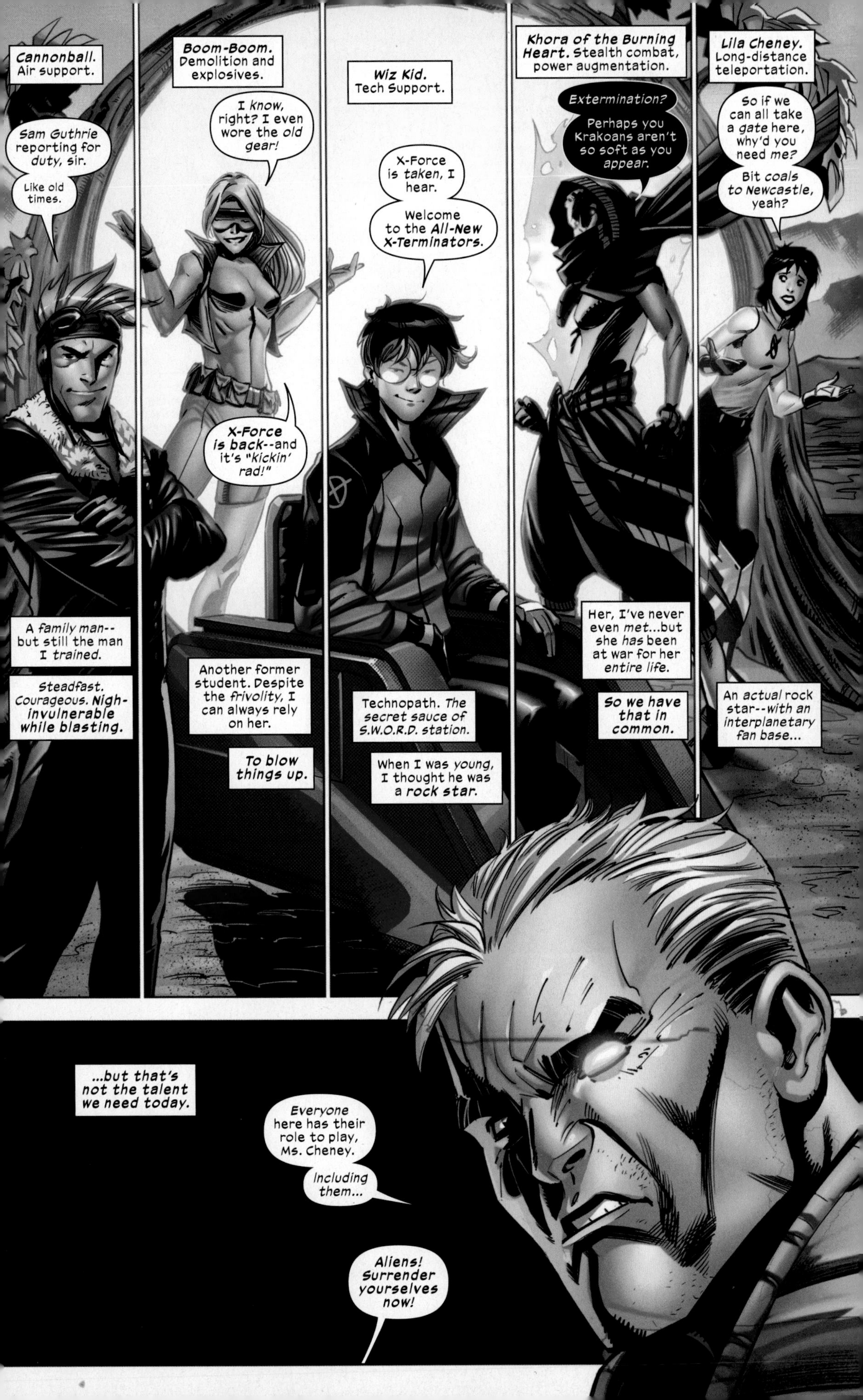

Cannonball. Air support.
Sam Guthrie reporting for duty, sir.
Like old times.
Boom-Boom. Demolition and explosives.
I know, right? I even wore the old gear!
X-Force is back--and it's "kickin' rad!"
Wiz Kid. Tech Support.
X-Force is taken, I hear.
Welcome to the All-New X-Terminators.
Khora of the Burning Heart. Stealth combat, power augmentation.
Extermination?
Perhaps you Krakoans aren't so soft as you appear.
Lila Cheney. Long-distance teleportation.
So if we can all take a gate here, why'd you need me?
Bit coals to Newcastle, yeah?
A family man--but still the man I trained.
Steadfast. Courageous. Nigh-invulnerable while blasting.
Another former student. Despite the frivolity, I can always rely on her.
To blow things up.
Technopath. The secret sauce of S.W.O.R.D. station.
When I was young, I thought he was a rock star.
Her, I've never even met...but she has been at war for her entire life.
So we have that in common.
An actual rock star--with an interplanetary fan base...
...but that's not the talent we need today.
Everyone here has their role to play, Ms. Cheney.
Including them...
Aliens! Surrender yourselves now!

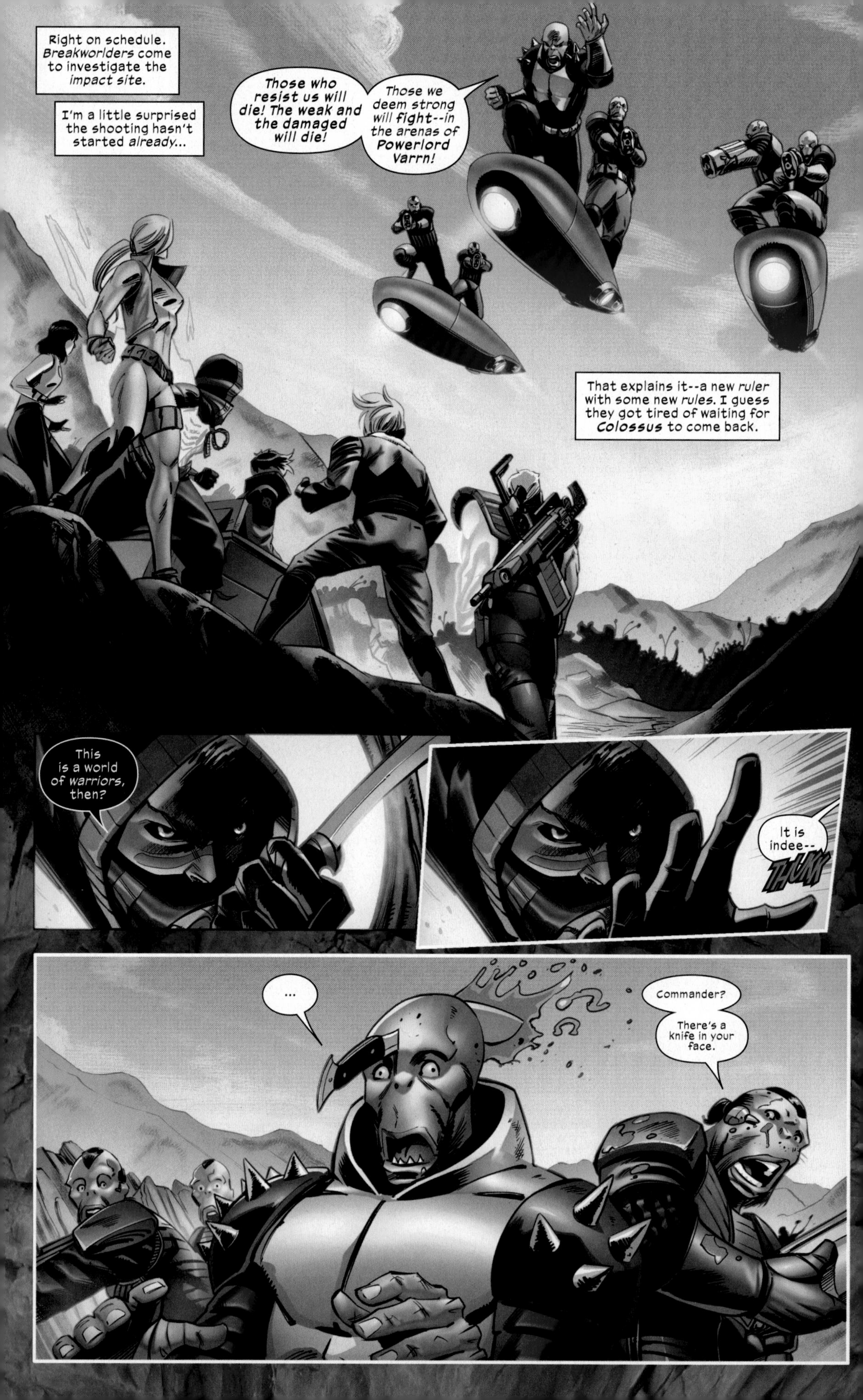
Right on schedule. Breakworlders come to investigate the impact site.
I'm a little surprised the shooting hasn't started already...
Those who resist us will die! The weak and the damaged will die!
Those we deem strong will fight--in the arenas of Powerlord Varrn!
That explains it--a new ruler with some new rules. I guess they got tired of waiting for Colossus to come back.
This is a world of warriors, then?
It is indee--
THUKK
...
Commander?
There's a knife in your face.

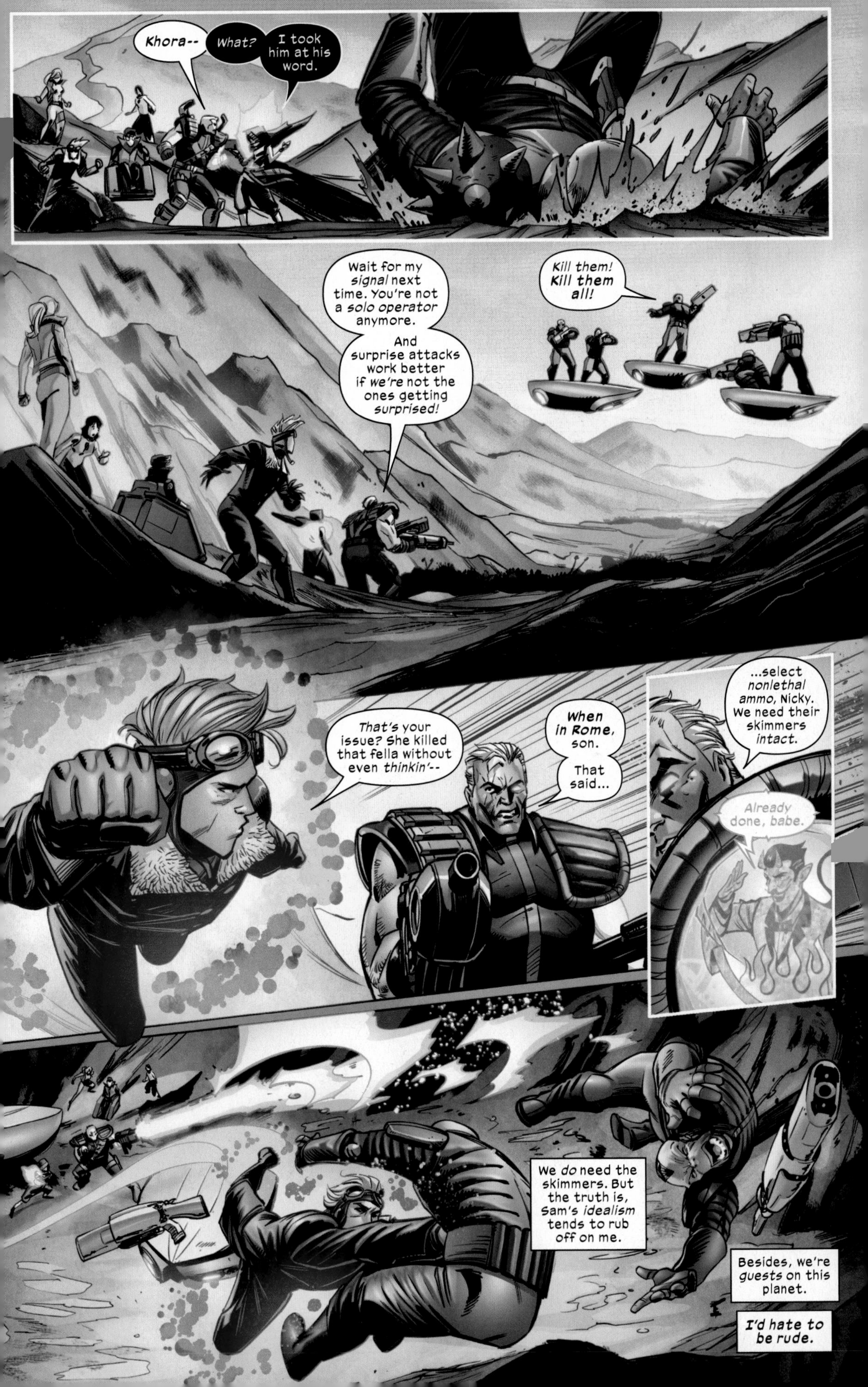

Khora--
What?
I took him at his word.
Wait for my *signal* next time. You're not a *solo operator* anymore.
And surprise attacks work better if *we're* not the ones getting *surprised!*
*Kill them!* **Kill them all!**
*That's* your issue? She killed that fella without even *thinkin'*--
**When in Rome,** son.
That said...
...select *nonlethal* ammo, Nicky. We need their skimmers *intact.*
*Already done, babe.*
We *do* need the skimmers. But the truth is, Sam's *idealism* tends to rub off on me.
Besides, we're *guests* on this planet.
***I'd hate to be rude.***

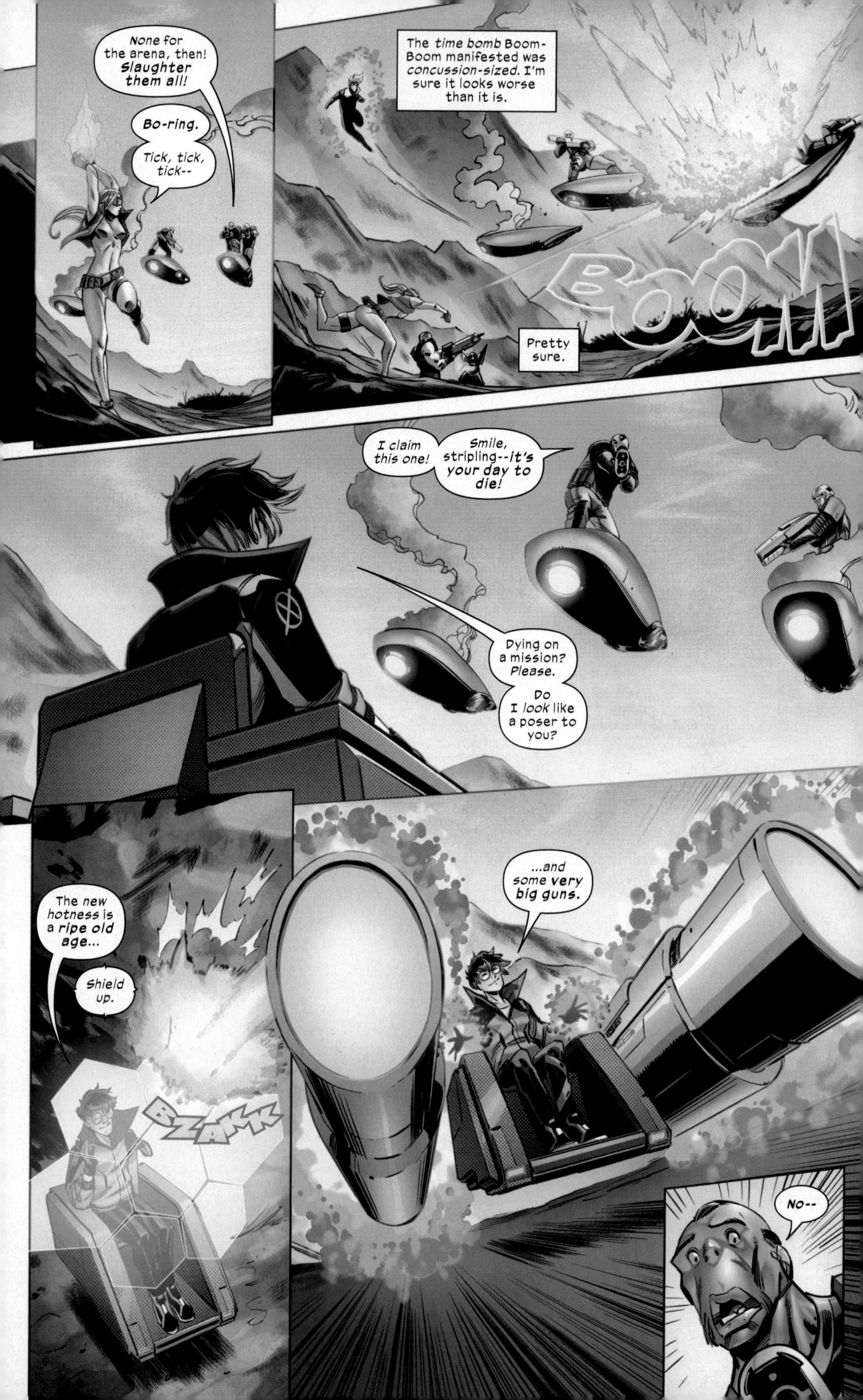
None for the arena, then! Slaughter them all!
Bo-ring.
Tick, tick, tick--
The time bomb Boom-Boom manifested was concussion-sized. I'm sure it looks worse than it is.
BOOM
Pretty sure.
I claim this one!
Smile, stripling--it's your day to die!
Dying on a mission? Please.
Do I look like a poser to you?
The new hotness is a ripe old age...
Shield up.
BZAKK
...and some very big guns.
No--

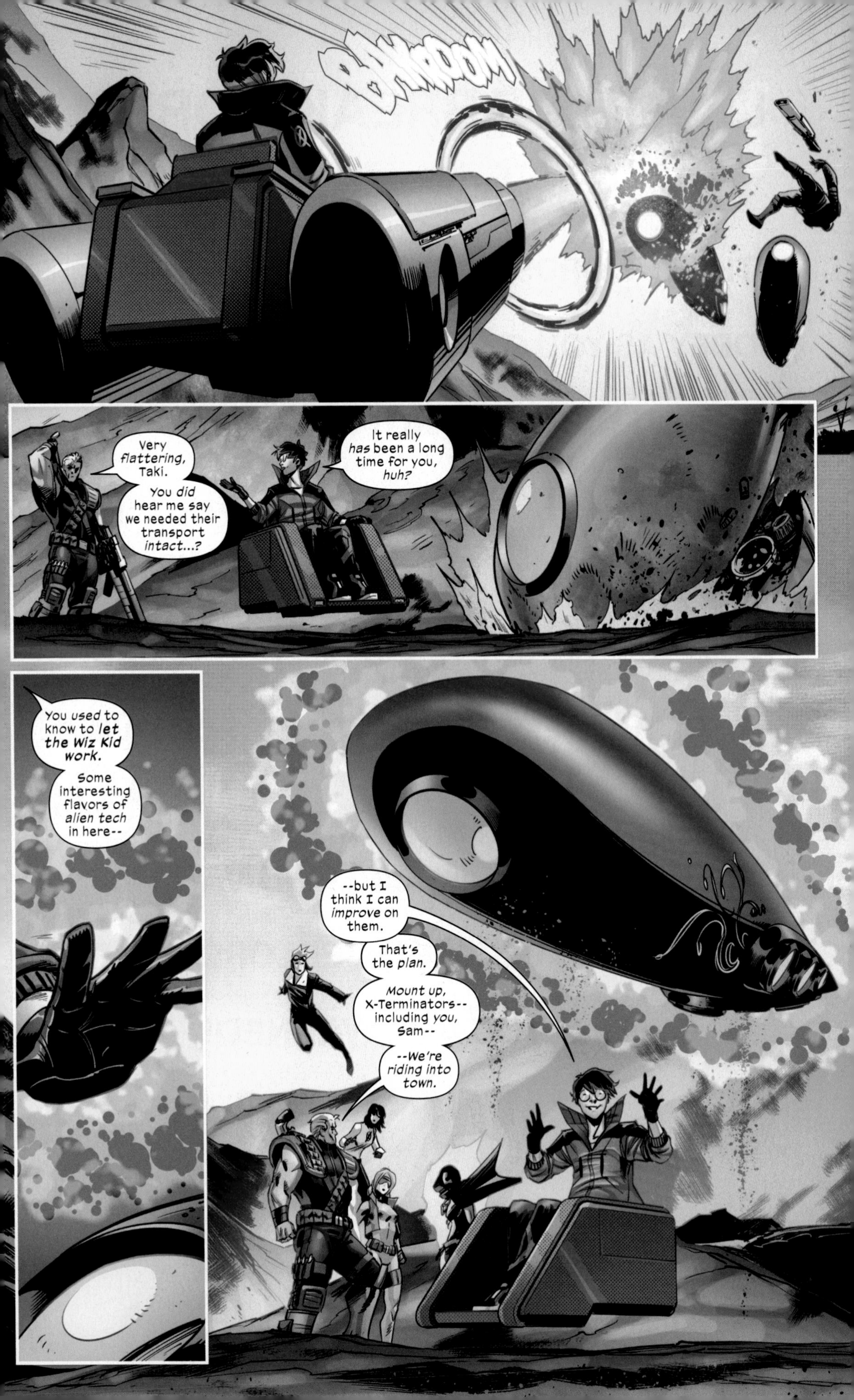
BAKROOM
Very flattering, Taki.
You did hear me say we needed their transport intact...?
It really has been a long time for you, huh?
You used to know to let the Wiz Kid work.
Some interesting flavors of alien tech in here--
--but I think I can improve on them.
That's the plan.
Mount up, X-Terminators-- including you, Sam--
--We're riding into town.

# LIVING OF BREAKWORLD!

## THIS NOTICE IS POWERLORD VARRN!

## THESE WORDS ARE POWERLORD VARRN!

## OBEY AS YOU OBEY POWERLORD VARRN!

## CITY SEVEN IS NOT FOR LIVING!

## TO ENTER CITY SEVEN IS NOT FOR LIVING!

## TO REMAIN IN CITY SEVEN IS NOT FOR LIVING!

## TO LEAVE CITY SEVEN IS ONLY FOR DEAD!

## THOSE WHO PERFORM ACTS NOT FOR LIVING
# WILL BE MADE DEAD!

## SO DECREES POWERLORD VARRN!

## OBEY AS YOU OBEY POWERLORD VARRN!

## NOW YOU ARE WARNED!

# NOW YOU
# OBEY!

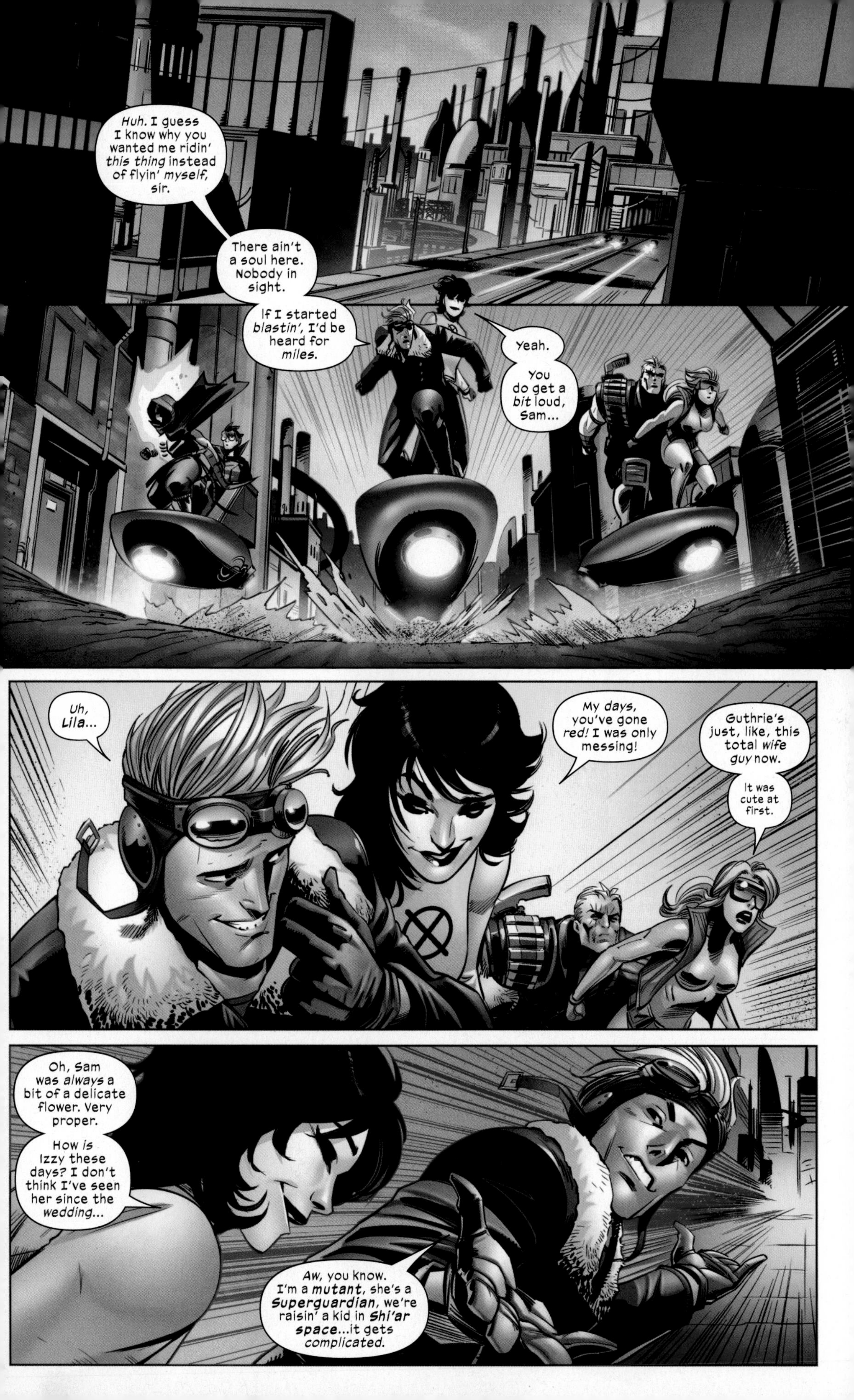

Huh. I guess I know why you wanted me ridin' this thing instead of flyin' myself, sir.
There ain't a soul here. Nobody in sight.
If I started blastin', I'd be heard for miles.
Yeah.
You do get a bit loud, Sam...
Uh, Lila...
My days, you've gone red! I was only messing!
Guthrie's just, like, this total wife guy now.
It was cute at first.
Oh, Sam was always a bit of a delicate flower. Very proper.
How is Izzy these days? I don't think I've seen her since the wedding...
Aw, you know. I'm a mutant, she's a Superguardian, we're raisin' a kid in Shi'ar space...it gets complicated.

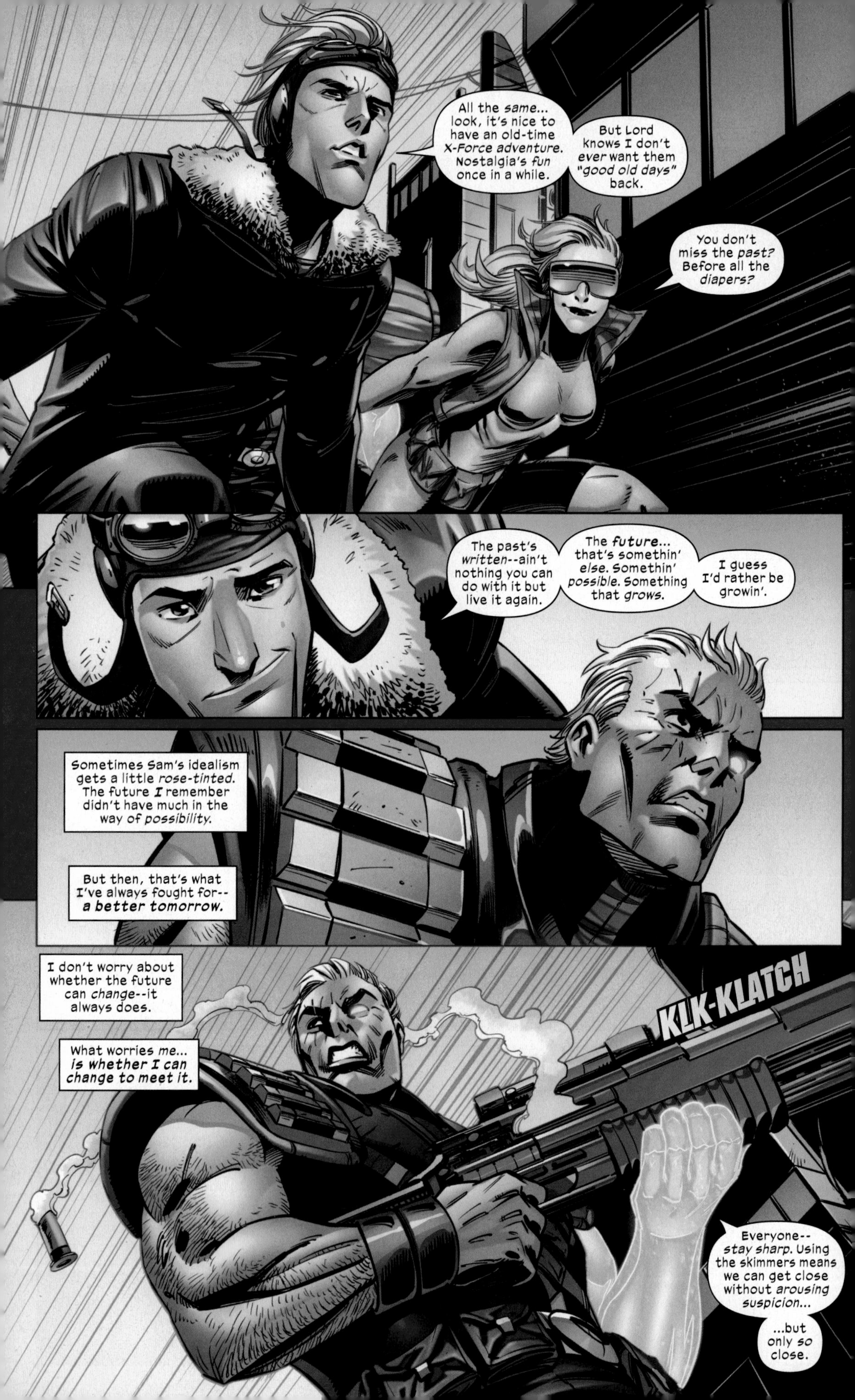

All the *same*... look, it's nice to have an old-time *X-Force adventure*. Nostalgia's *fun* once in a while.
But Lord knows I don't *ever* want them *"good old days"* back.
You don't miss the *past*? Before all the *diapers*?
The past's *written*--ain't nothing you can do with it but live it again.
The ***future***... that's somethin' *else*. Somethin' *possible*. Something that *grows*.
I guess I'd rather be growin'.
Sometimes Sam's idealism gets a little *rose-tinted*. The future ***I*** remember didn't have much in the way of *possibility*.
But then, that's what I've always fought for-- ***a better tomorrow.***
I don't worry about whether the future can *change*--it always does.
What worries *me*... ***is whether I can change to meet it.***
KLK-KLATCH
Everyone-- *stay sharp*. Using the skimmers means we can get close without *arousing suspicion*...
...but only so close.

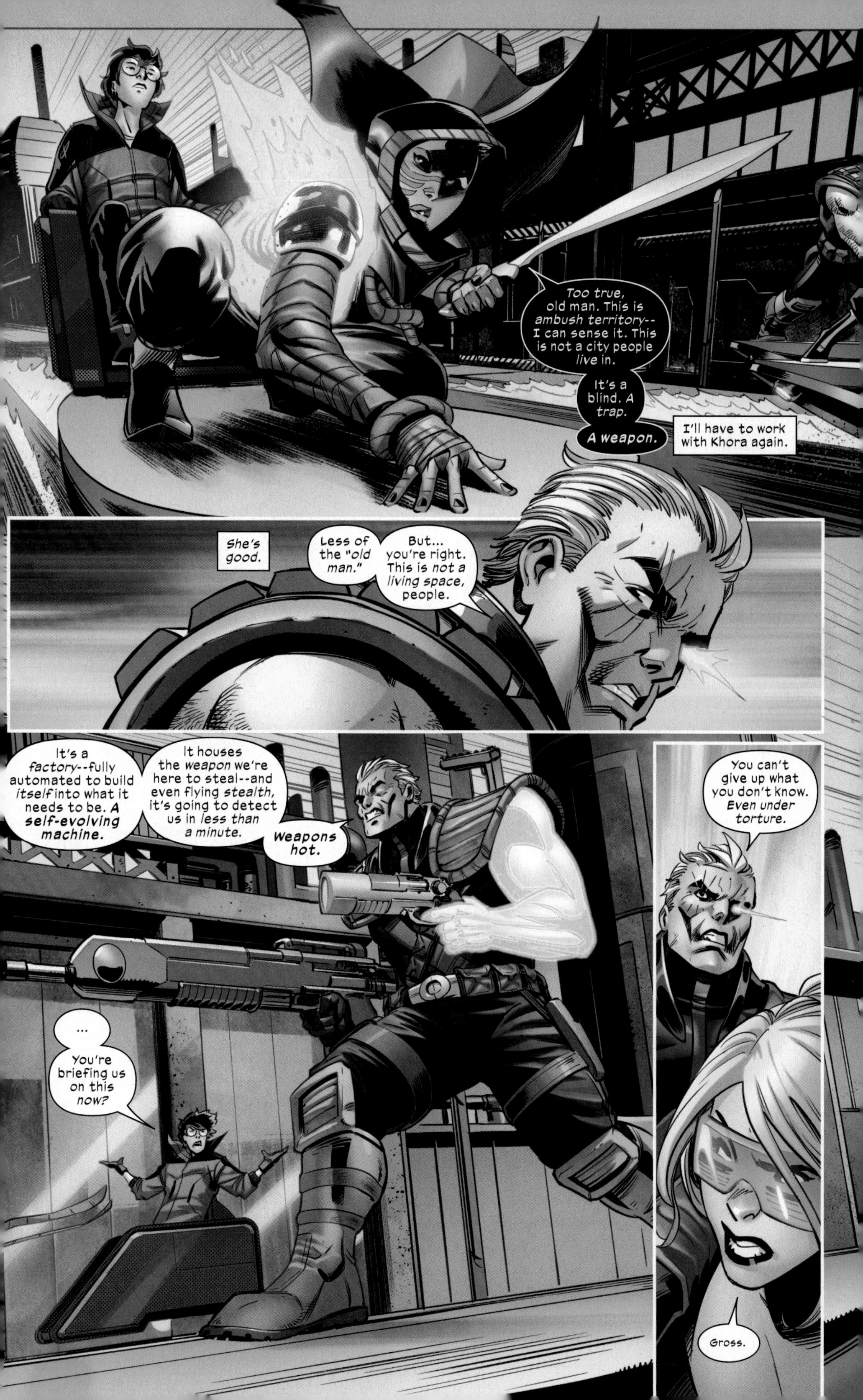

Too true, old man. This is ambush territory--I can sense it. This is not a city people live in.
It's a blind. A trap.
A weapon.
I'll have to work with Khora again.
She's good.
Less of the "old man."
But... you're right. This is not a living space, people.
It's a factory--fully automated to build itself into what it needs to be. A self-evolving machine.
It houses the weapon we're here to steal--and even flying stealth, it's going to detect us in less than a minute.
Weapons hot.
...
You're briefing us on this now?
You can't give up what you don't know. Even under torture.
Gross.

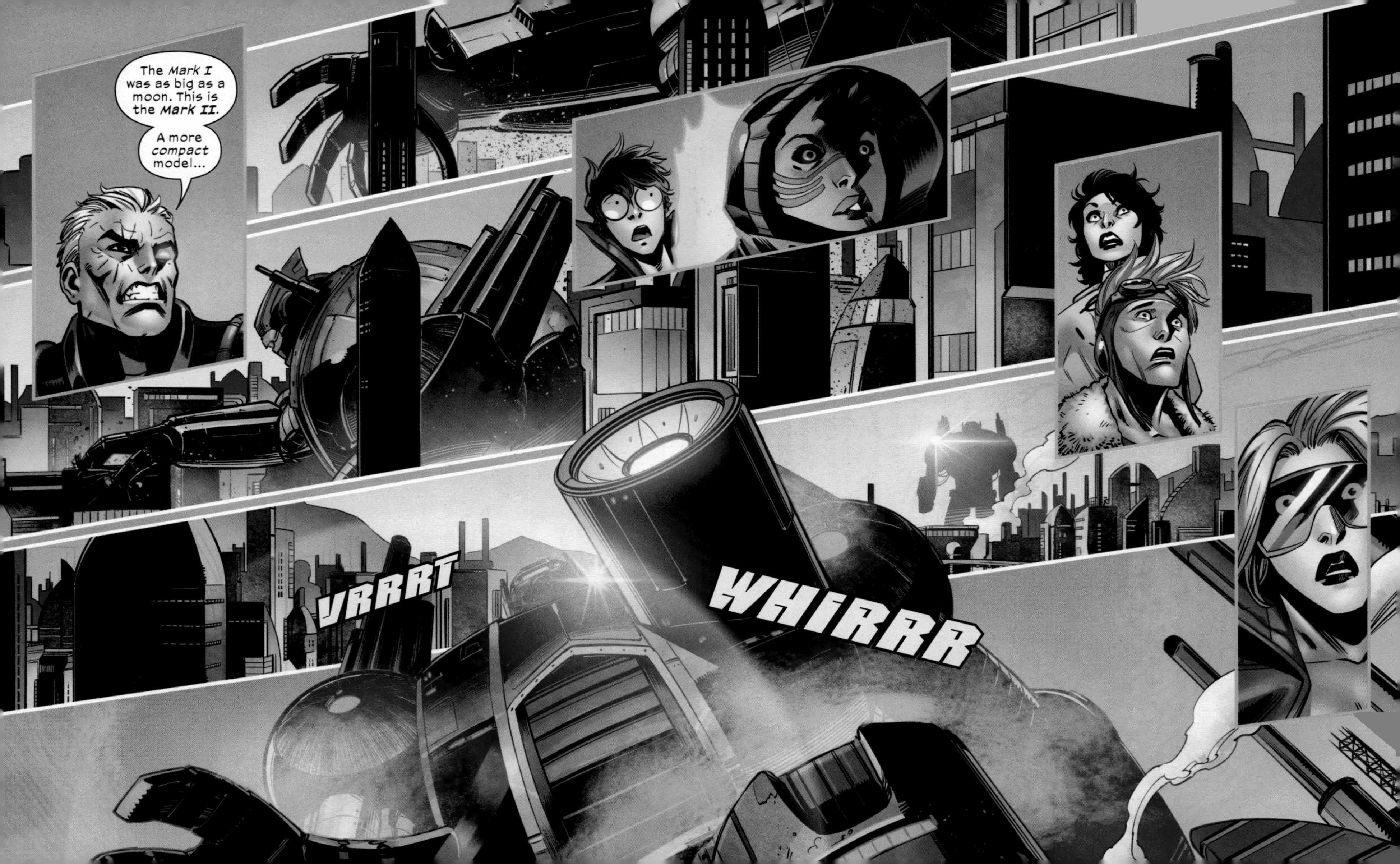
The *Mark I* was as big as a moon. This is the ***Mark II***.
A more *compact* model...
VRRRT
WHIRRR

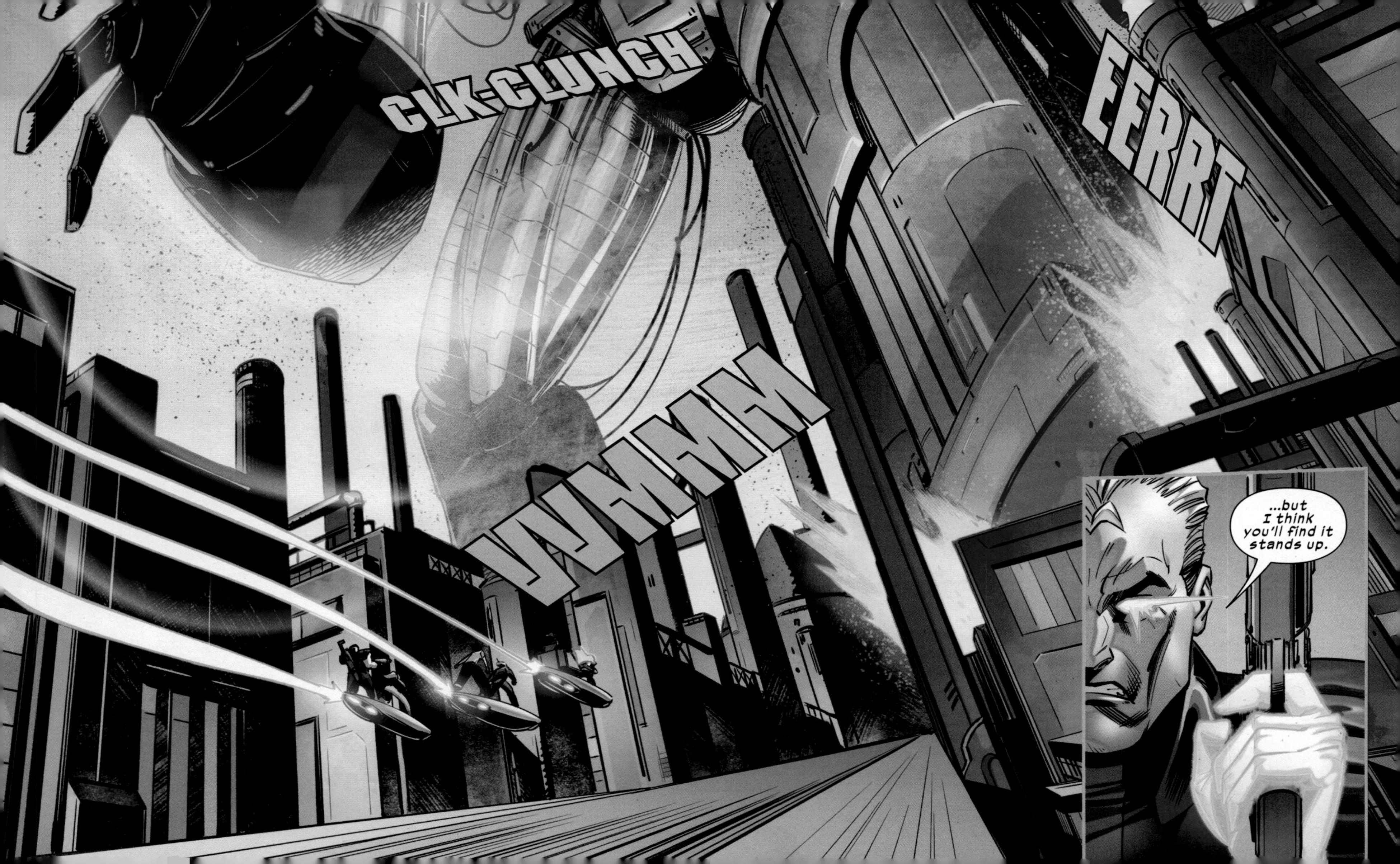
CLK-CLUNCH
EERRT
VVMMMM
...but I think you'll find it stands up.

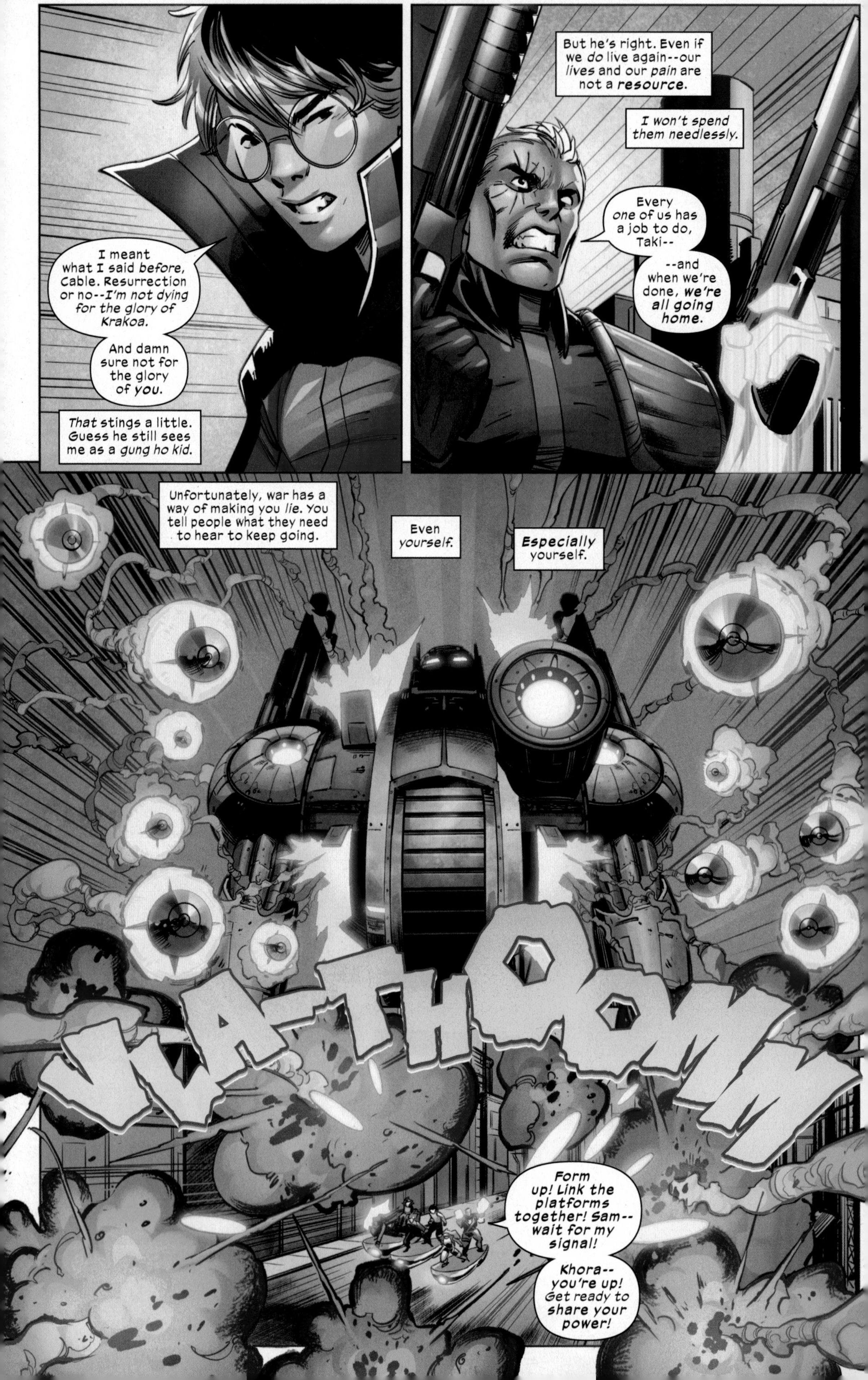

I meant what I said *before*, Cable. Resurrection or no--*I'm not dying for the glory of Krakoa.*
And damn sure not for the glory of *you.*
*That* stings a little. Guess he still sees me as a *gung ho kid.*
But he's right. Even if we *do* live again--our *lives* and our *pain* are not a ***resource.***
*I won't spend them needlessly.*
Every one of us has a job to do, Taki--
--and when we're done, ***we're all going home.***
Unfortunately, war has a way of making you *lie*. You tell people what they need to hear to keep going.
Even *yourself.*
***Especially*** yourself.
VA-THOOM
*Form up! Link the platforms together! Sam--wait for my signal!*
*Khora--you're up! Get ready to share your power!*

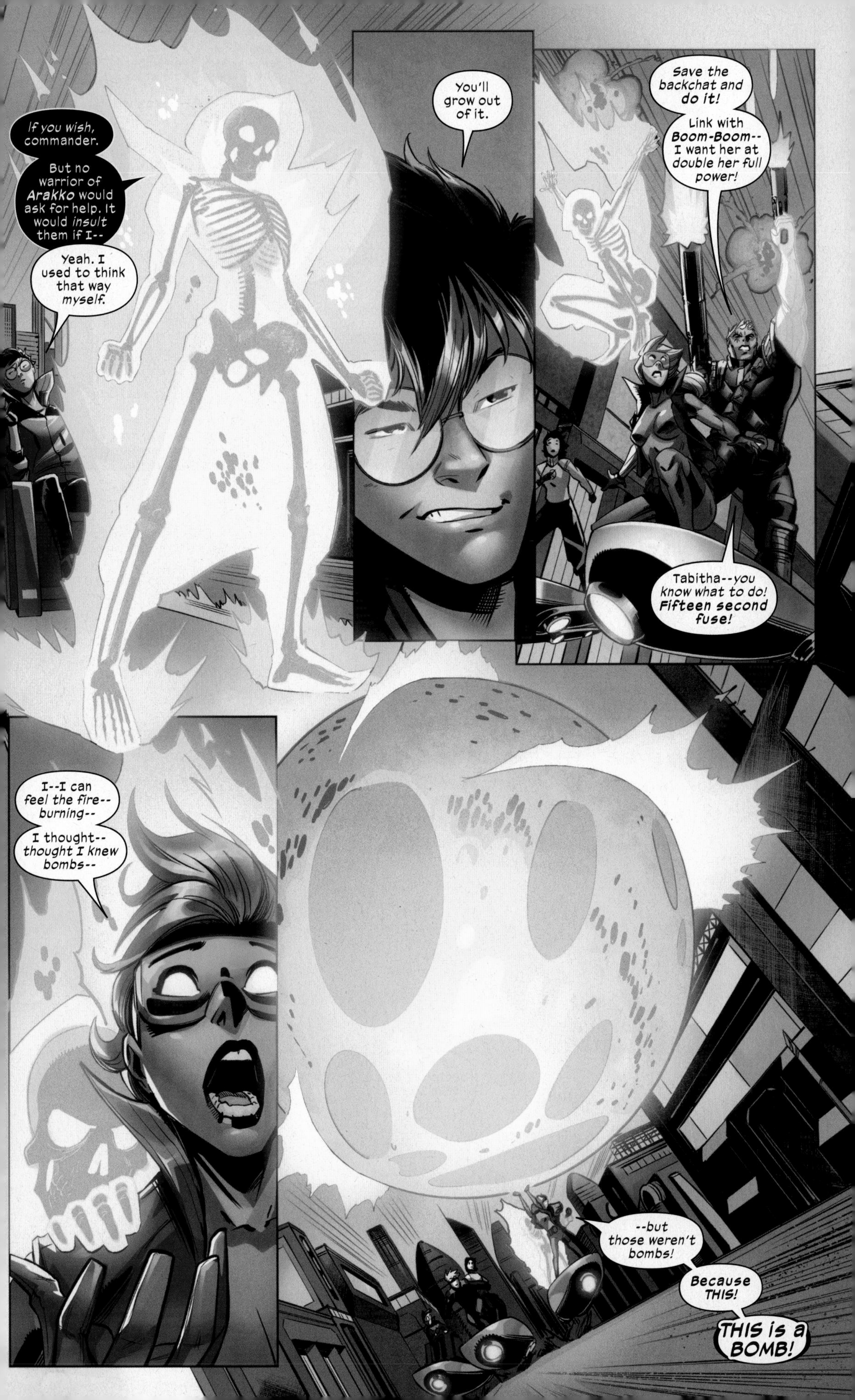

If you wish, commander.
But no warrior of Arakko would ask for help. It would insult them if I--
Yeah. I used to think that way myself.
You'll grow out of it.
Save the backchat and do it!
Link with Boom-Boom-- I want her at double her full power!
Tabitha--you know what to do! Fifteen second fuse!
I--I can feel the fire-- burning--
I thought-- thought I knew bombs--
--but those weren't bombs!
Because THIS!
THIS is a BOMB!

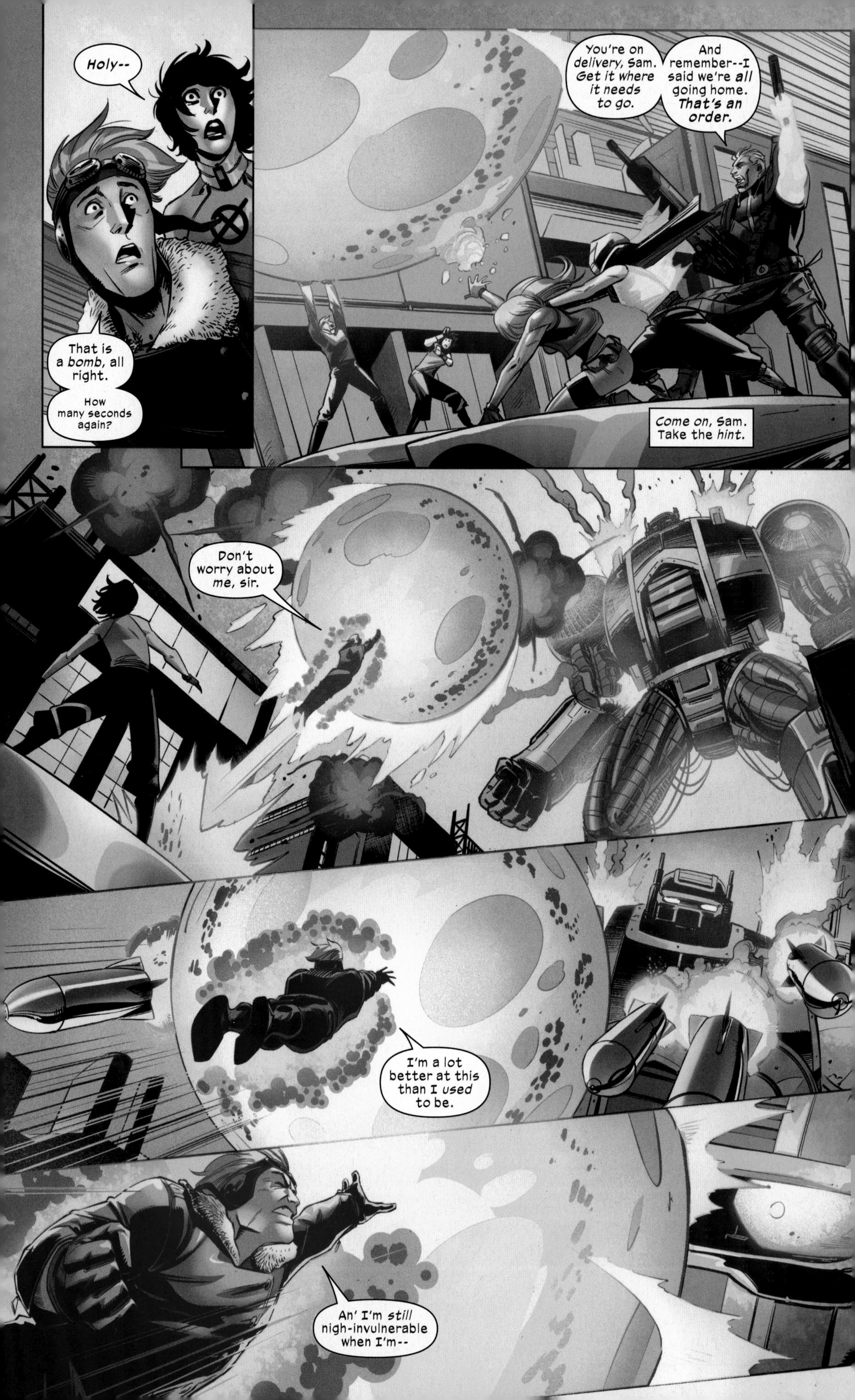
Holy--
That is a *bomb,* all right.
How many seconds again?
You're on delivery, Sam. Get it where it needs to go.
And remember--I said we're *all* going home. *That's an order.*
Come on, Sam. Take the *hint.*
Don't worry about *me,* sir.
I'm a lot better at this than I *used* to be.
An' I'm *still* nigh-invulnerable when I'm--

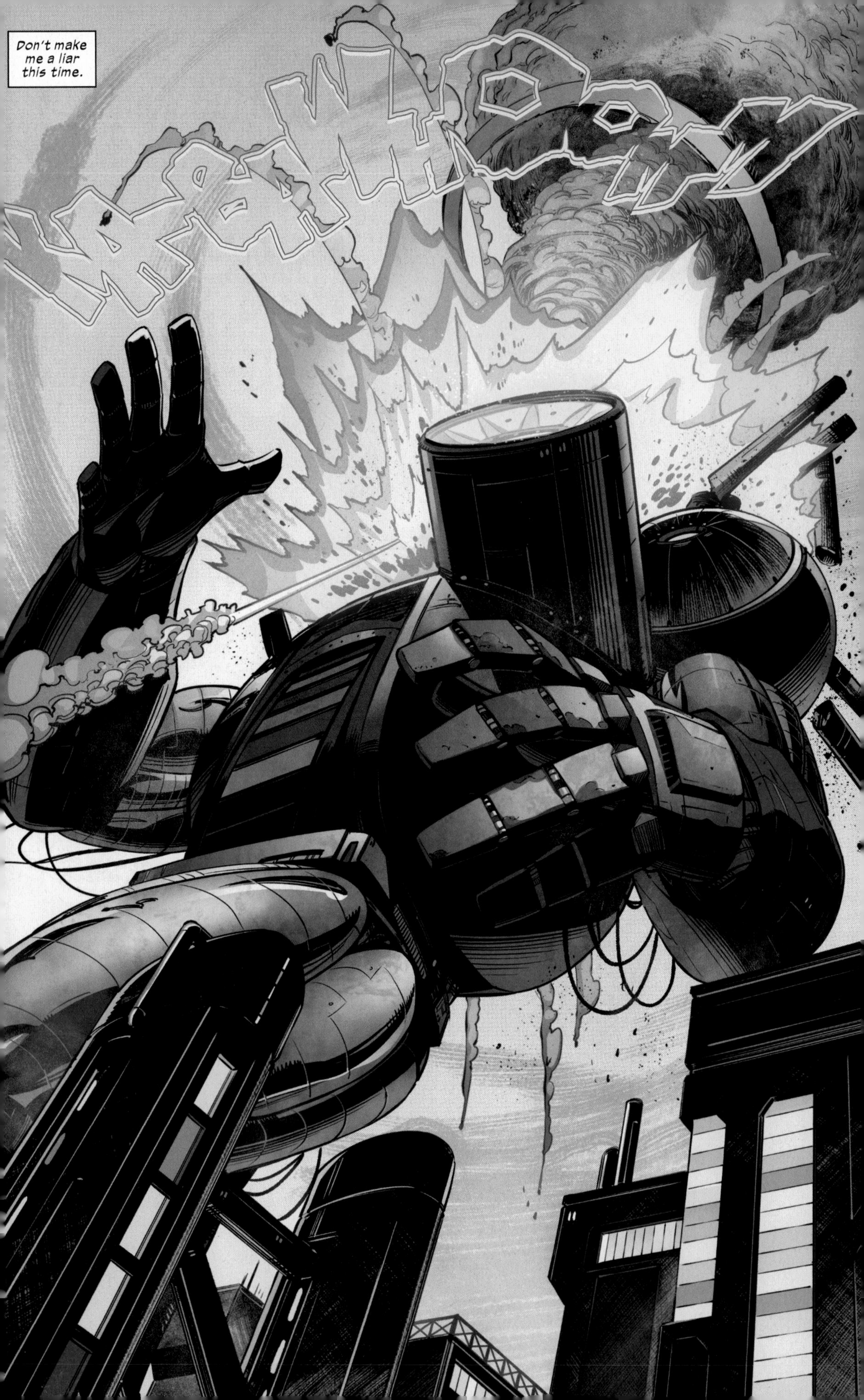
Don't make me a liar this time.

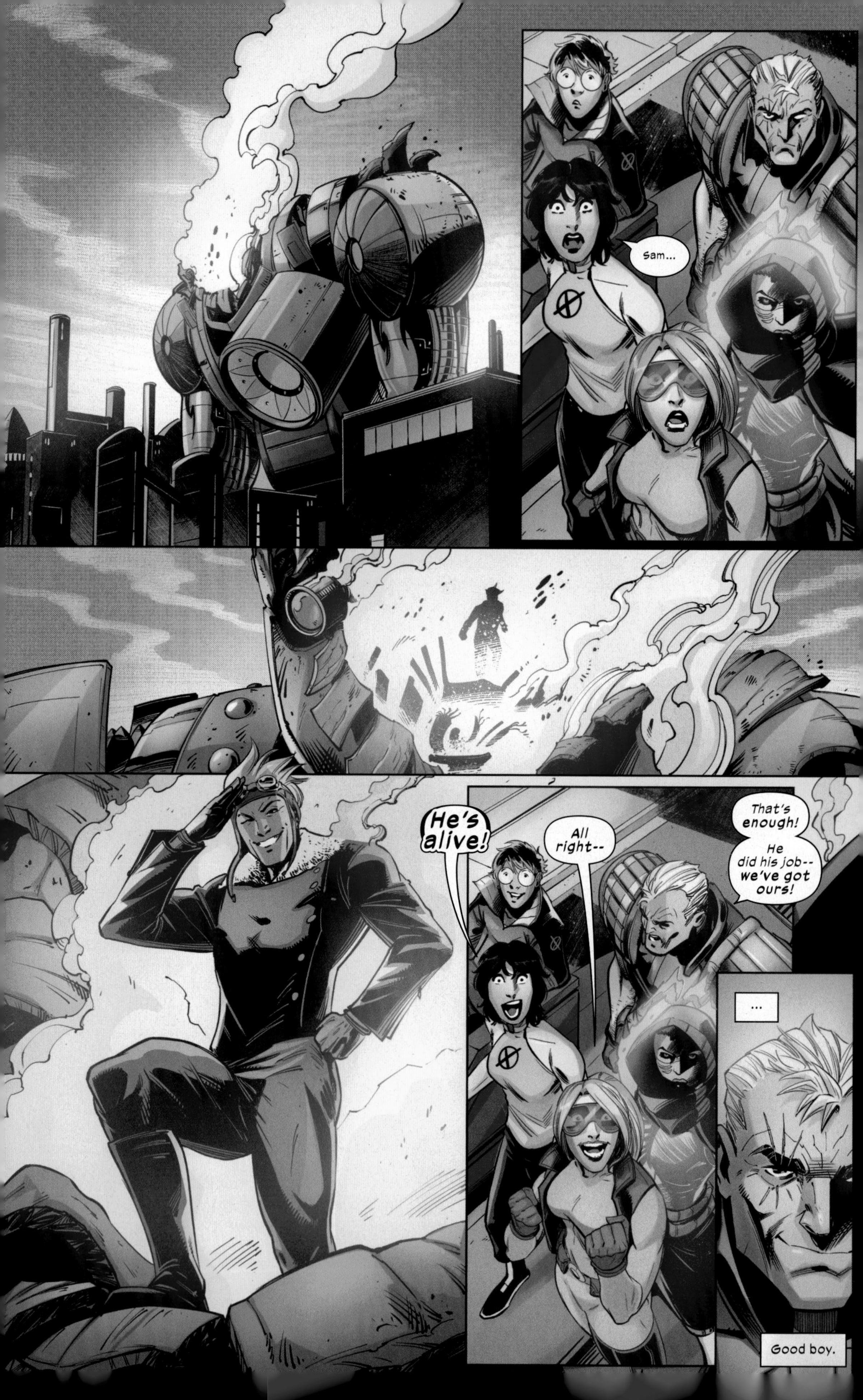
Sam...
He's alive!
All right--
That's enough!
He did his job-- we've got ours!
...
Good boy.

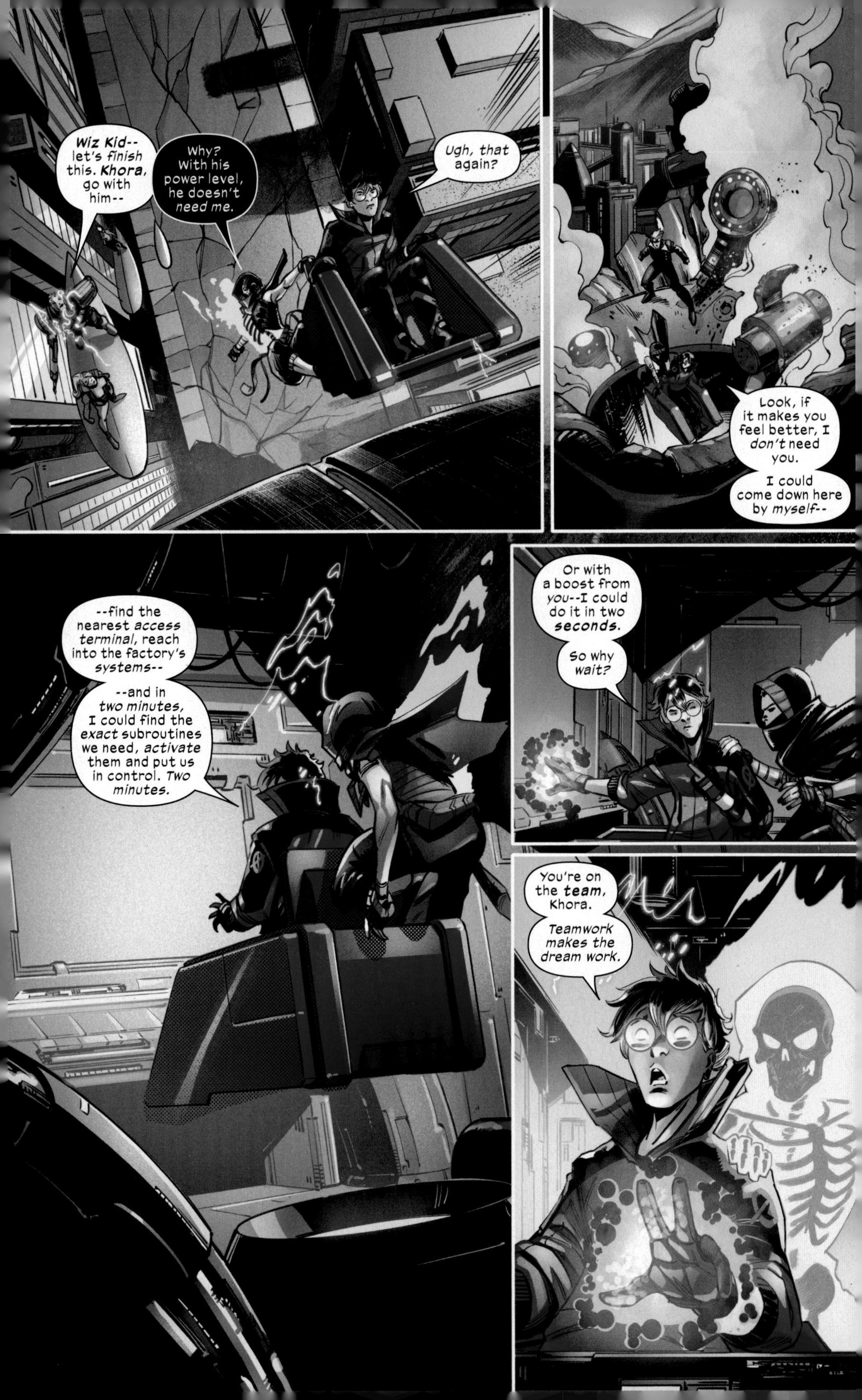

Wiz Kid-- let's finish this. Khora, go with him--
Why? With his power level, he doesn't need me.
Ugh, that again?
Look, if it makes you feel better, I don't need you.
I could come down here by myself--
--find the nearest access terminal, reach into the factory's systems--
--and in two minutes, I could find the exact subroutines we need, activate them and put us in control. Two minutes.
Or with a boost from you--I could do it in two seconds.
So why wait?
You're on the team, Khora.
Teamwork makes the dream work.

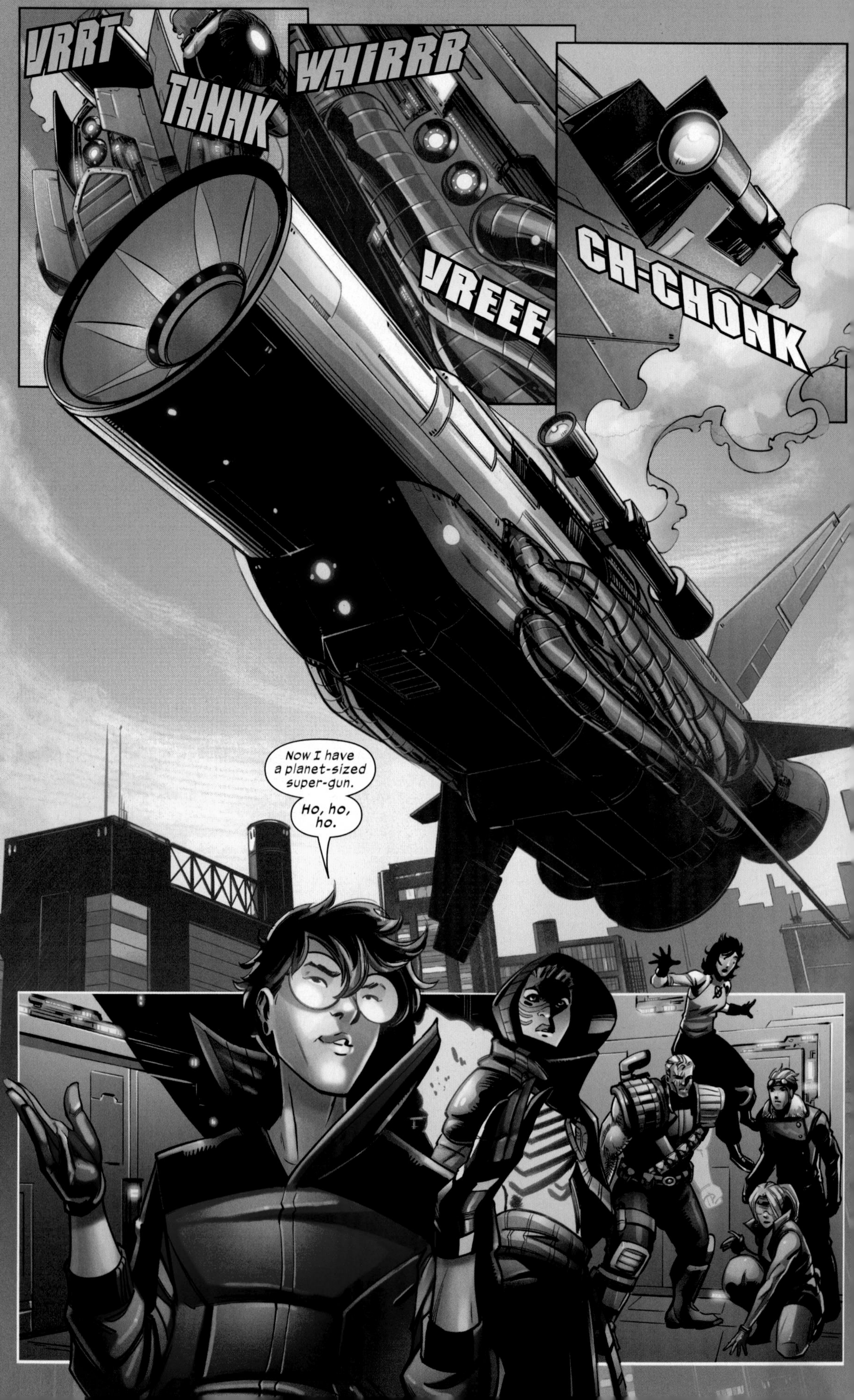

VRRT
THNNK
WHIRRR
VREEE
CH-CHONK
Now I have a planet-sized super-gun.
Ho, ho, ho.

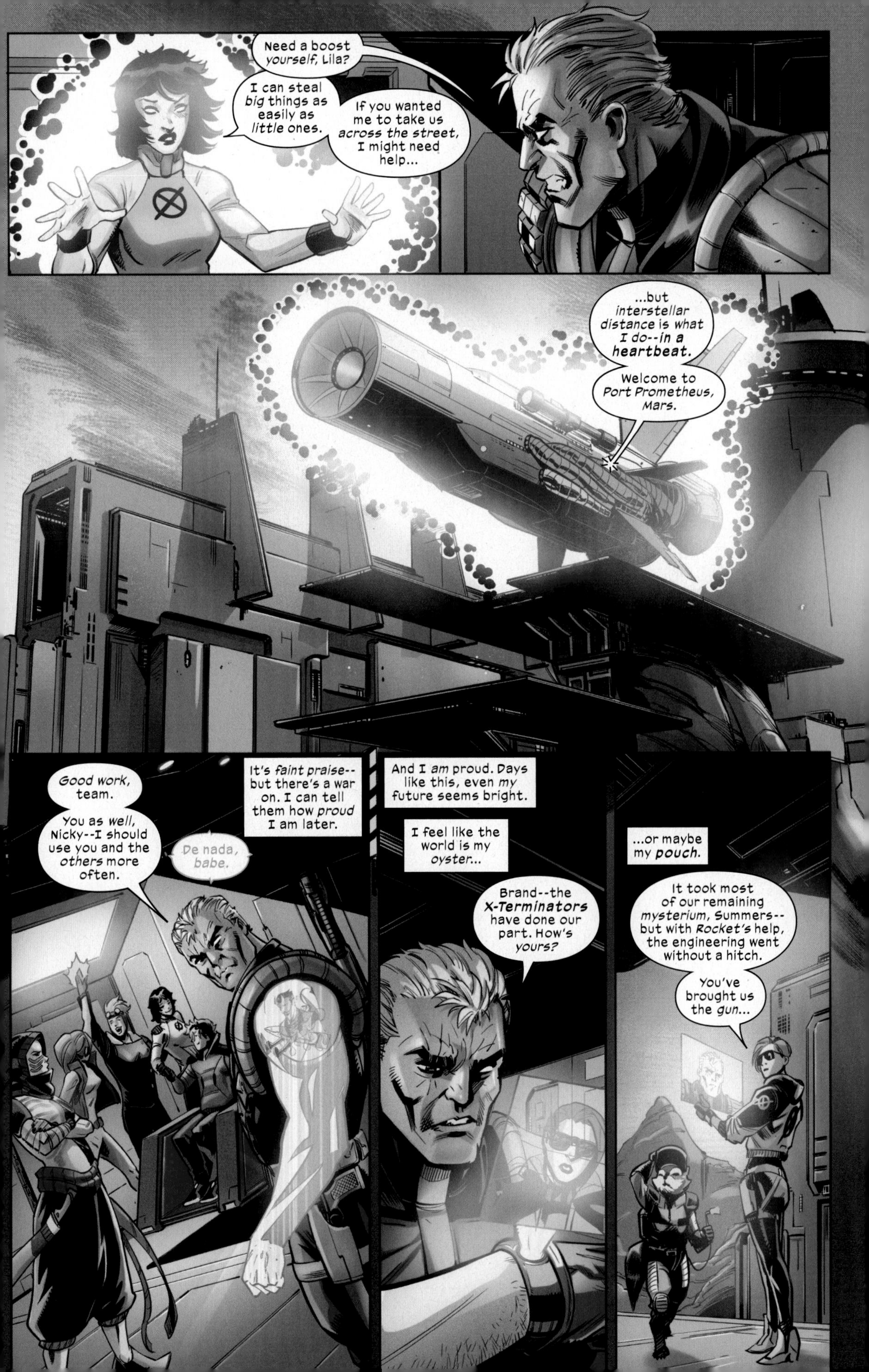
Need a boost yourself, Lila?
I can steal big things as easily as little ones.
If you wanted me to take us across the street, I might need help...
...but interstellar distance is what I do--in a heartbeat.
Welcome to Port Prometheus, Mars.
Good work, team.
You as well, Nicky--I should use you and the others more often.
It's faint praise--but there's a war on. I can tell them how proud I am later.
De nada, babe.
And I am proud. Days like this, even my future seems bright.
I feel like the world is my oyster...
Brand--the X-Terminators have done our part. How's yours?
...or maybe my pouch.
It took most of our remaining mysterium, Summers--but with Rocket's help, the engineering went without a hitch.
You've brought us the gun...

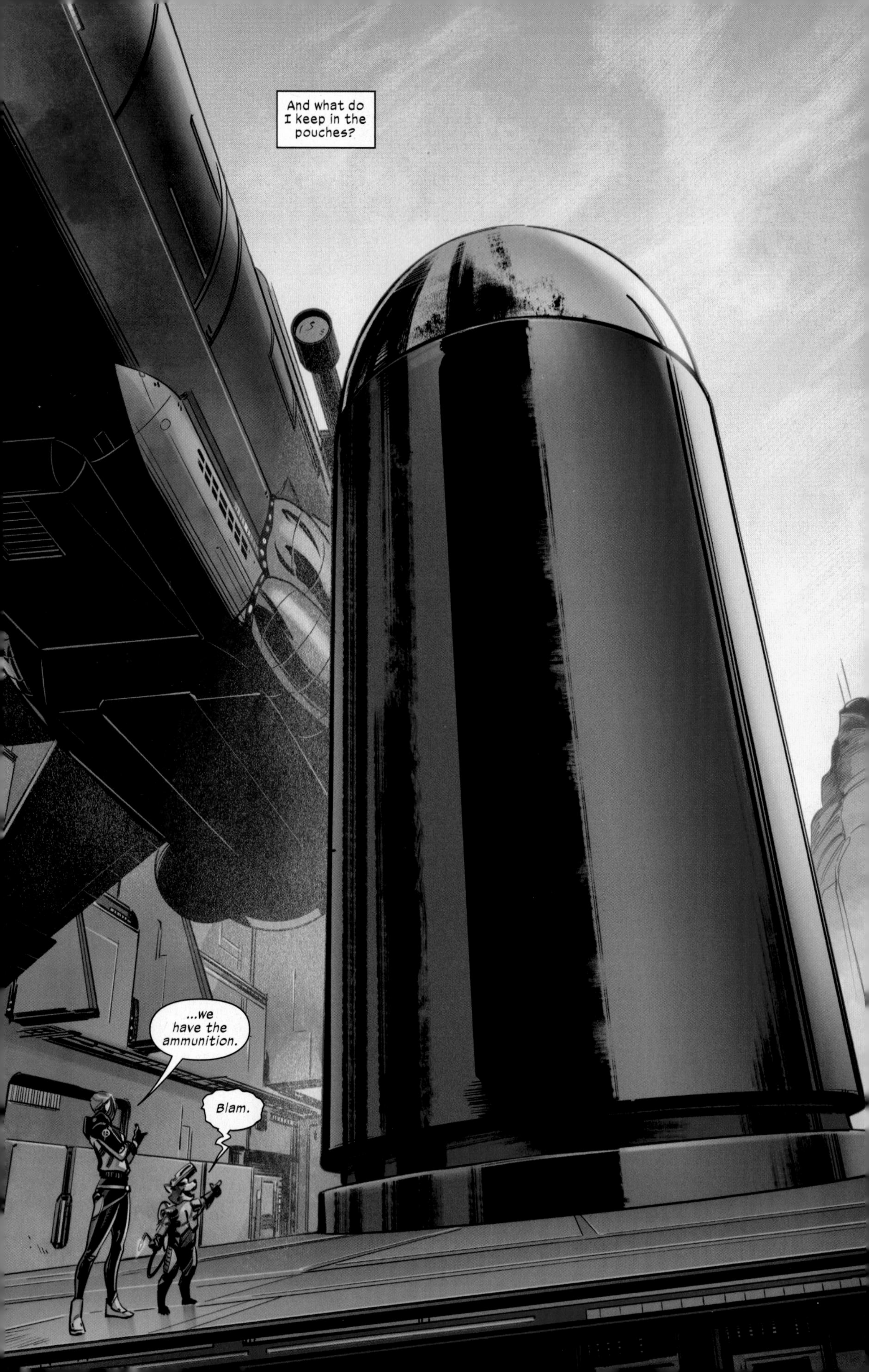
And what do I keep in the pouches?
...we have the ammunition.
Blam.

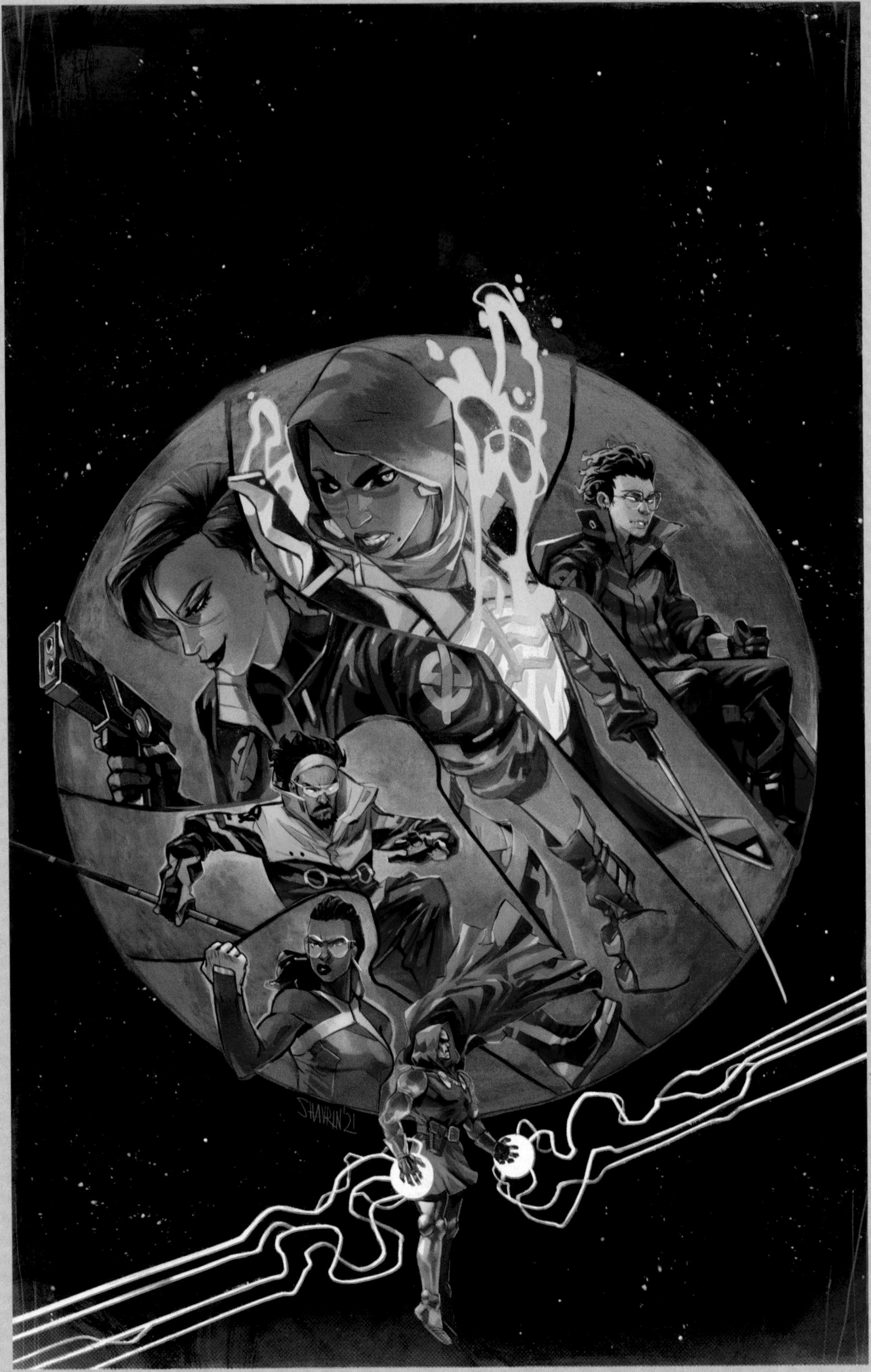
SHAVRIN '21

**S.W.O.R.D. #7 Variant** by Ivan Shavrin

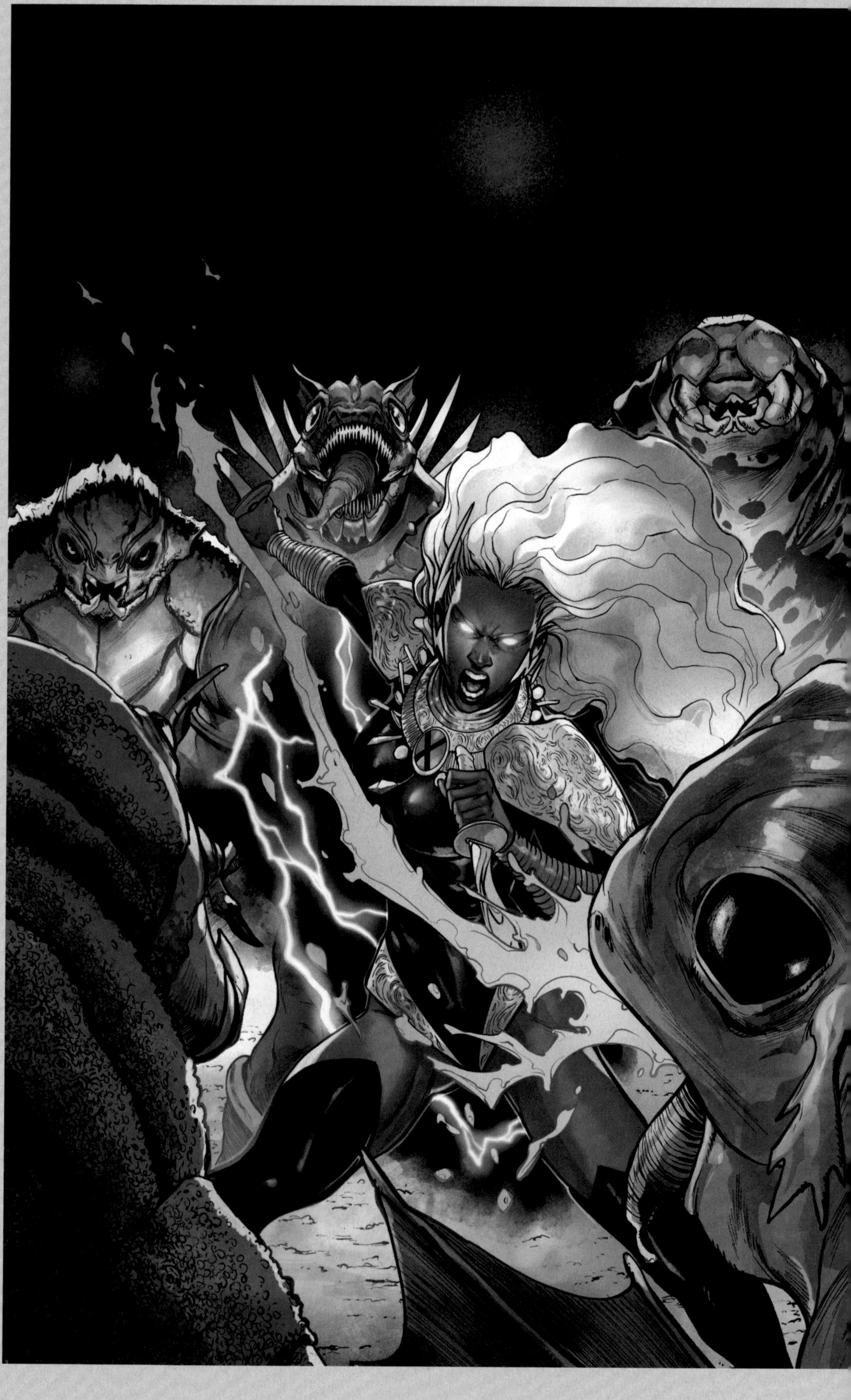

Chapter 08

# Unbroken

8

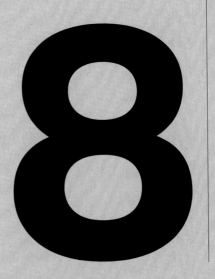

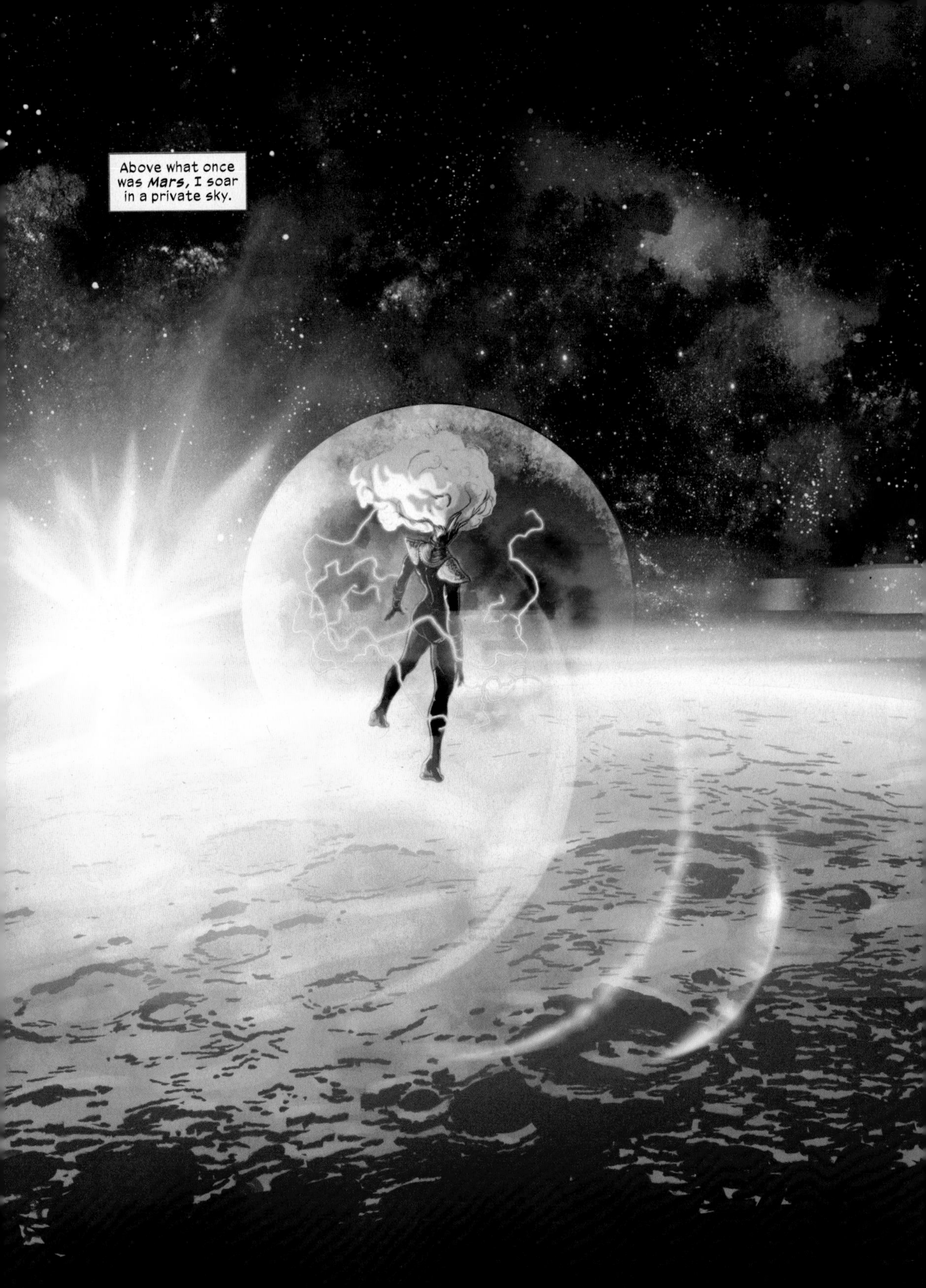
Above what once was *Mars*, I soar in a private sky.

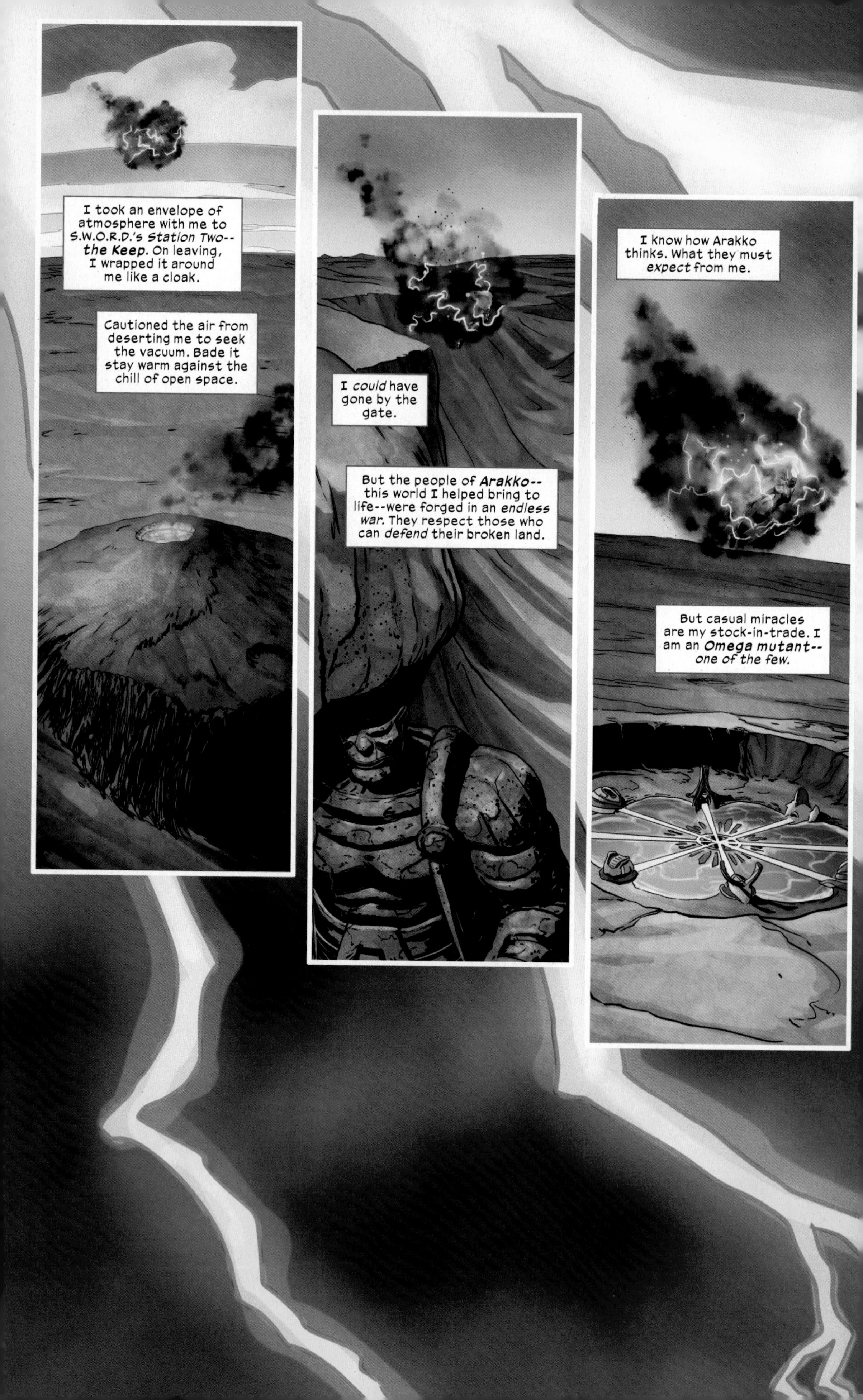
I took an envelope of atmosphere with me to S.W.O.R.D.'s *Station Two*-- ***the Keep***. On leaving, I wrapped it around me like a cloak.
Cautioned the air from deserting me to seek the vacuum. Bade it stay warm against the chill of open space.
I *could* have gone by the gate.
But the people of ***Arakko***-- this world I helped bring to life--were forged in an *endless war*. They respect those who can *defend* their broken land.
I know how Arakko thinks. What they must *expect* from me.
But casual miracles are my stock-in-trade. I am an ***Omega mutant***-- *one of the few.*

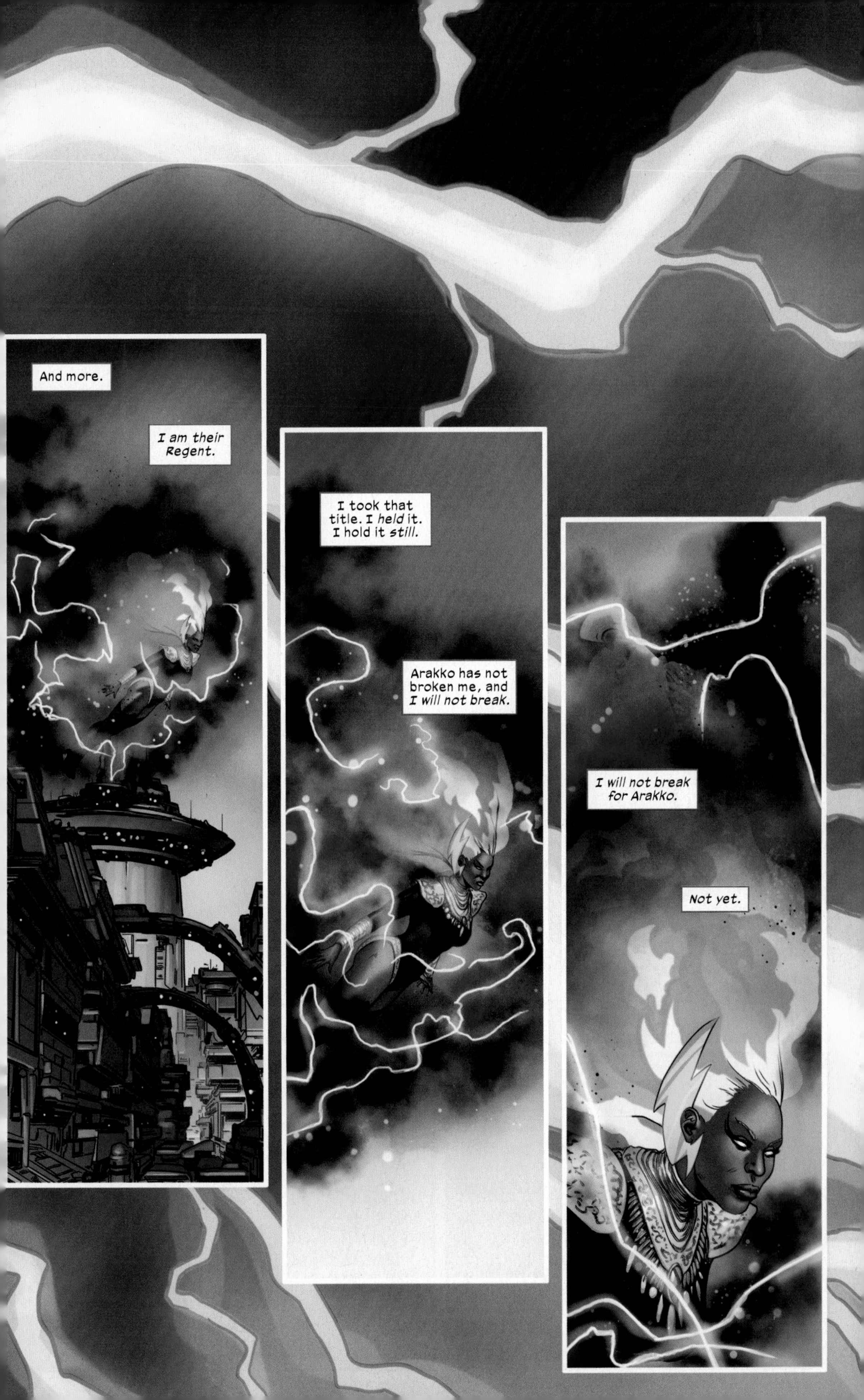
And more.
*I am their Regent.*
I took that title. I *held* it. I hold it *still.*
Arakko has not broken me, and *I will not break.*
*I will not break for Arakko.*
*Not yet.*

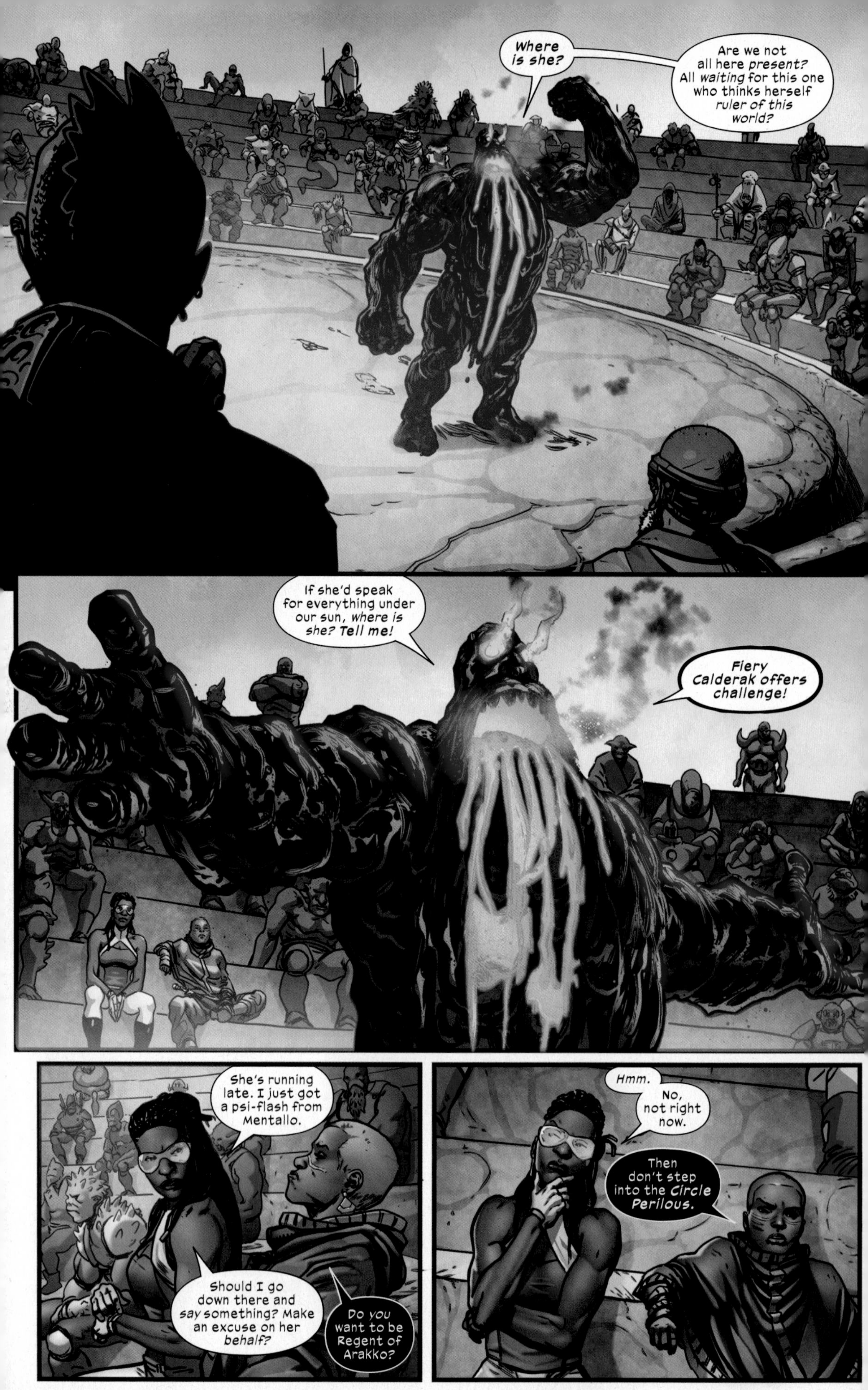
Where is she?
Are we not all here present? All waiting for this one who thinks herself ruler of this world?
If she'd speak for everything under our sun, where is she? Tell me!
Fiery Calderak offers challenge!
She's running late. I just got a psi-flash from Mentallo.
Should I go down there and say something? Make an excuse on her behalf?
Do you want to be Regent of Arakko?
Hmm.
No, not right now.
Then don't step into the Circle Perilous.

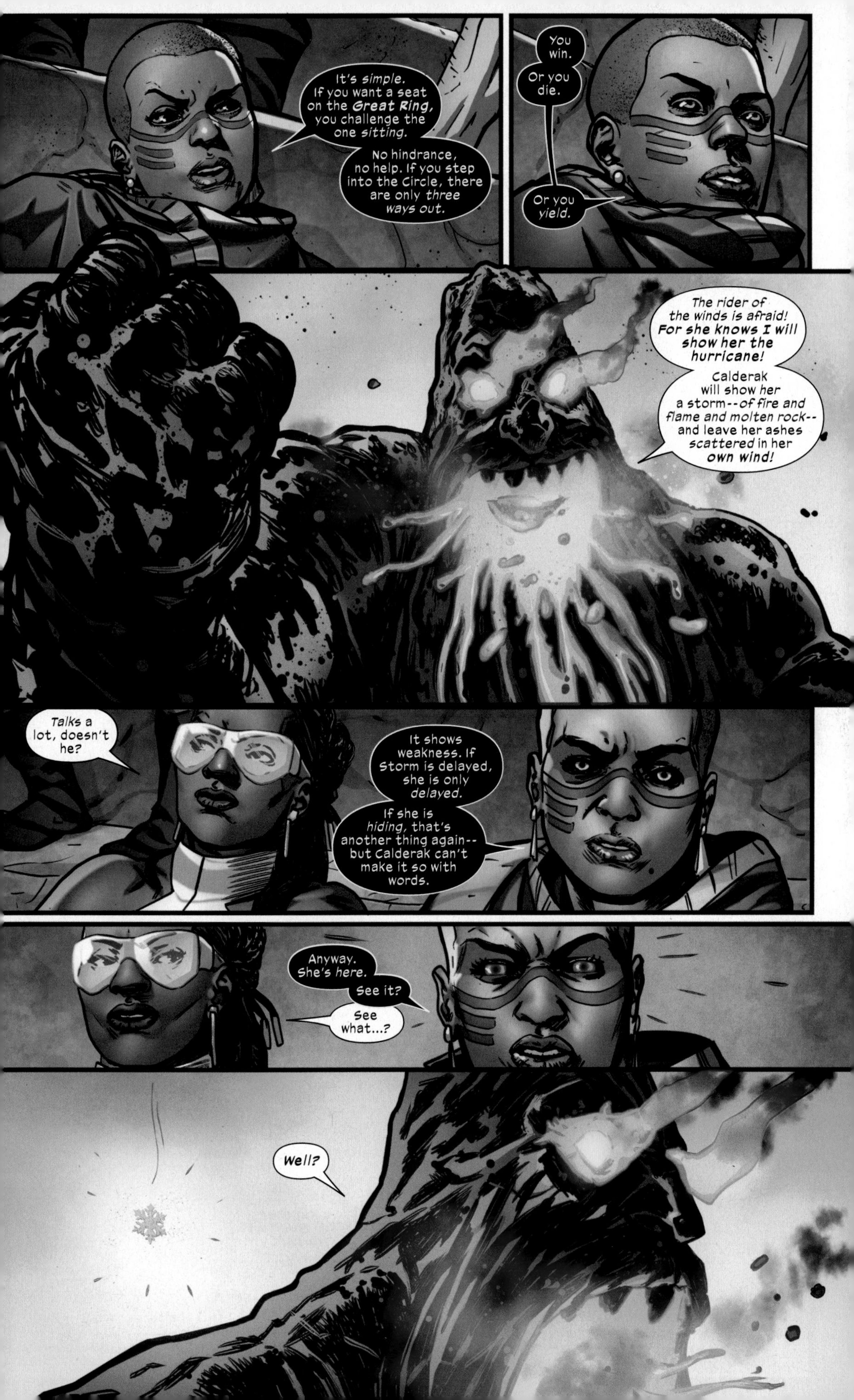
It's simple. If you want a seat on the Great Ring, you challenge the one sitting.
No hindrance, no help. If you step into the Circle, there are only three ways out.
You win.
Or you die.
Or you yield.
The rider of the winds is afraid! For she knows I will show her the hurricane!
Calderak will show her a storm--of fire and flame and molten rock--and leave her ashes scattered in her own wind!
Talks a lot, doesn't he?
It shows weakness. If Storm is delayed, she is only delayed.
If she is hiding, that's another thing again--but Calderak can't make it so with words.
Anyway. She's here.
See it?
See what...?
Well?

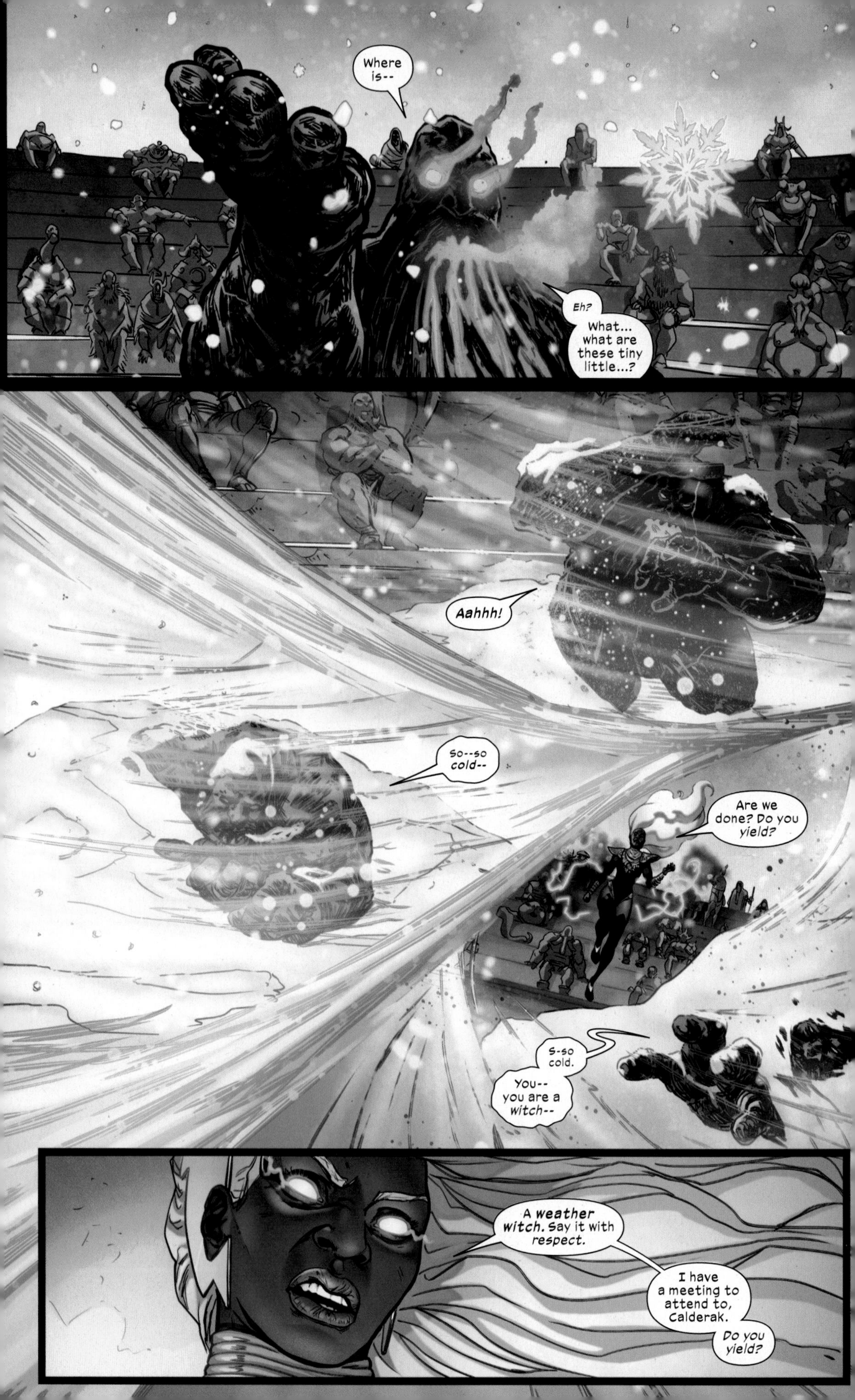

Where is--
Eh?
What... what are these tiny little...?
Aahhh!
So--so cold--
Are we done? Do you yield?
S-so cold.
You-- you are a witch--
A weather witch. Say it with respect.
I have a meeting to attend to, Calderak.
Do you yield?

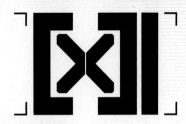

# THE NINE SEATS OF THE GREAT RING

**THE THREE SEATS OF THE DAWN.** These three seats plan for the three outcomes of any conflict. *They are deferred to in time of* ***WAR.***

**01 - THE SEAT OF** VICTORY. When the battle is won, this seat plans the next. Because it is traditionally the seat most consulted, it is also called the **Head of the Great Ring.**

Once, this was the seat of **Genesis.** Now **ISCA THE UNBEATEN** sits here.

**02 - THE SEAT OF** STALEMATE. Not all battles are won or lost. When there is no clear winner, this seat is consulted.

**IDYLL** sits here.

**03 - THE SEAT OF** LOSS. This seat is consulted in dark times of humiliation and pain, when the world has fallen.

**TARN THE UNCARING** sits here.

**THE THREE SEATS OF THE DAY.** The seats of the world and of what can be seen and touched. *They are deferred to in time of* ***PEACE.*** *They are deferred to now.*

**04 - THE SEAT OF** ABOVE-US. Consulted on matters of the heavens.

**LACTUCA** sits here.

**05 - THE SEAT OF** ALL-AROUND-US. The central seat is consulted on matters of the land, the people, the weather and the turn of the world. As a matter of unbreakable law, this seat has an **additional casting vote** -- thus, whoever claims the responsibility of sitting here is known as **Regent of Arakko.**

**STORM** sits here.

**06 - THE SEAT OF** BELOW-US. Consulted on matters of the deep.

**SOBUNAR** sits here.

**THE THREE SEATS OF THE DUSK.** These seats are consulted on what cannot be seen and cannot be touched. *This table, though necessary in both war and peace, is **NEVER DEFERRED TO.***

**07 - THE SEAT OF LAW.** Consulted on all legal matters. The laws of Arakko are few and do not change easily. But when they do, this seat is the **final arbiter.**

**ORA SERRATA** sits here.

**08 - THE SEAT OF HISTORY.** Consulted on matters of lore. This seat records -- *and decides* -- the history of Arakko.

**XILO WHO-WAS-STULGID** sits here.

**09 - THE SEAT OF DREAMS.** Consulted on matters of art, poetry and song. Few challenge for this seat, but those who do are the most dangerous -- *for they never yield.*

**LODUS LOGOS** sits here.

**THE GROUND ON WHICH ALL SEATS REST.**

**00 - THE VOICE OF ARAKKO.** Arakko itself -- *the island that fights like a man* -- is always present. However, in the ongoing absence of **REDROOT,** direct consultation is difficult. Arakko has little to say on this or on any other thing. ***But Arakko is listening.***

***Always.***

> **No mutant who was not an Omega-level mutant has ever sat on the Great Ring.**
>
> **Not once.**
>
> **It has never happened -- *it never will.***
>
> **But the Great Ring has only nine recognized seats.**

*There are rumors of three more.*

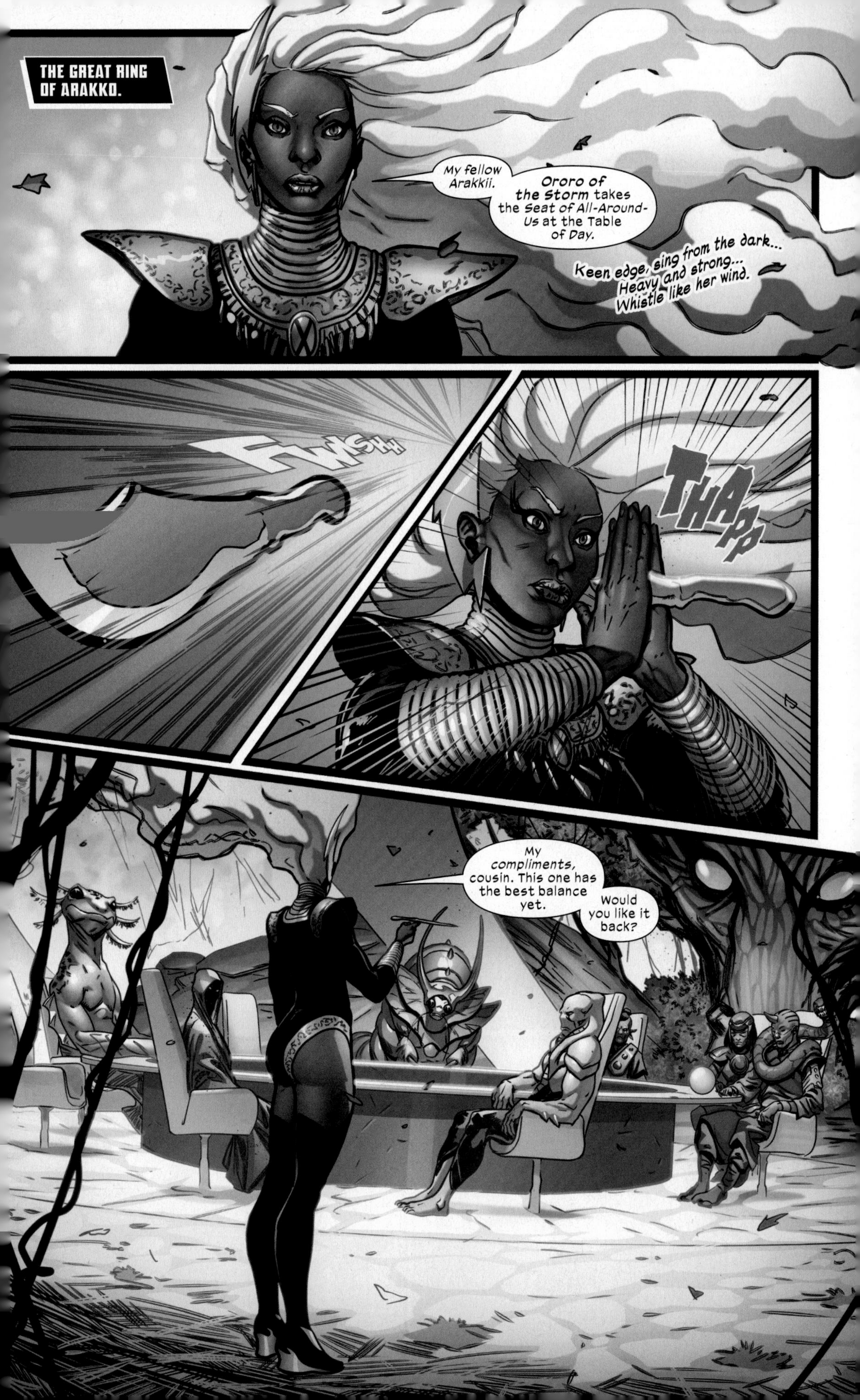
THE GREAT RING OF ARAKKO.
My fellow Arakkii.
Ororo of the Storm takes the Seat of All-Around-Us at the Table of Day.
Keen edge, sing from the dark... Heavy and strong... Whistle like her wind.
FWSHH
THAPP
My compliments, cousin. This one has the best balance yet.
Would you like it back?

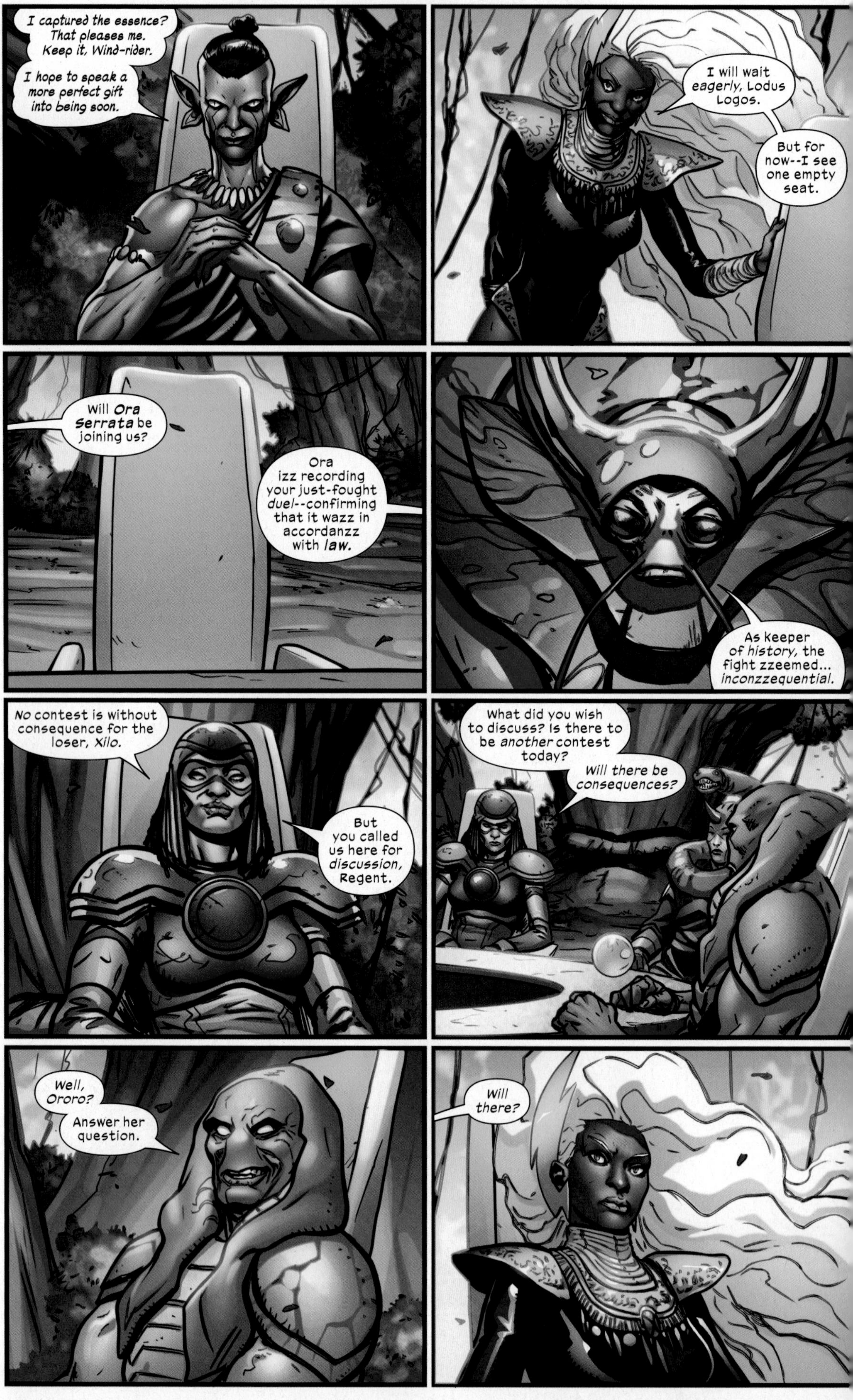
I captured the essence? That pleases me. Keep it, Wind-rider.
I hope to speak a more perfect gift into being soon.
I will wait eagerly, Lodus Logos.
But for now--I see one empty seat.
Will Ora Serrata be joining us?
Ora izz recording your just-fought duel--confirming that it wazz in accordanzz with law.
As keeper of history, the fight zzeemed... inconzzequential.
No contest is without consequence for the loser, Xilo.
But you called us here for discussion, Regent.
What did you wish to discuss? Is there to be another contest today?
Will there be consequences?
Well, Ororo?
Answer her question.
Will there?

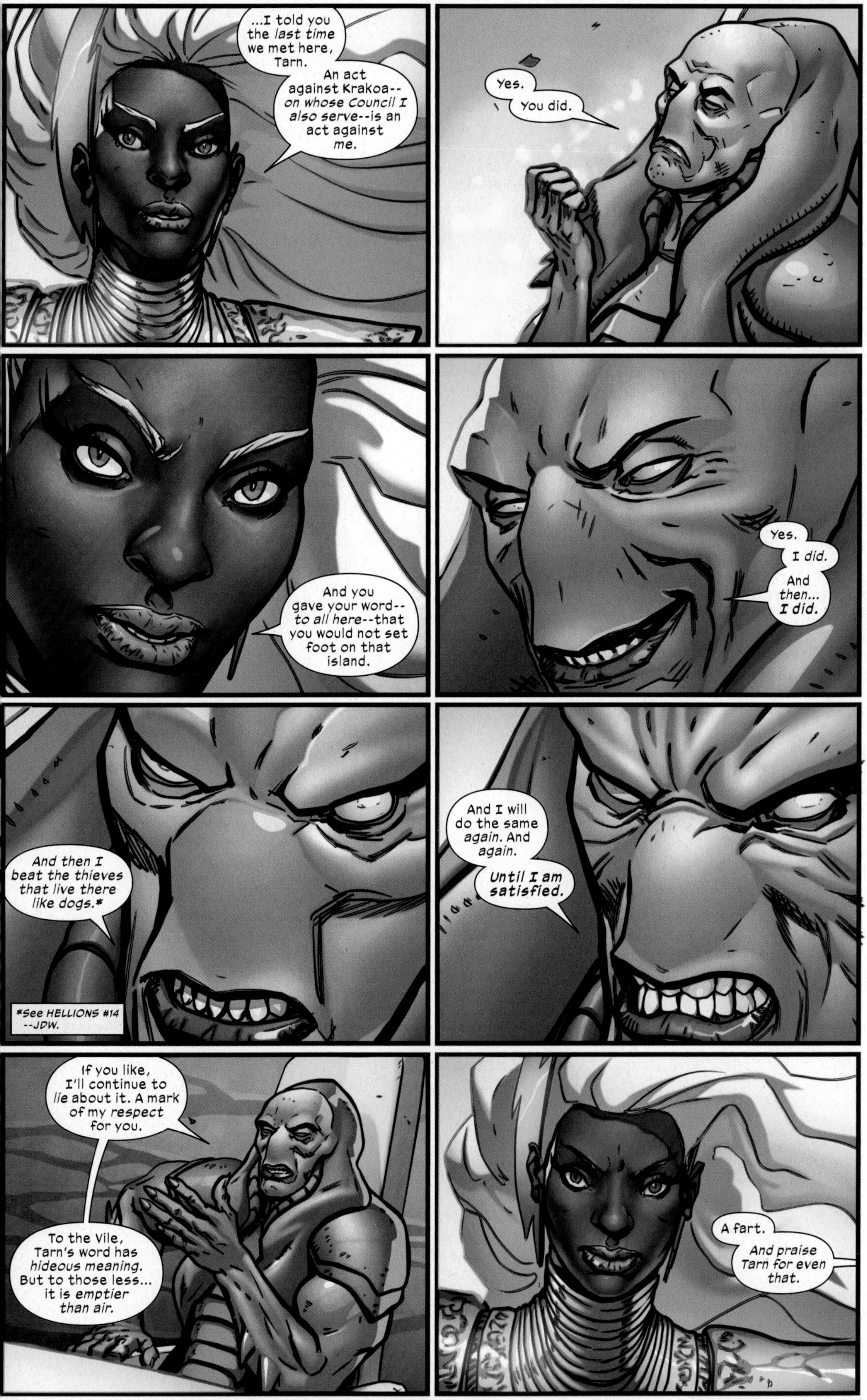
...I told you the *last time* we met here, Tarn.
An act against Krakoa--*on whose Council I also serve*--is an act against *me.*
Yes.
You did.
And you gave your word--*to all here*--that you would not set foot on that island.
Yes.
I *did.*
And *then... **I did.***
*And then I beat the thieves that live there like dogs.**
*See HELLIONS #14 --JDW.
And I will do the same *again.* And *again.*
***Until I am satisfied.***
If you like, I'll continue to *lie* about it. A mark of my *respect* for you.
To the Vile, Tarn's word has *hideous meaning.* But to those less... it is *emptier than air.*
A fart.
*And praise Tarn for even that.*

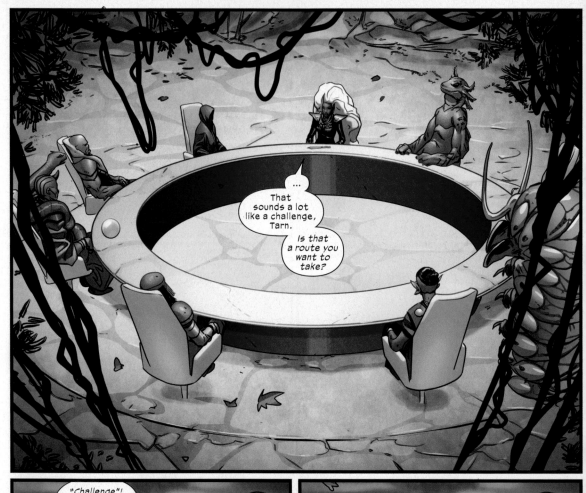

...That sounds a lot like a challenge, Tarn.

Is that a route you want to take?

"Challenge"! You speak the word with such... *gravitas.*

But you are on *Arakko,* Ororo-of-many-names. Challenges fall here like *rain* or *blood.*

How did you get to sit *here* without knowing *that?*

I AMM YUU.

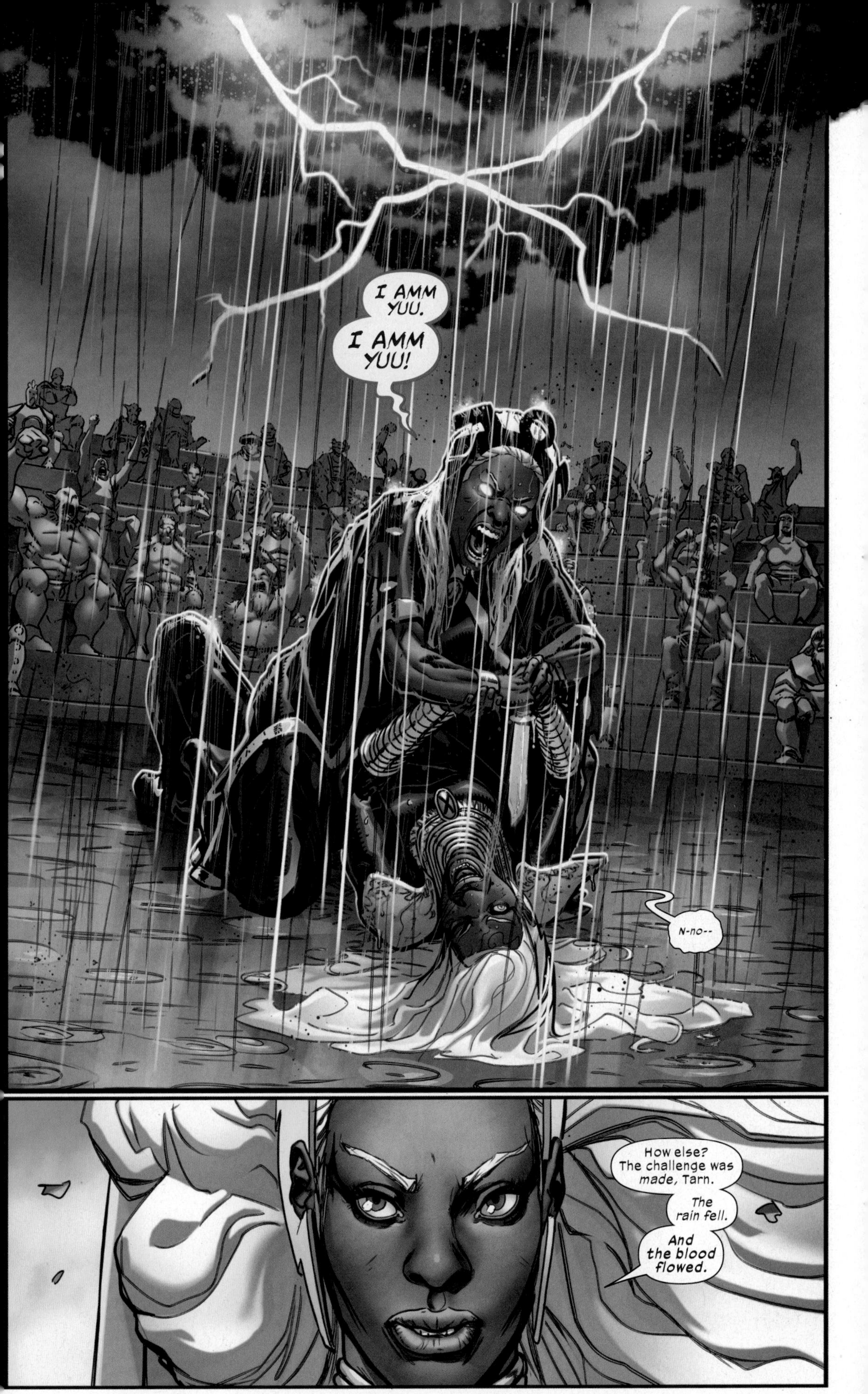
I AMM YUU.
I AMM YUU!
N-no--
How else? The challenge was made, Tarn.
The rain fell.
And the blood flowed.

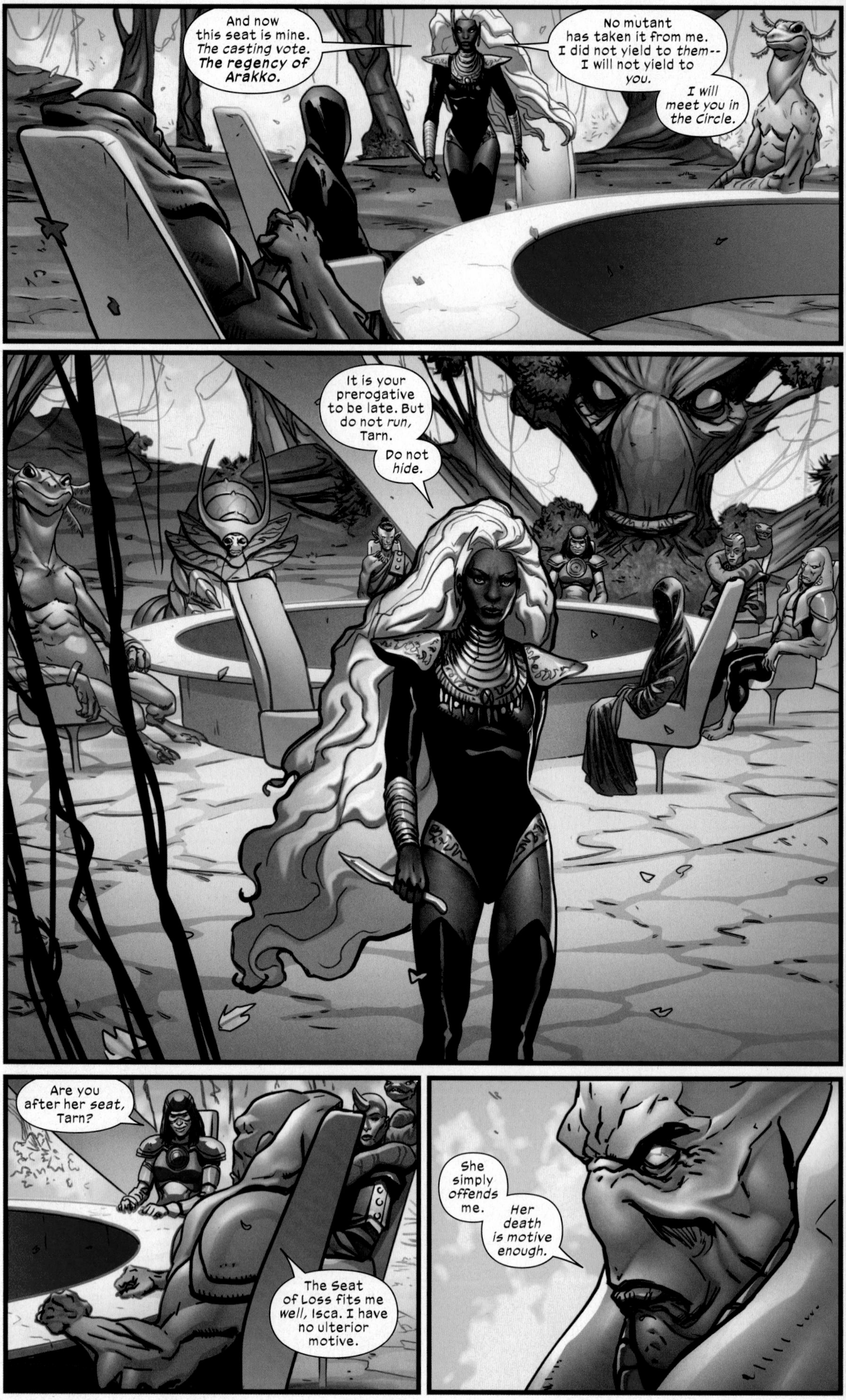

And now this seat is mine. The casting vote. The regency of Arakko.
No mutant has taken it from me. I did not yield to them-- I will not yield to you.
I will meet you in the Circle.
It is your prerogative to be late. But do not run, Tarn.
Do not hide.
Are you after her seat, Tarn?
The Seat of Loss fits me well, Isca. I have no ulterior motive.
She simply offends me.
Her death is motive enough.

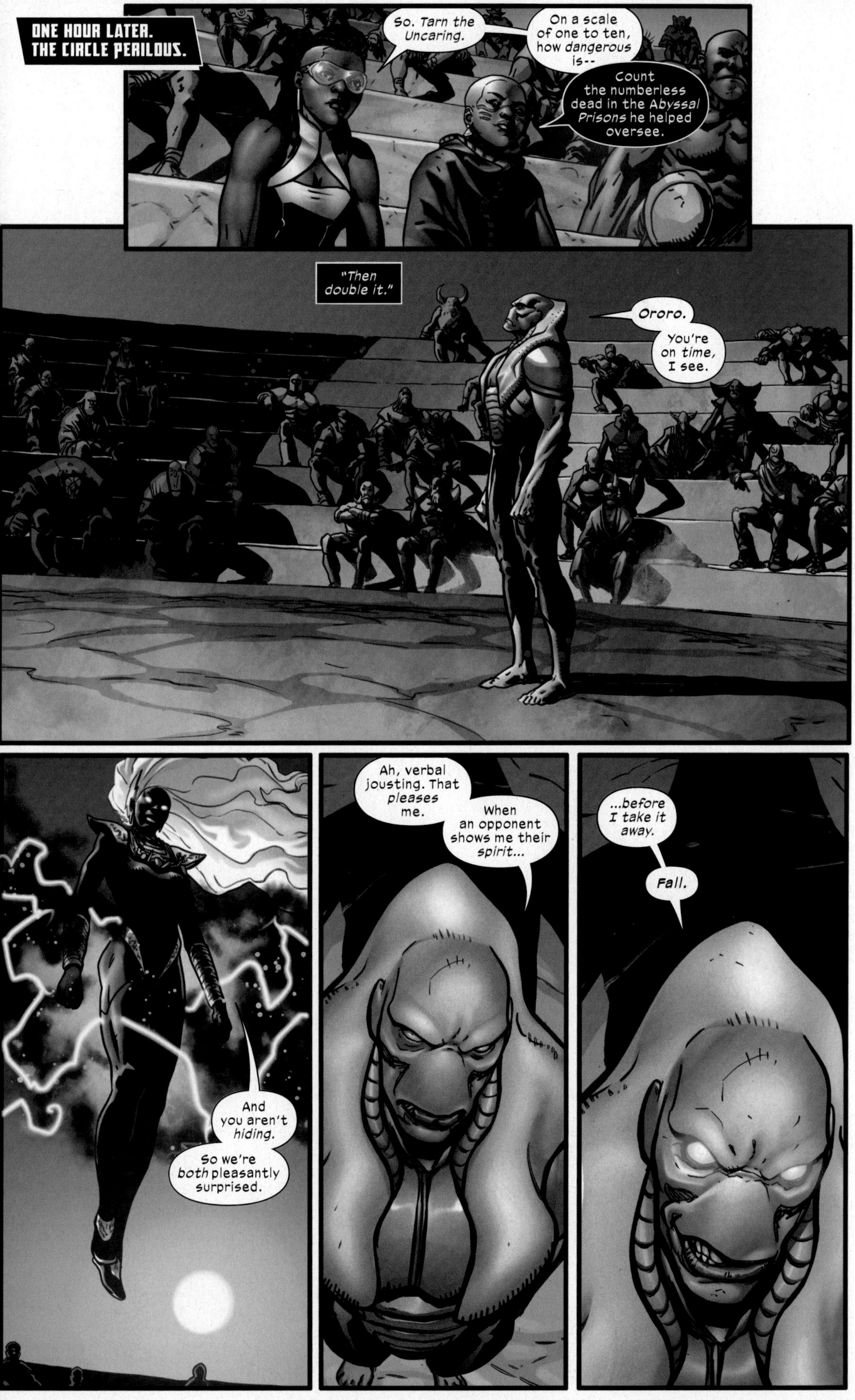
ONE HOUR LATER. THE CIRCLE PERILOUS.
So. Tarn the Uncaring.
On a scale of one to ten, how dangerous is--
Count the numberless dead in the Abyssal Prisons he helped oversee.
"Then double it."
Ororo.
You're on time, I see.
And you aren't hiding.
So we're both pleasantly surprised.
Ah, verbal jousting. That pleases me.
When an opponent shows me their spirit...
...before I take it away.
Fall.

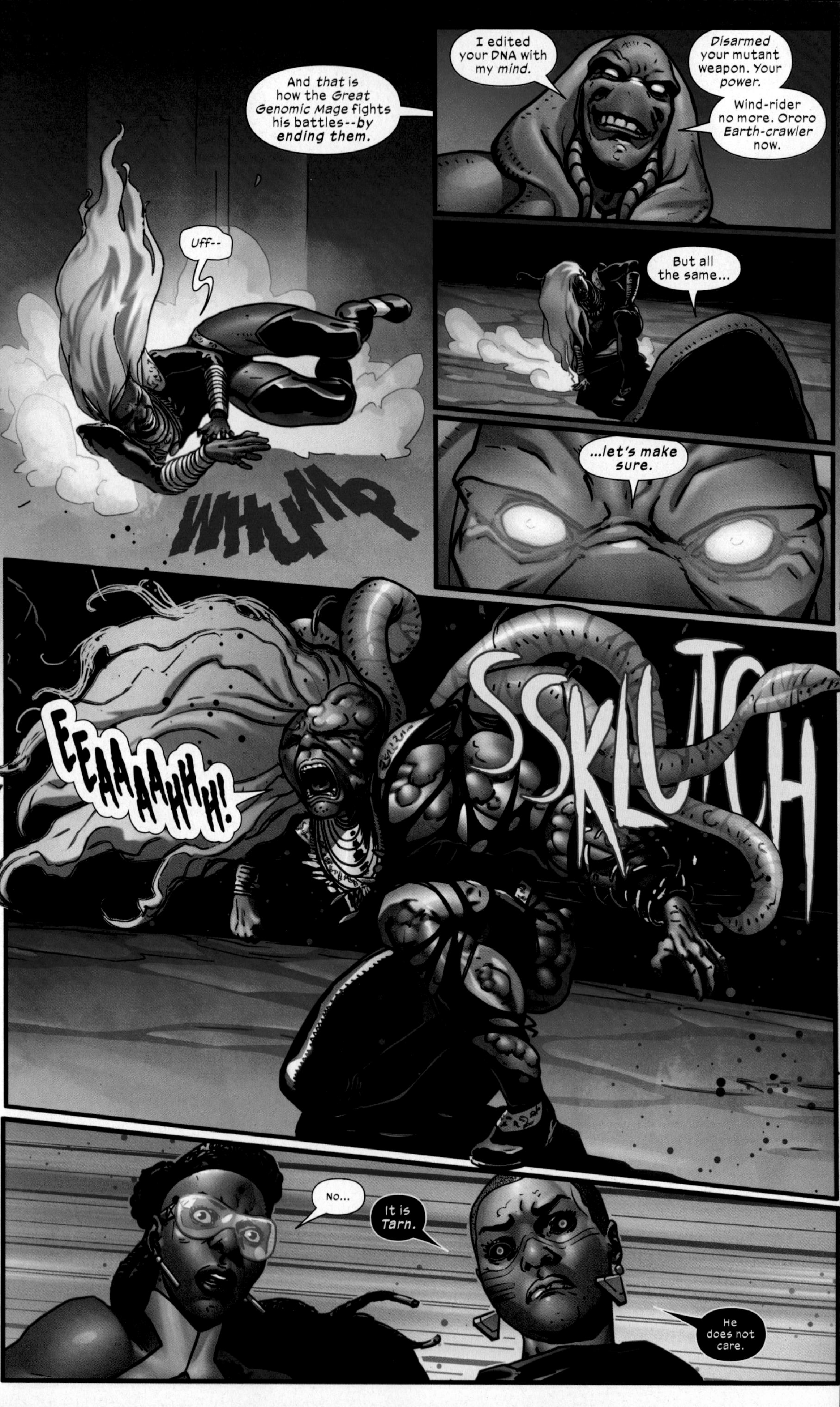

And that is how the Great Genomic Mage fights his battles--by ending them.
I edited your DNA with my mind.
Disarmed your mutant weapon. Your power.
Wind-rider no more. Ororo Earth-crawler now.
Uff--
WHUMP
But all the same...
...let's make sure.
EEAAAAHHH!
SSKLUTCH
No...
It is Tarn.
He does not care.

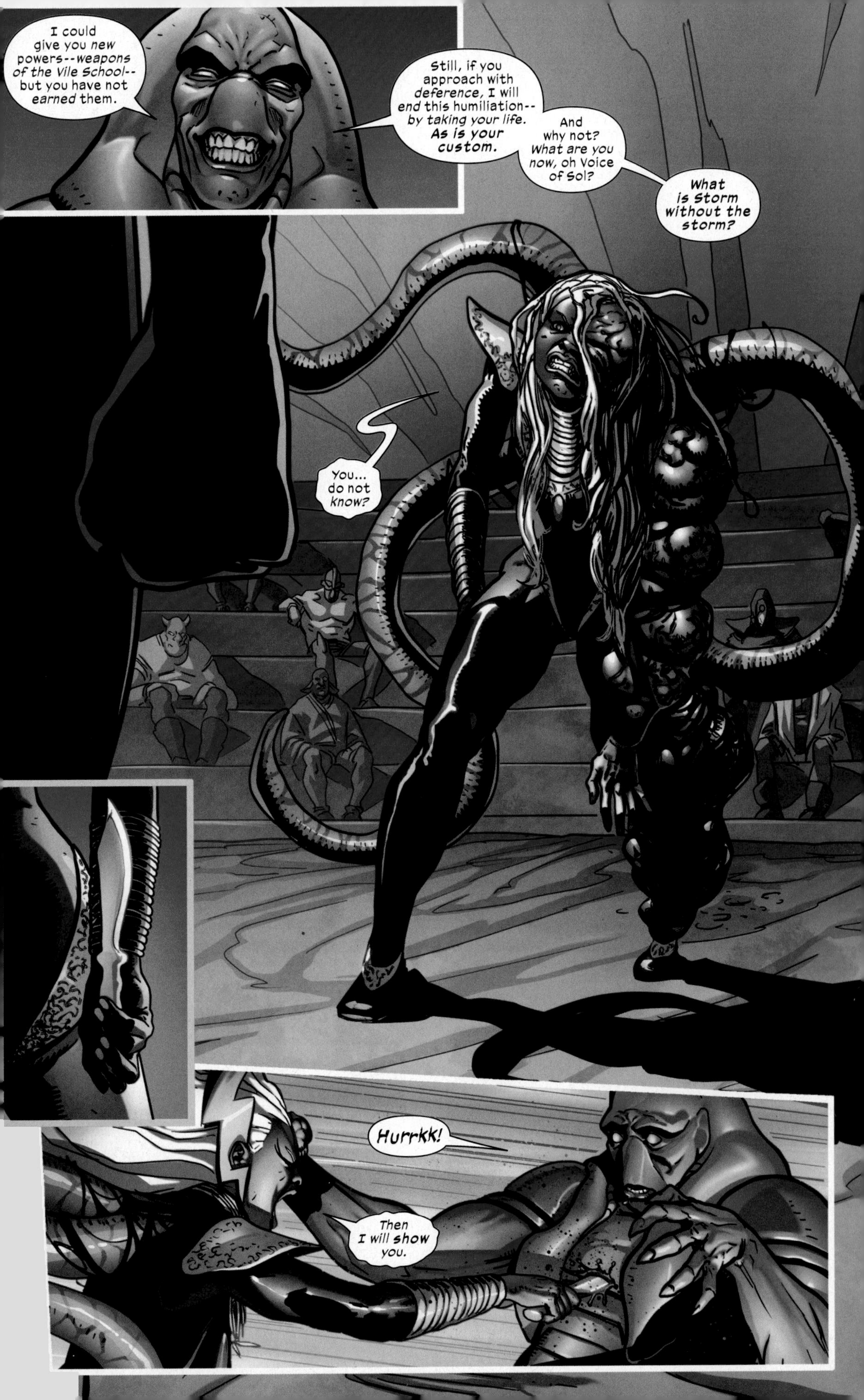
I could give you new powers--*weapons of the Vile School*--but you have not *earned* them.
Still, if you approach with *deference*, I will end this humiliation--by *taking your life.* **As is your custom.**
And why not? What are you now, oh Voice of Sol?
**What is Storm without the storm?**
You... do not know?
***Hurrkk!***
Then I will **show** you.

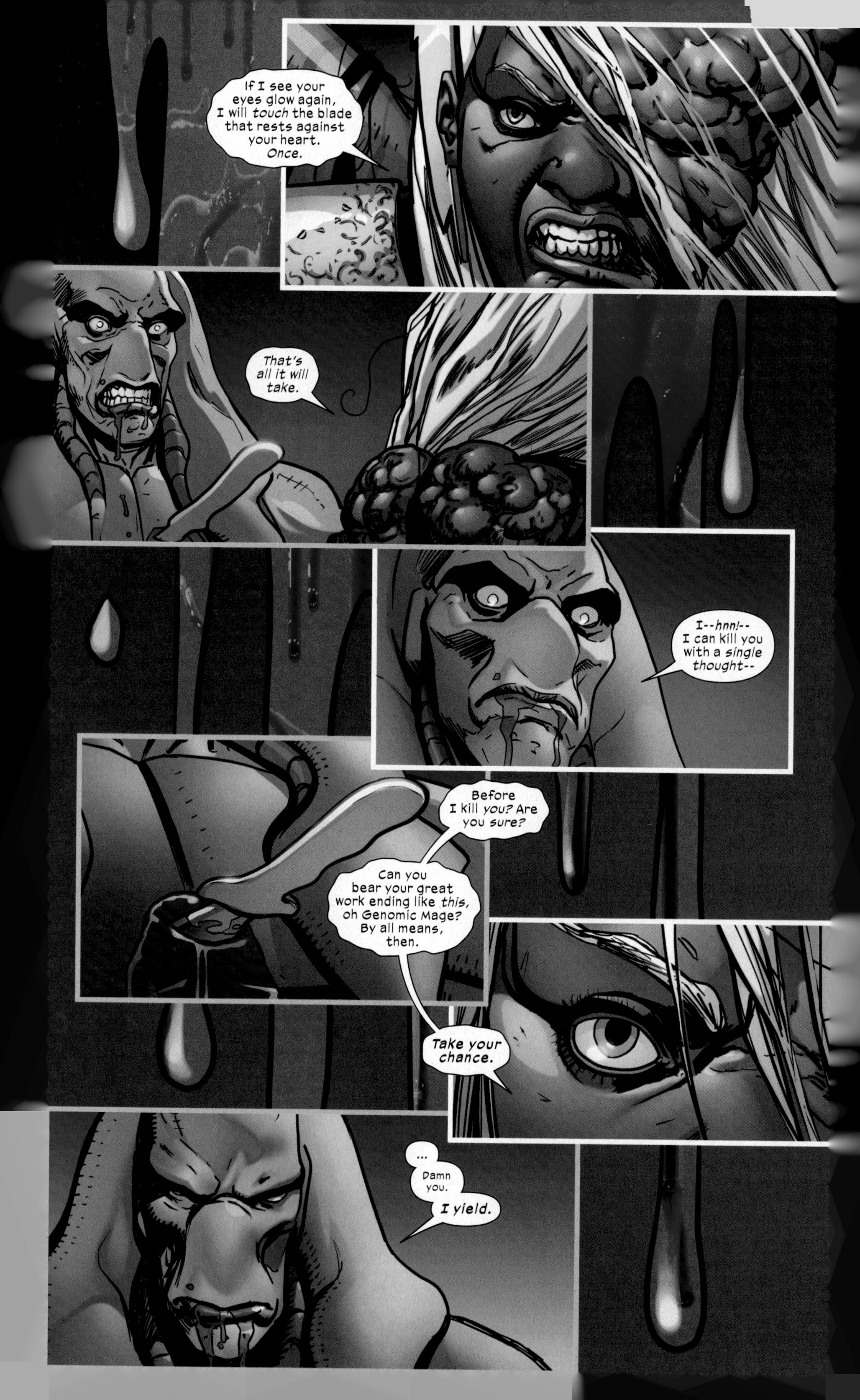
If I see your eyes glow again, I will *touch* the blade that rests against your heart. *Once.*
*That's all it will take.*
I--*hnn!*-- I can kill you with a *single thought*--
Before I kill *you?* Are you *sure?*
Can you bear your great work ending like *this,* oh Genomic Mage? By all means, then.
*Take your chance.*
...
Damn you.
**I yield.**

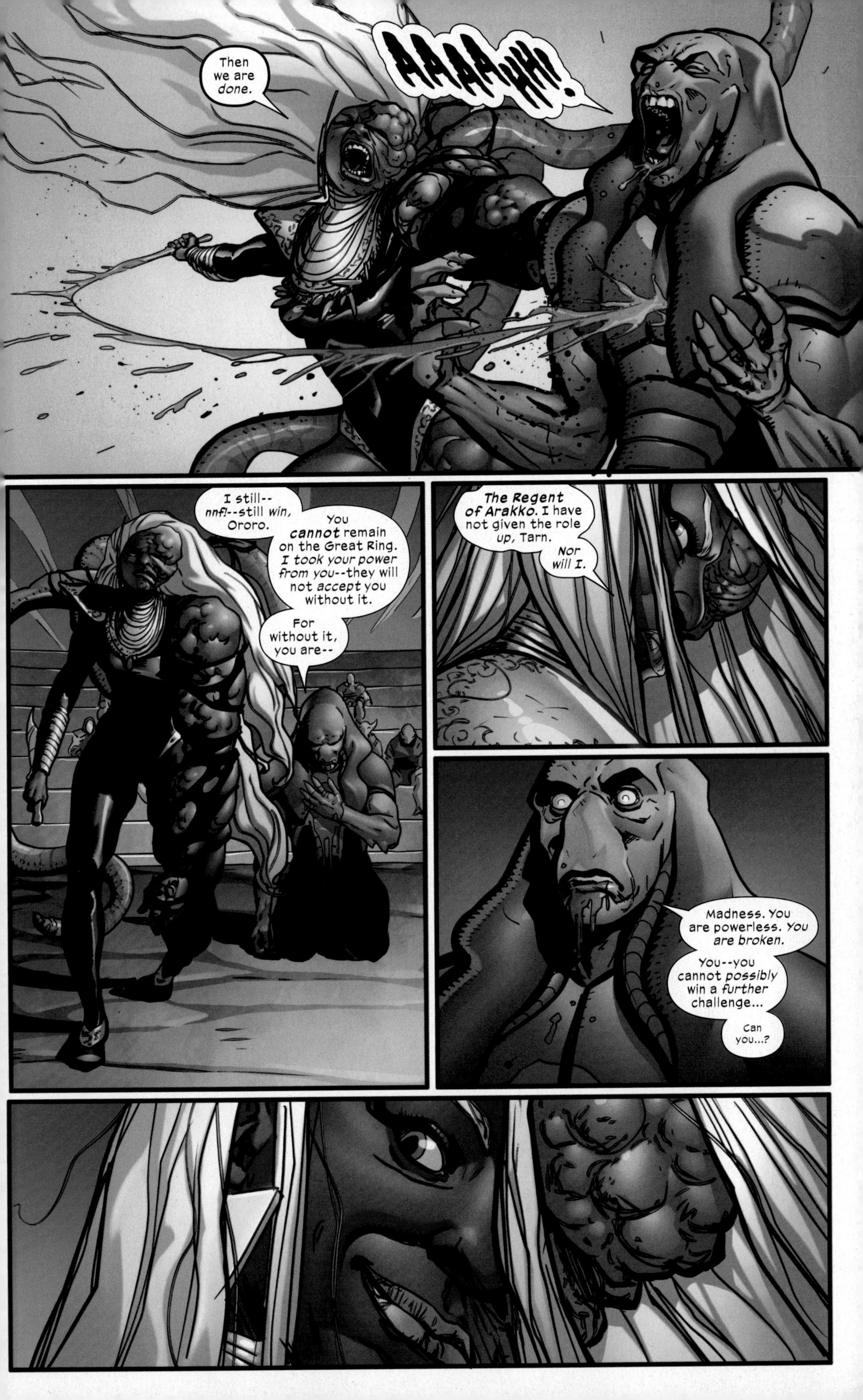

Then we are *done.*
AAAAAHH!
I still-- *nnf!*--still *win,* Ororo.
You *cannot* remain on the Great Ring. *I took your power from you*--they will not *accept* you without it.
For without it, you are--
*The Regent of Arakko.* I have not given the role *up,* Tarn.
*Nor will I.*
Madness. You are *powerless. You are broken.*
You--you cannot *possibly* win a *further* challenge...
Can you...?

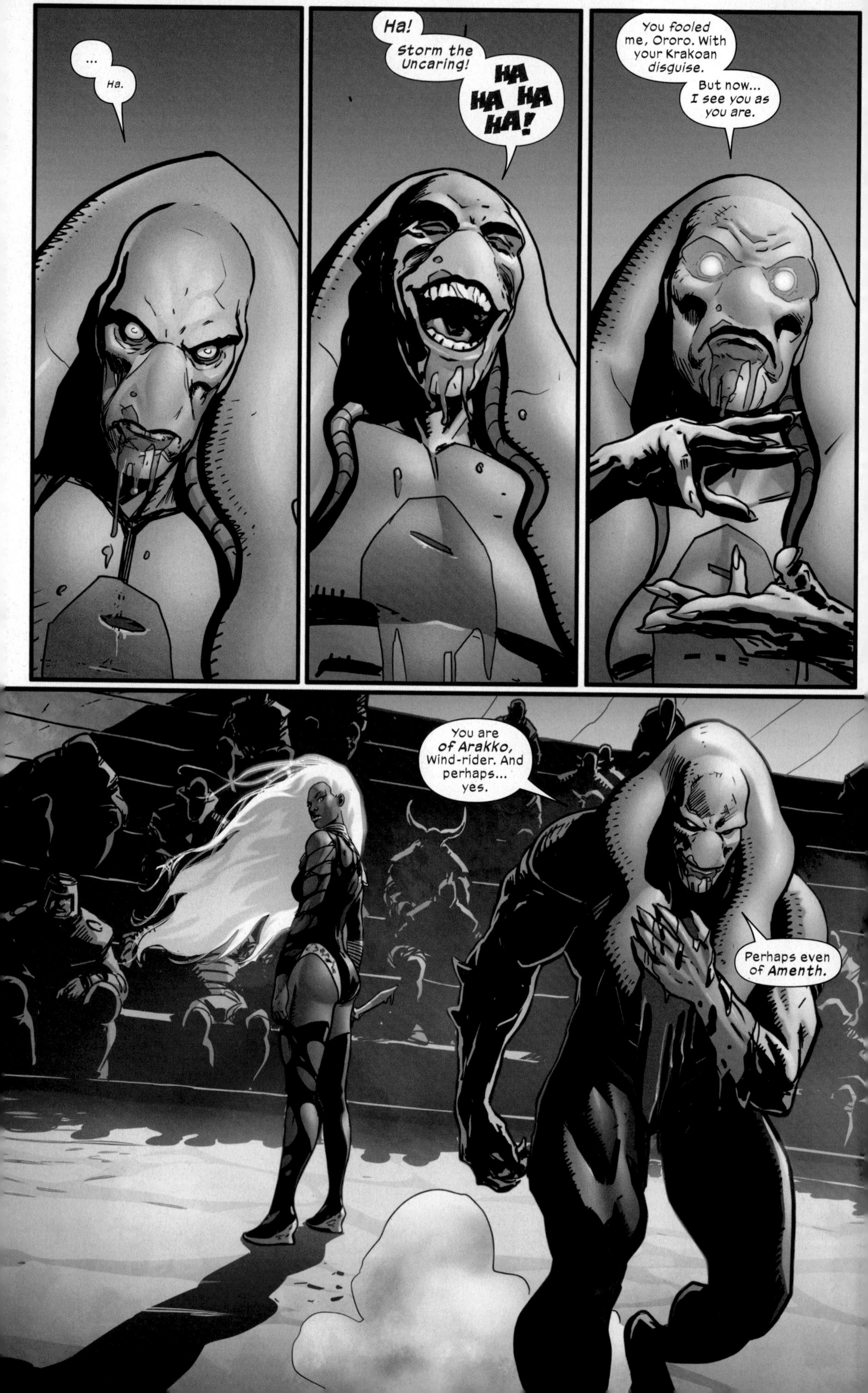
...
Ha.
Ha! Storm the Uncaring!
HA HA HA HA!
You fooled me, Ororo. With your Krakoan disguise.
But now... I see you as you are.
You are of Arakko, Wind-rider. And perhaps... yes.
Perhaps even of Amenth.

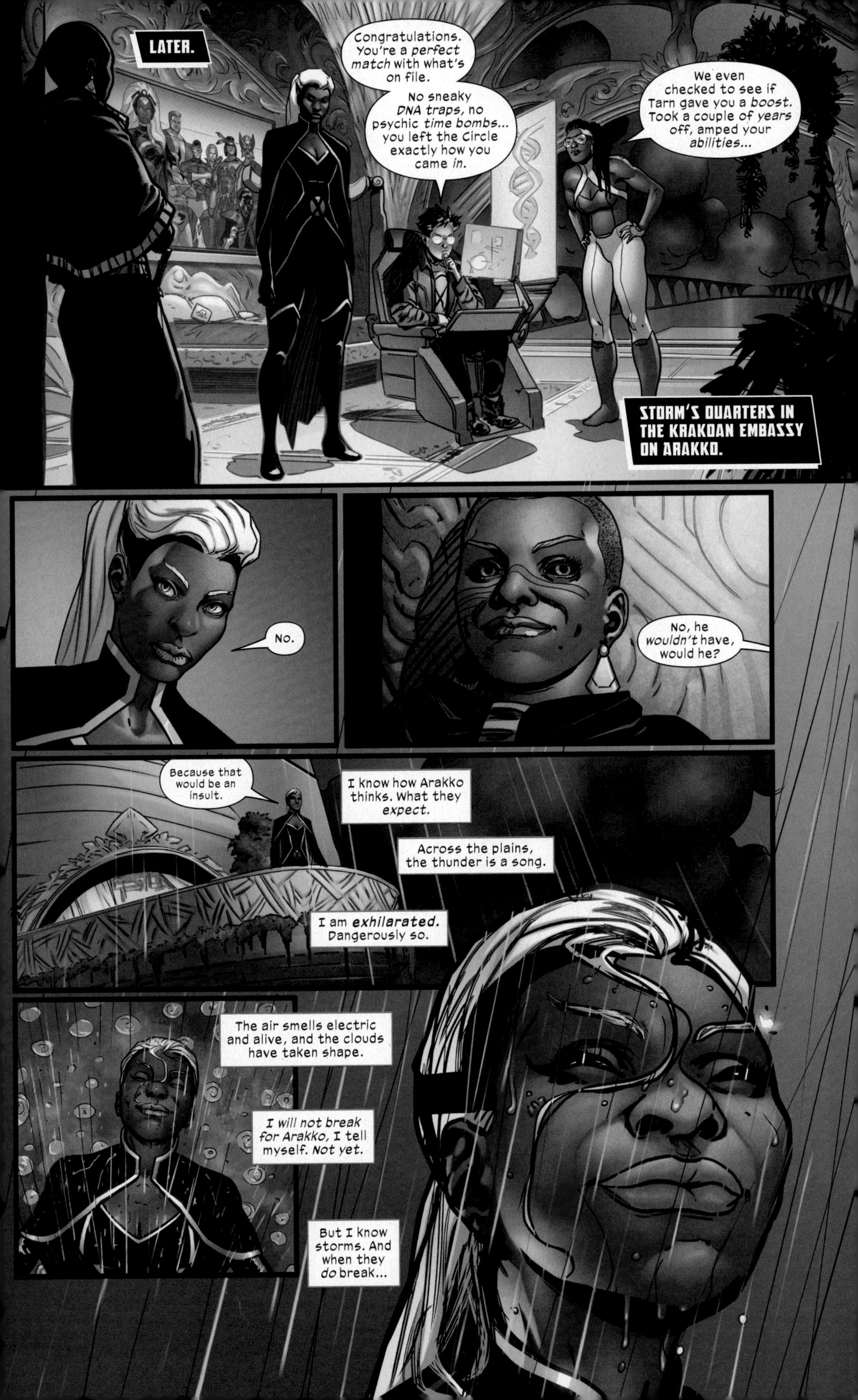
LATER.
Congratulations. You're a *perfect match* with what's on file.
No sneaky *DNA traps*, no psychic *time bombs*... you left the Circle exactly how you came *in*.
We even checked to see if Tarn gave you a *boost*. Took a couple of *years* off, amped your *abilities*...
STORM'S QUARTERS IN THE KRAKOAN EMBASSY ON ARAKKO.
No.
No, he *wouldn't* have, would he?
Because that would be an insult.
I know how Arakko thinks. What they *expect*.
Across the plains, the thunder is a song.
I am **exhilarated.** Dangerously so.
The air smells electric and alive, and the clouds have taken shape.
*I will not break for Arakko*, I tell myself. *Not yet.*
But I know storms. And when they *do* break...

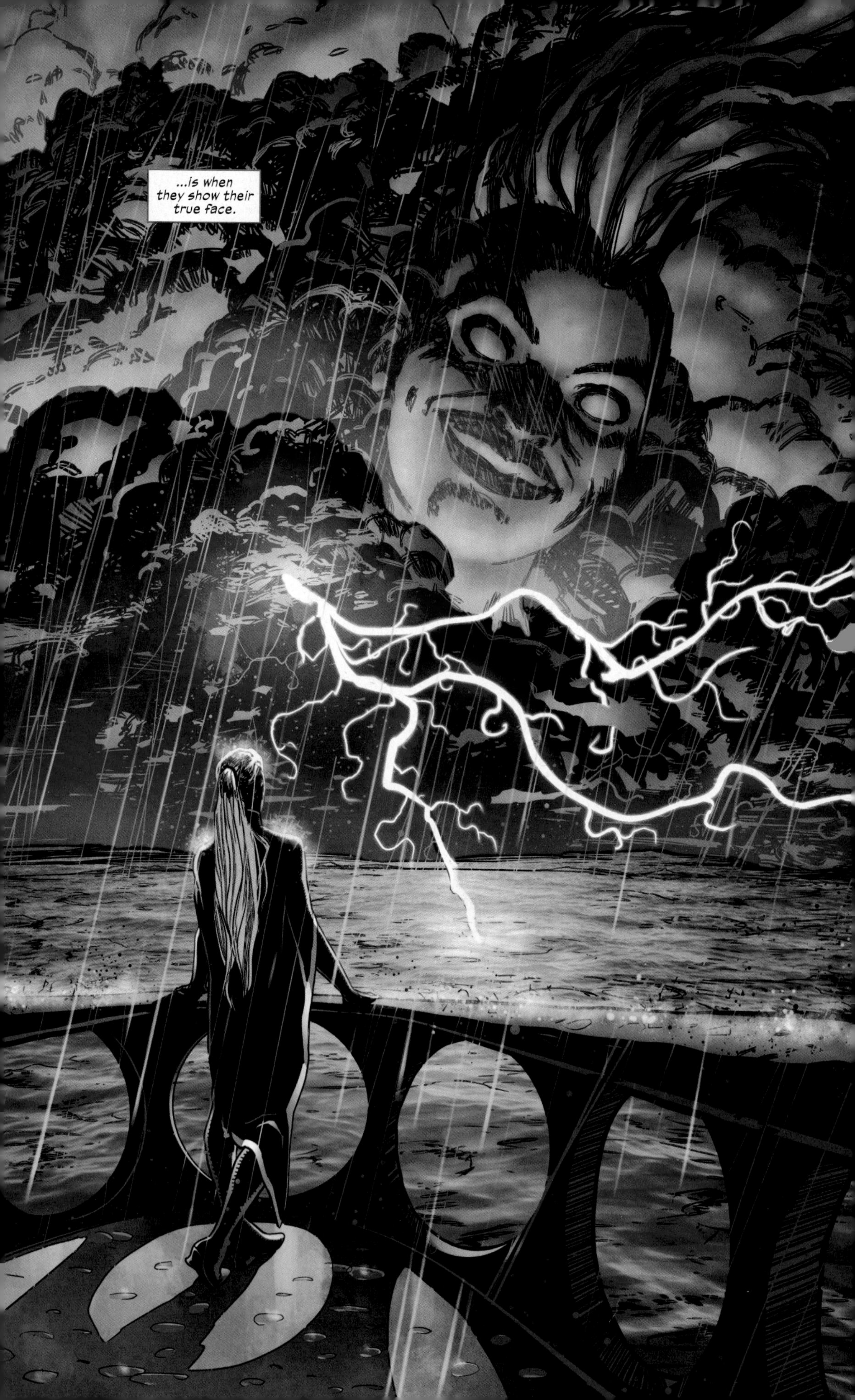
...is when
they show their
true face.

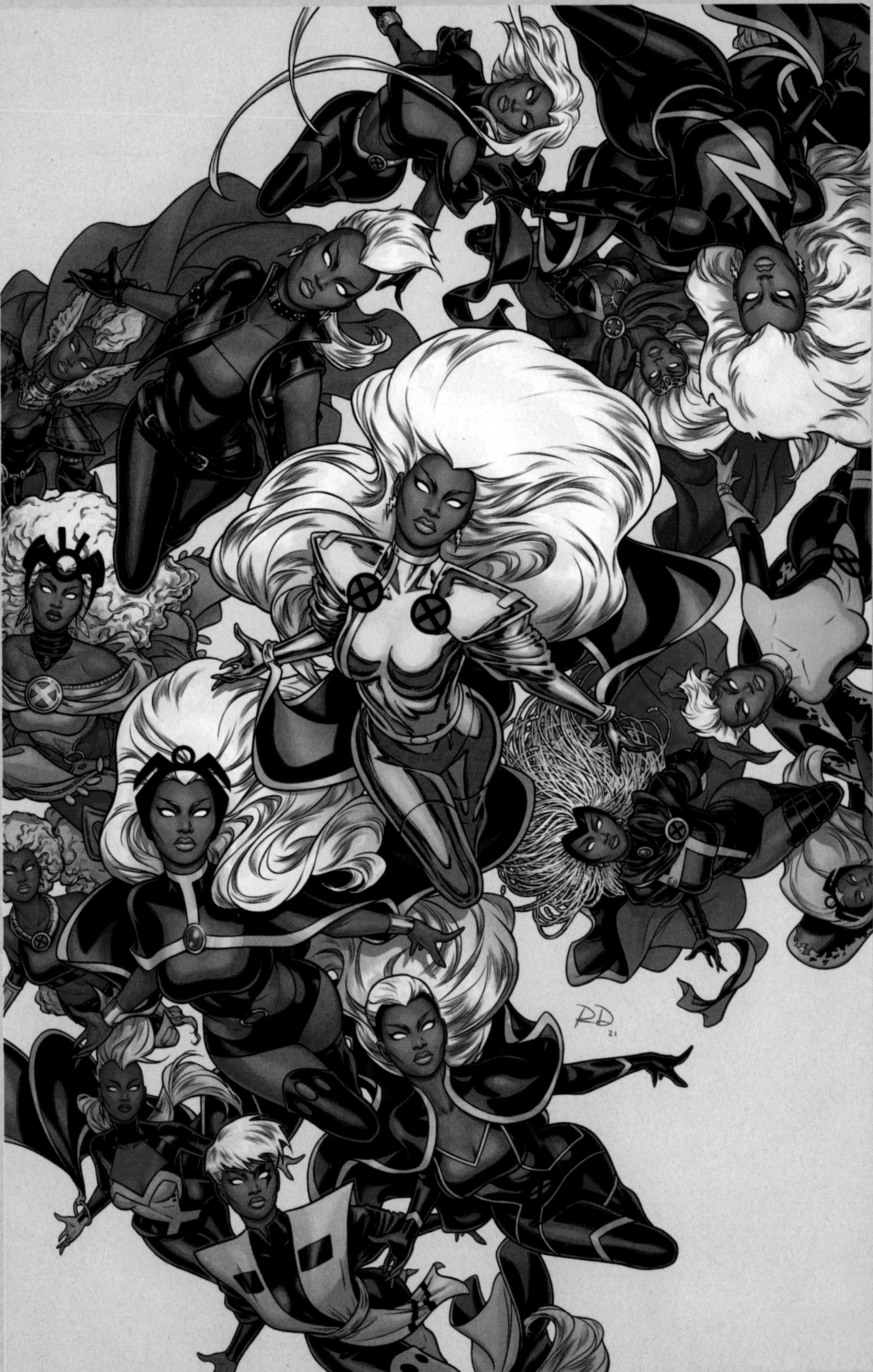

**S.W.O.R.D. #8 Variant** by Russell Dauterman

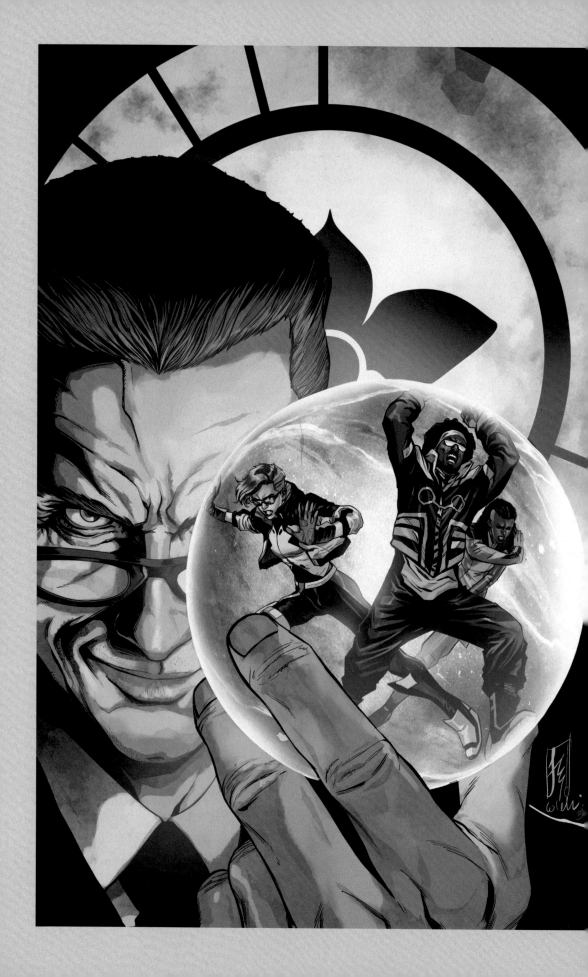

Friends in High Places

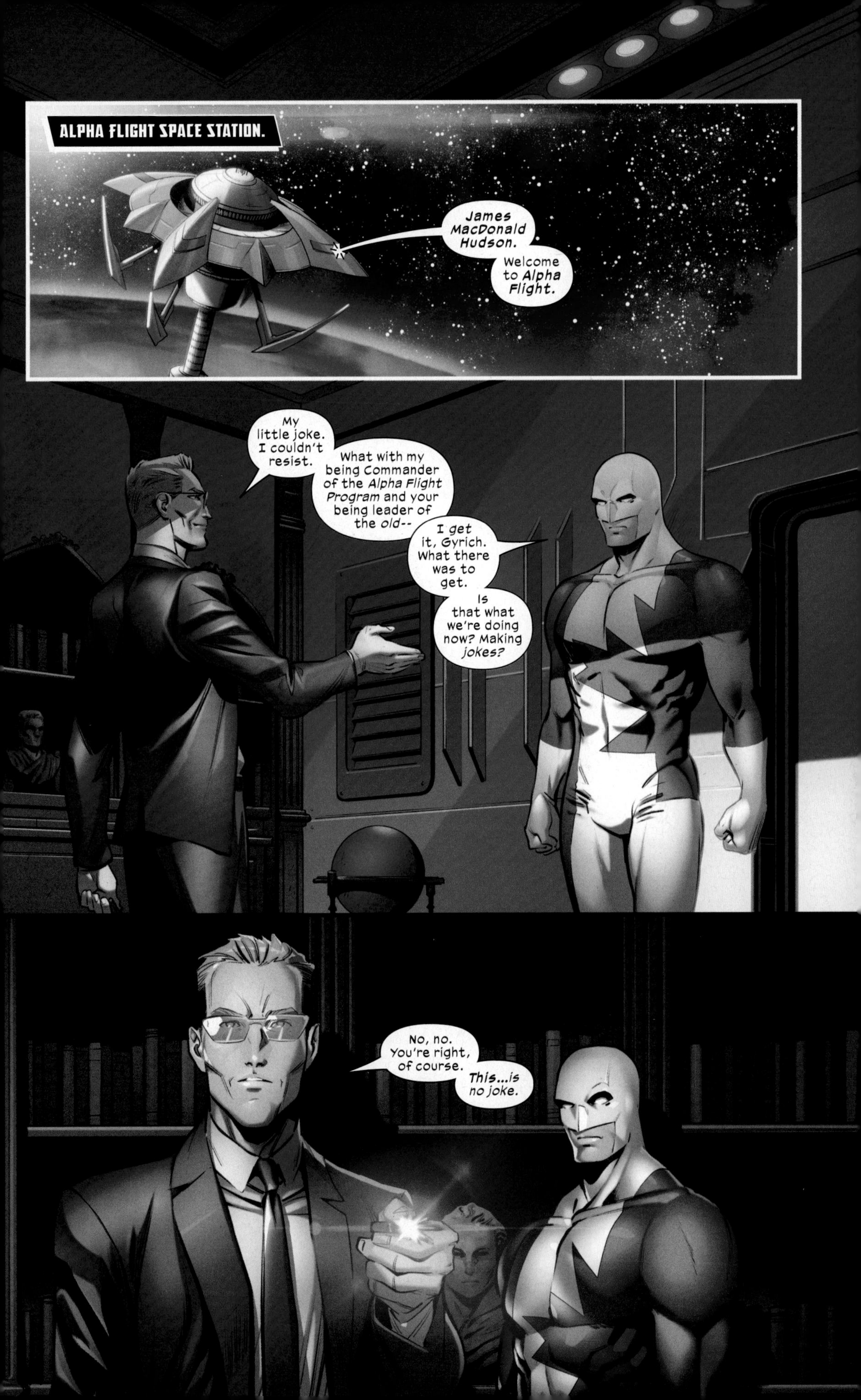
ALPHA FLIGHT SPACE STATION.
James MacDonald Hudson.
Welcome to Alpha Flight.
My little joke. I couldn't resist.
What with my being Commander of the Alpha Flight Program and your being leader of the old--
I get it, Gyrich. What there was to get.
Is that what we're doing now? Making jokes?
No, no. You're right, of course.
This...is no joke.

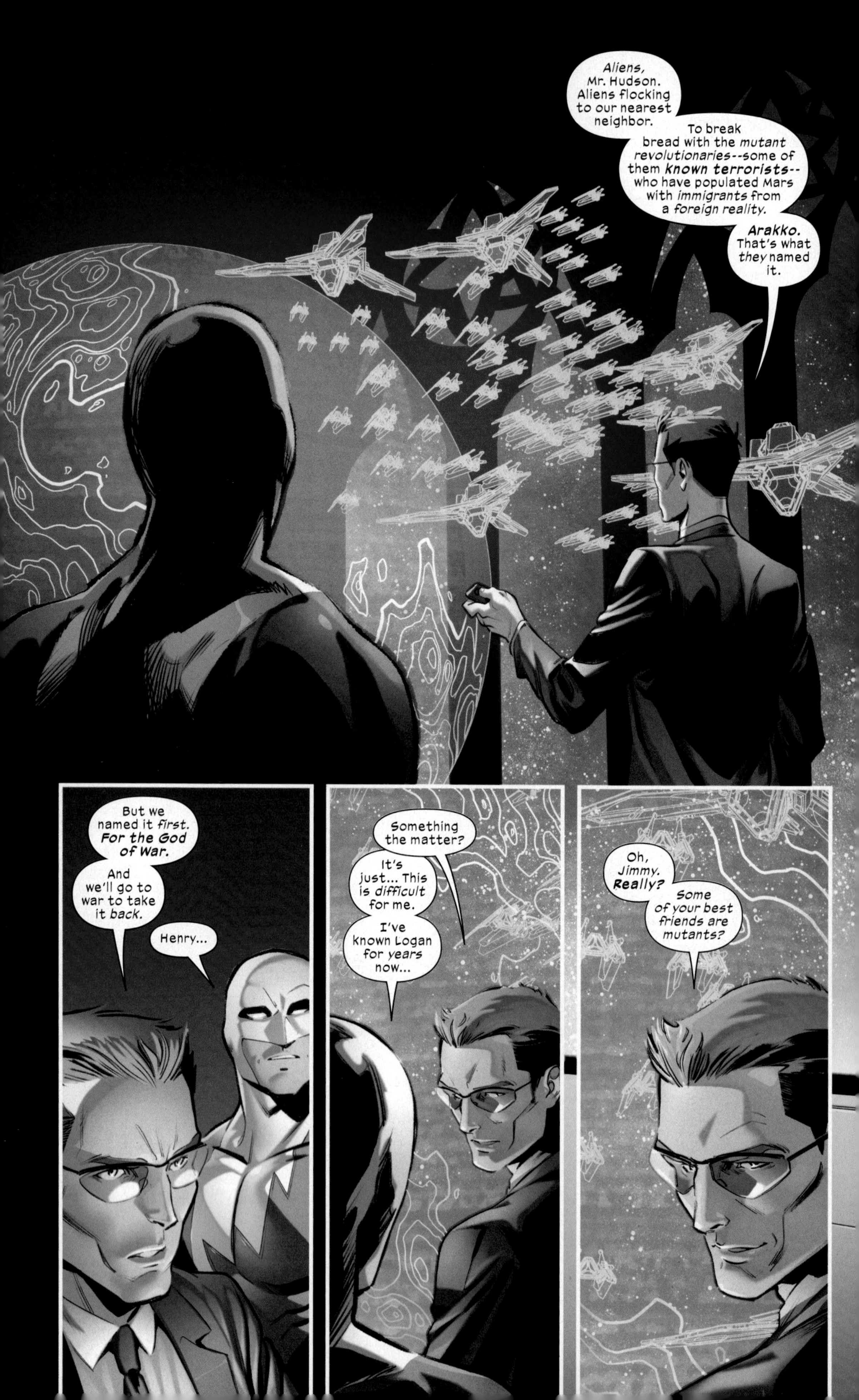

Aliens, Mr. Hudson. Aliens flocking to our nearest neighbor.
To break bread with the *mutant revolutionaries*--some of them ***known terrorists***--who have populated Mars with *immigrants* from a *foreign reality.*
***Arakko.*** That's what *they* named it.
But we named it *first.* ***For the God of War.***
And we'll go to war to take it *back.*
Henry...
Something the matter?
It's just... This is *difficult* for me.
I've known Logan for *years* now...
Oh, Jimmy. ***Really?***
Some of *your best friends* are *mutants?*

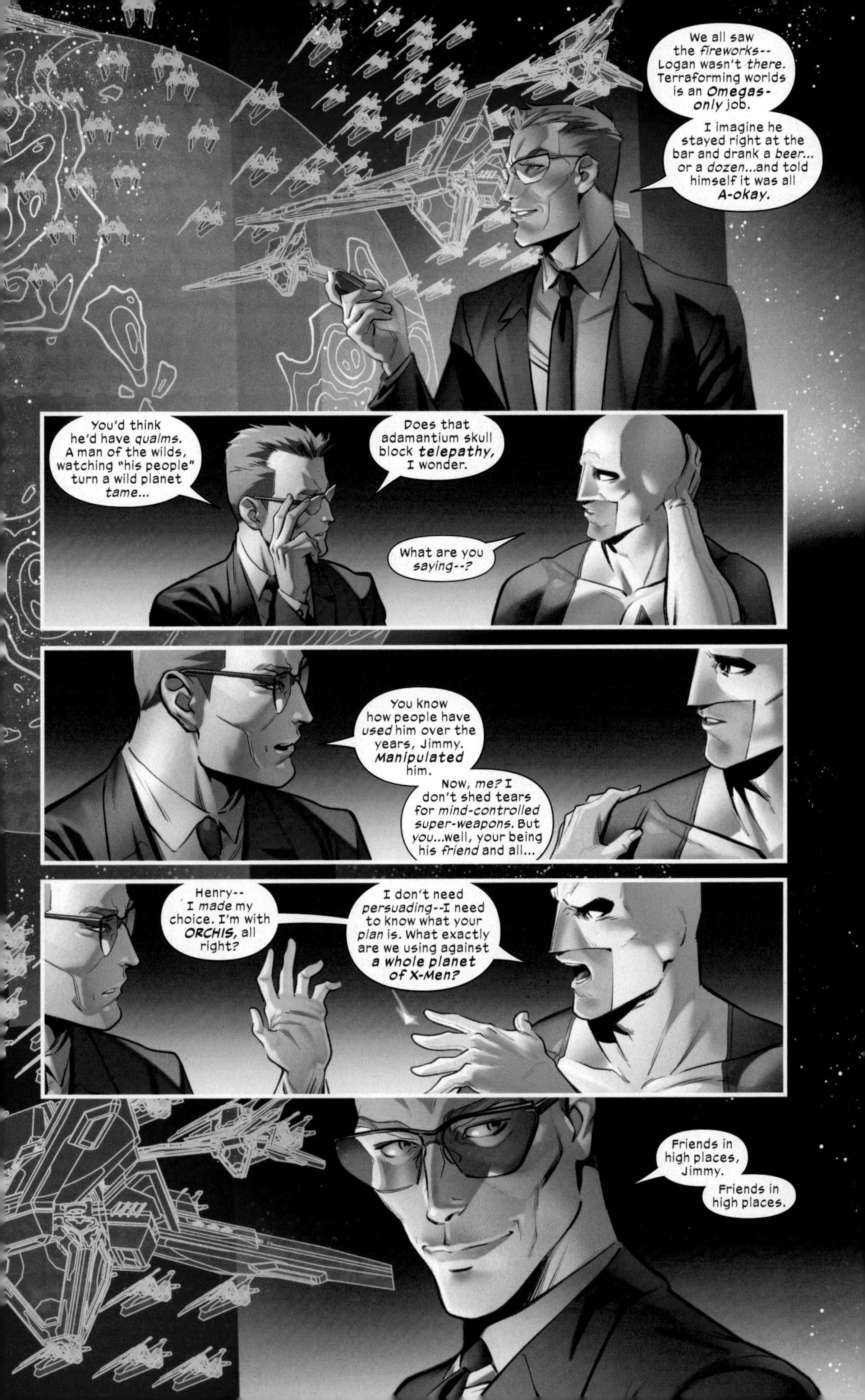
We all saw the *fireworks*--Logan wasn't *there.* Terraforming worlds is an ***Omegas-only*** job.
I imagine he stayed right at the bar and drank a *beer*... or a *dozen*...and told himself it was all ***A-okay.***
You'd think he'd have *qualms.* A man of the wilds, watching "his people" turn a wild planet *tame*...
Does that adamantium skull block ***telepathy,*** I wonder.
What are you *saying--?*
You know how people have *used* him over the years, Jimmy. ***Manipulated*** him.
Now, *me?* I don't shed tears for *mind-controlled super-weapons.* But *you*...well, your being his *friend* and all...
Henry--I *made* my choice. I'm with ***ORCHIS,*** all right?
I don't need *persuading*--I need to know what your *plan* is. What exactly are we using against ***a whole planet of X-Men?***
Friends in high places, Jimmy.
Friends in high places.

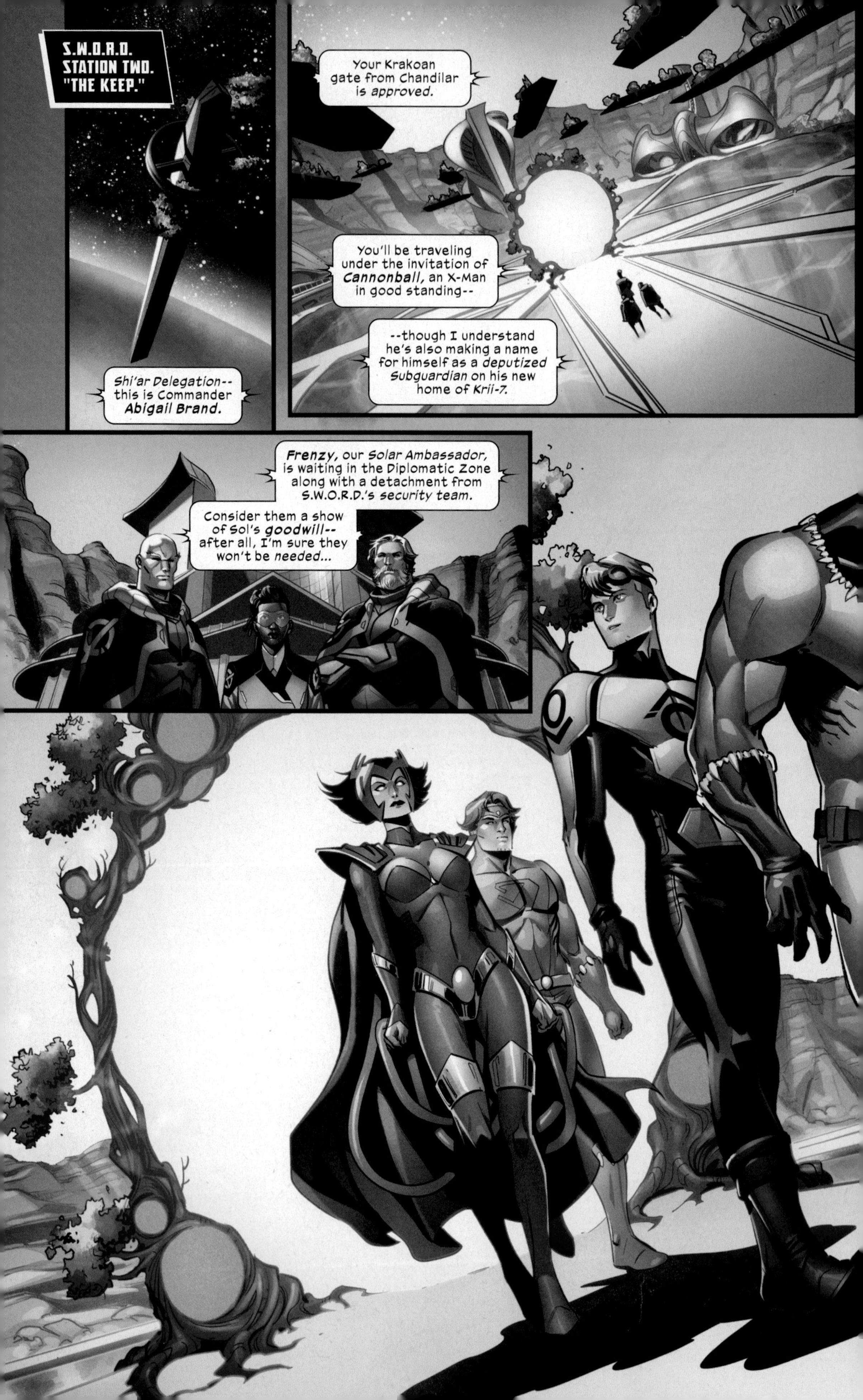

S.W.O.R.D. STATION TWO. "THE KEEP."
Shi'ar Delegation-- this is Commander Abigail Brand.
Your Krakoan gate from Chandilar is approved.
You'll be traveling under the invitation of Cannonball, an X-Man in good standing--
--though I understand he's also making a name for himself as a deputized Subguardian on his new home of Krii-7.
Frenzy, our Solar Ambassador, is waiting in the Diplomatic Zone along with a detachment from S.W.O.R.D.'s security team.
Consider them a show of Sol's goodwill-- after all, I'm sure they won't be needed...

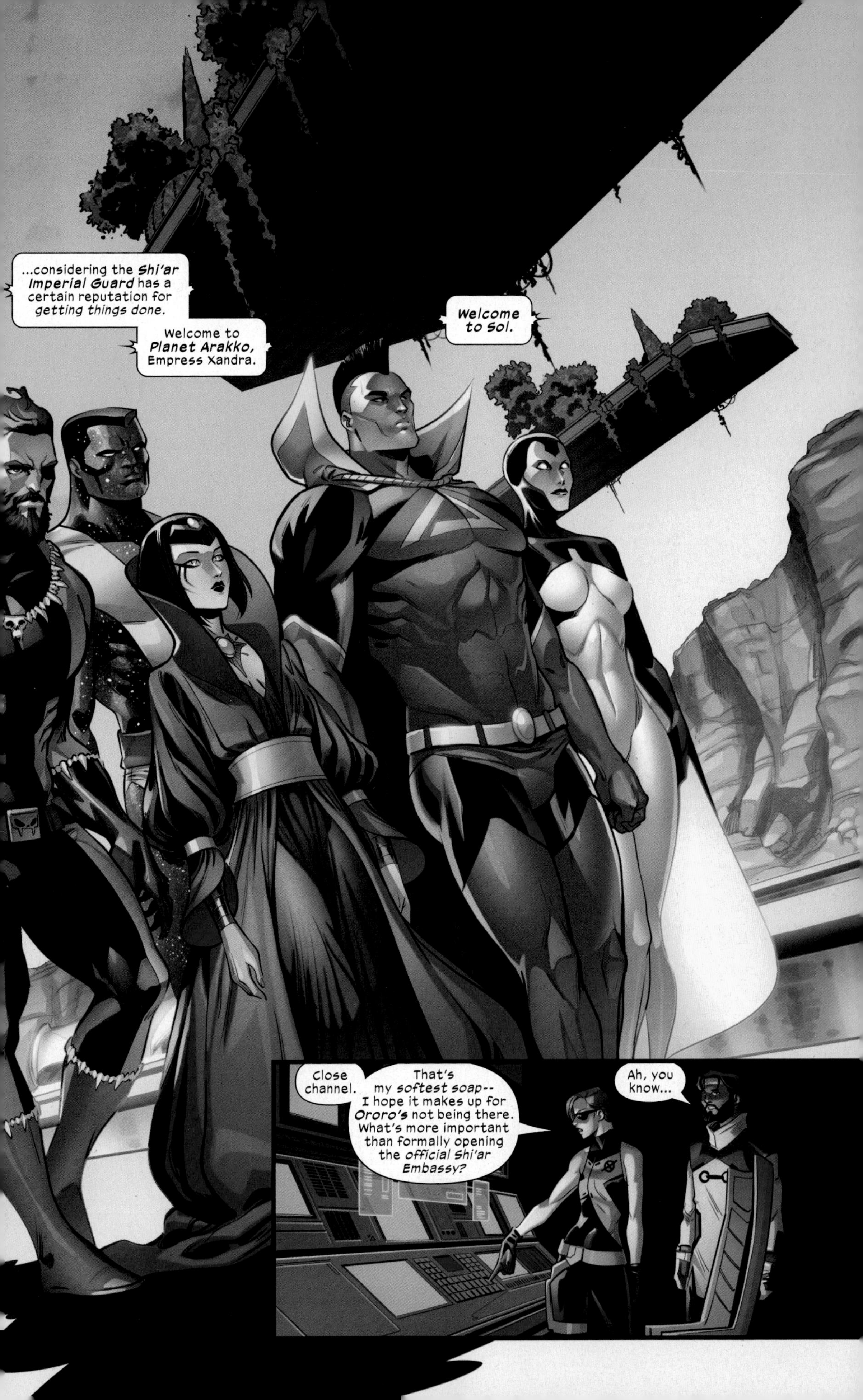

...considering the Shi'ar Imperial Guard has a certain reputation for getting things done.
Welcome to Planet Arakko, Empress Xandra.
Welcome to Sol.
Close channel.
That's my softest soap--I hope it makes up for Ororo's not being there. What's more important than formally opening the official Shi'ar Embassy?
Ah, you know...

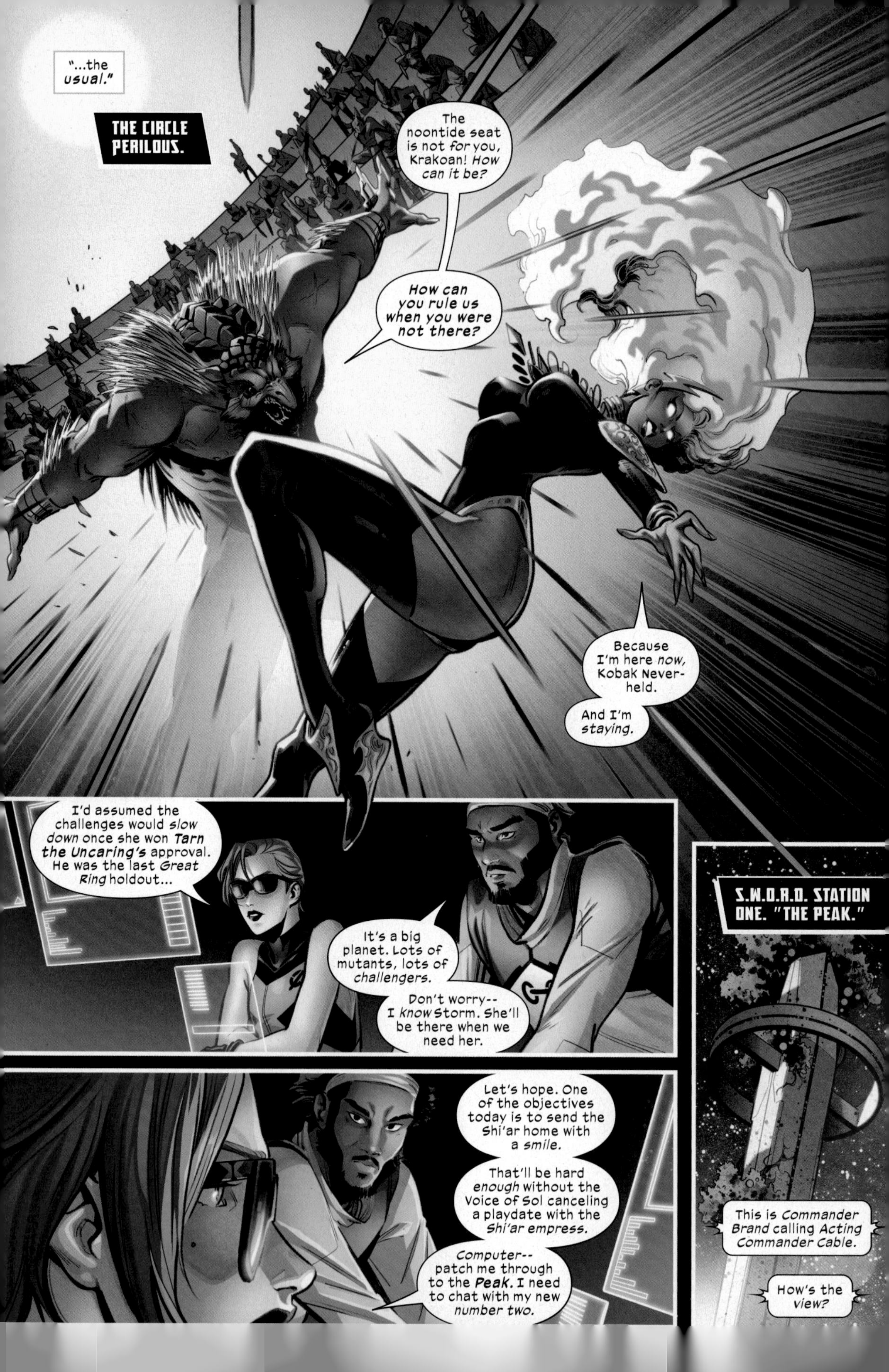
"...the usual."
THE CIRCLE PERILOUS.
The noontide seat is not for you, Krakoan! How can it be?
How can you rule us when you were not there?
Because I'm here now, Kobak Never-held.
And I'm staying.
I'd assumed the challenges would slow down once she won Tarn the Uncaring's approval. He was the last Great Ring holdout...
It's a big planet. Lots of mutants, lots of challengers.
Don't worry-- I know Storm. She'll be there when we need her.
Let's hope. One of the objectives today is to send the Shi'ar home with a smile.
That'll be hard enough without the Voice of Sol canceling a playdate with the Shi'ar empress.
Computer-- patch me through to the Peak. I need to chat with my new number two.
S.W.O.R.D. STATION ONE. "THE PEAK."
This is Commander Brand calling Acting Commander Cable.
How's the view?

# EYES ONLY :: PERSONNEL NOTES
# NATHAN SUMMERS / CABLE :: EYES ONLY

[DE...[ep]__0X]
[SEC..[ret]_09]

## ABIGAIL BRAND :: Z-2-08 :: GSTC 1010

There were two excellent reasons to pick Cable as my security chief. Unfortunately, they were both his parents.

Jean Grey was a Quiet Council member in the very best standing. Scott Summers was Captain Commander. And their son was a distracted teenager playing at being the Old Man he'd one day become -- enough combat skill to be useful, but not enough tactical and strategic know-how to become difficult. There was every chance he was going to stay that way too -- as I heard it, he'd come to our time as a fresh-faced youngster to prune the branch of his timeline that became the Old Man in the first place. New Cable, new future.

Except the new future didn't pan out -- not for him and not for me. Summers and Grey have excised themselves neatly from Krakoan politics, so putting their kid on my team no longer gives me even secondhand pull with the Council. And as for young Nathan... Well, the Old Man's back again.

Older, wiser and smarter. He looks at me through that glowing eye of his like he knows everything I'm about to do -- and maybe he does. For all I know, he read it in a history book.

And Glorp knows how history will tell the story of what I've got planned. They'll acknowledge the necessity of it, I'm sure.

But I doubt they'll be kind.

[D_[en]Y........[0]
[EVE_r[yth]ING..[9]

## /// DEEP SECRET :: ABOVE EYES ONLY ///

**Private note:** That glowing eye? It's not the window to Cable's soul, but, all the same, it might be a window of opportunity. Nathan Summers is infected with the Techno-Organic Virus -- what Warlock's species, the Phalanx, use to commune with (and consume) organic life. It's generally in his full control -- he uses it as an interface with his various prosthetic arms, but he can form a prosthesis entirely out of techno-organic material, and has done so for years at a time. His control of the virus is beyond anything I've ever seen, outside of the Phalanx themselves.

That all comes down to Cable's telekinesis, which is vastly overpowered -- to the point that it could burn his system out if controlling the virus didn't keep it occupied. So the TK controls the TO and the TO controls the TK -- a balance as delicate as a house of cards. Playing the right ace could bring the whole thing down on him... Too bad I deal from the bottom of the deck.

(Which is exactly the kind of strained metaphor turned dad joke he uses all the time. It's kind of a shame he'll never read this. I think he'd appreciate

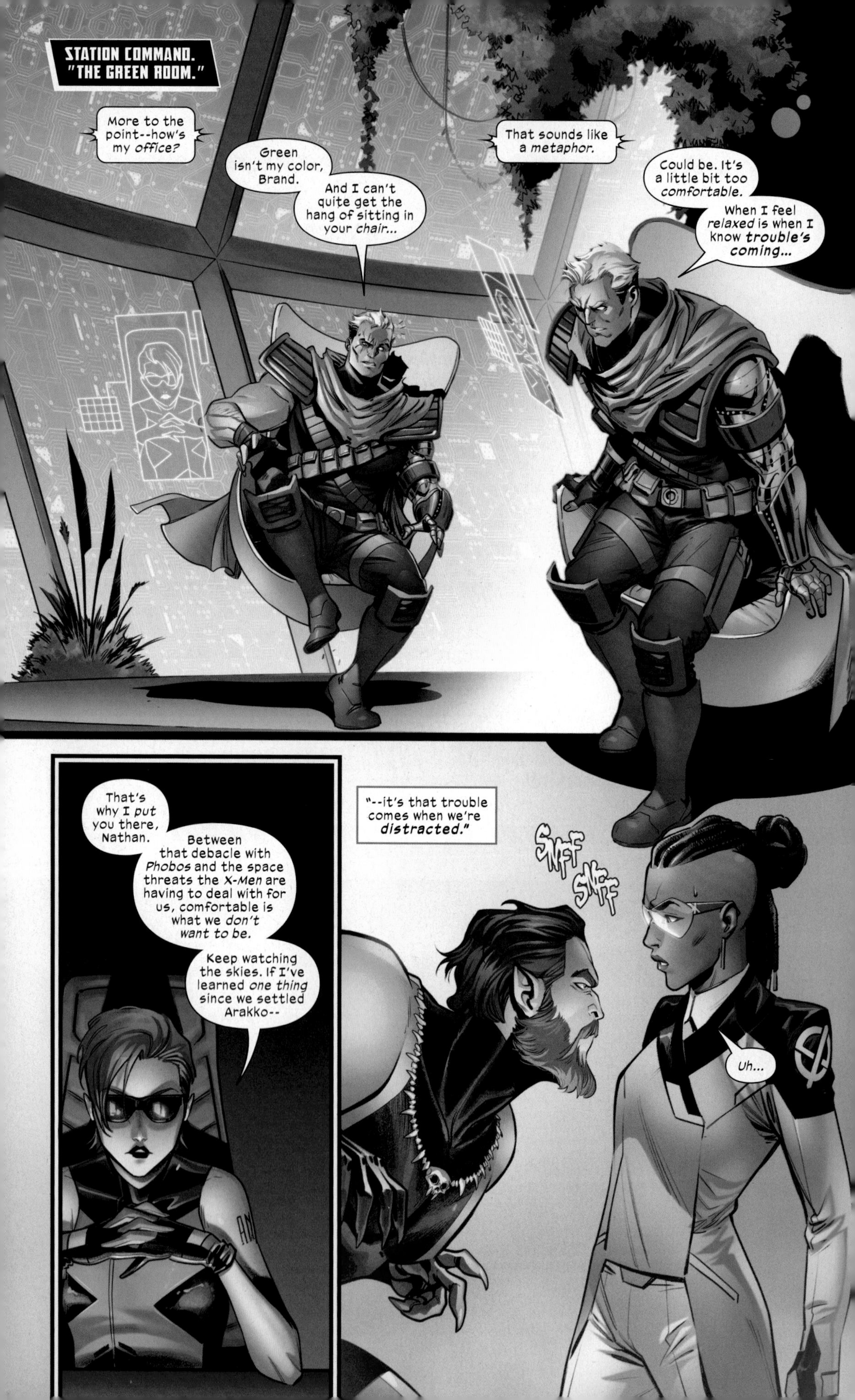

STATION COMMAND. "THE GREEN ROOM."
More to the point--how's my office?
Green isn't my color, Brand.
And I can't quite get the hang of sitting in your chair...
That sounds like a metaphor.
Could be. It's a little bit too comfortable.
When I feel relaxed is when I know trouble's coming...
That's why I put you there, Nathan.
Between that debacle with Phobos and the space threats the X-Men are having to deal with for us, comfortable is what we don't want to be.
Keep watching the skies. If I've learned one thing since we settled Arakko--
"--it's that trouble comes when we're distracted."
SNFF SNFF
Uh...

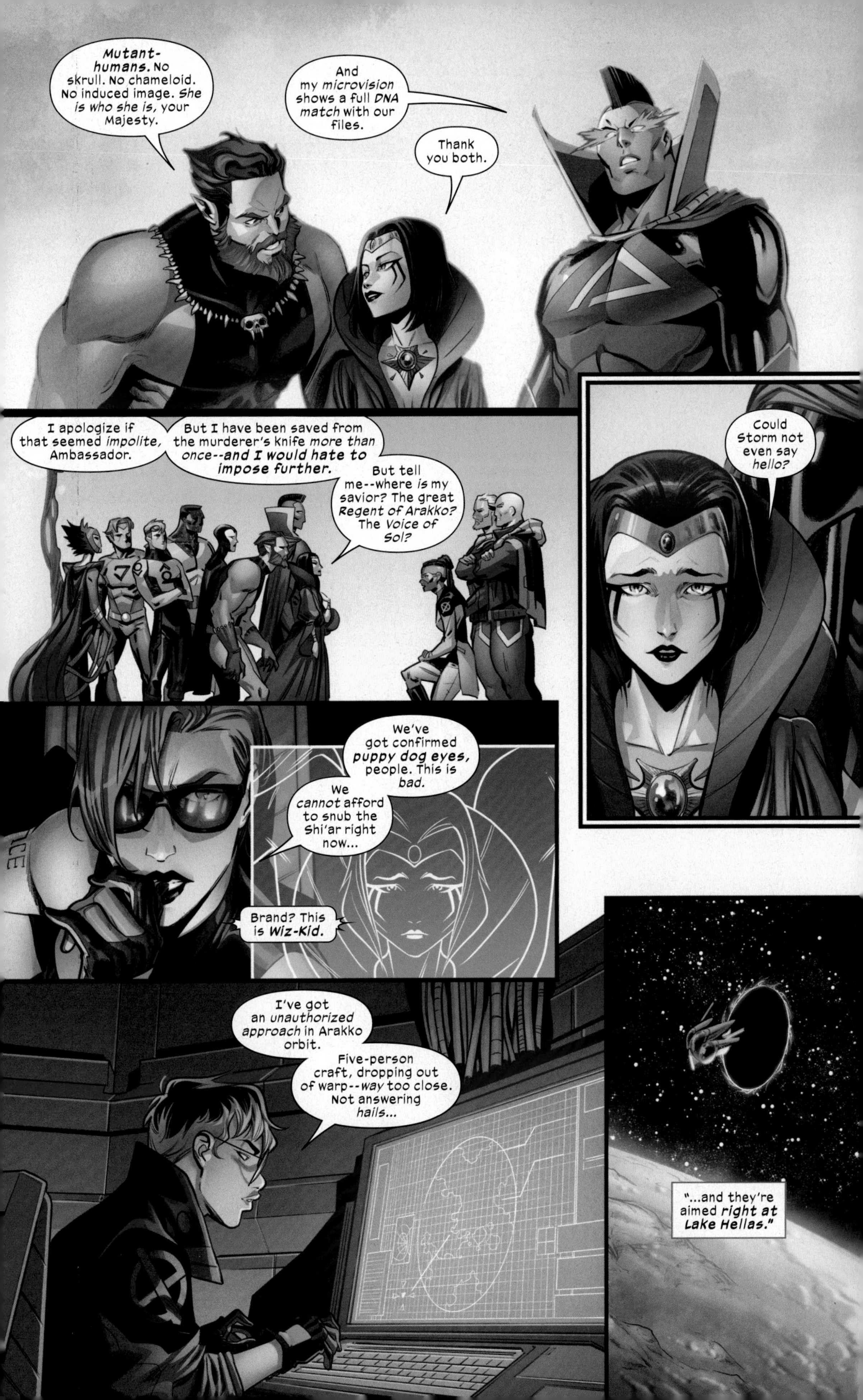
*Mutant-humans.* No skrull. No chameloid. No induced image. *She is who she is,* your Majesty.
And my *microvision* shows a full *DNA match* with our files.
Thank you both.
I apologize if that seemed *impolite,* Ambassador.
But I have been saved from the murderer's knife *more than once*--**and I would hate to impose further.**
But tell me--where *is* my savior? The great *Regent of Arakko?* The *Voice of Sol?*
Could Storm not even say *hello?*
We've got confirmed **puppy dog eyes,** people. This is *bad.*
We *cannot* afford to snub the Shi'ar right now...
Brand? This is **Wiz-Kid.**
I've got an *unauthorized approach* in Arakko orbit.
Five-person craft, dropping out of warp--*way* too close. Not answering *hails...*
"...and they're aimed **right at Lake Hellas."**

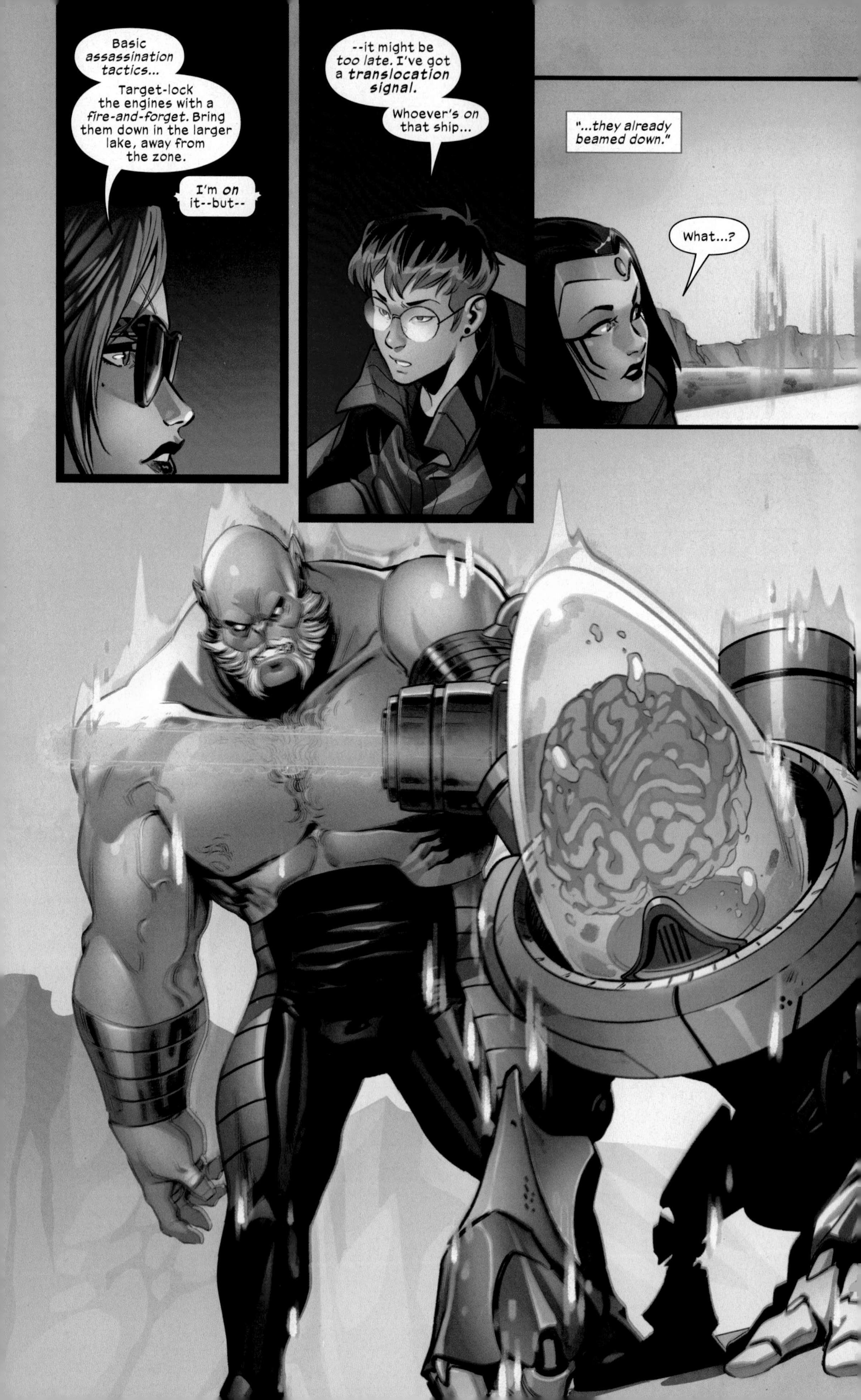
Basic *assassination tactics...*
Target-lock the engines with a *fire-and-forget*. Bring them down in the larger lake, away from the zone.
I'm *on* it--but--
--it might be *too late*. I've got a ***translocation signal.***
Whoever's *on* that ship...
*"...they already beamed down."*
What...?

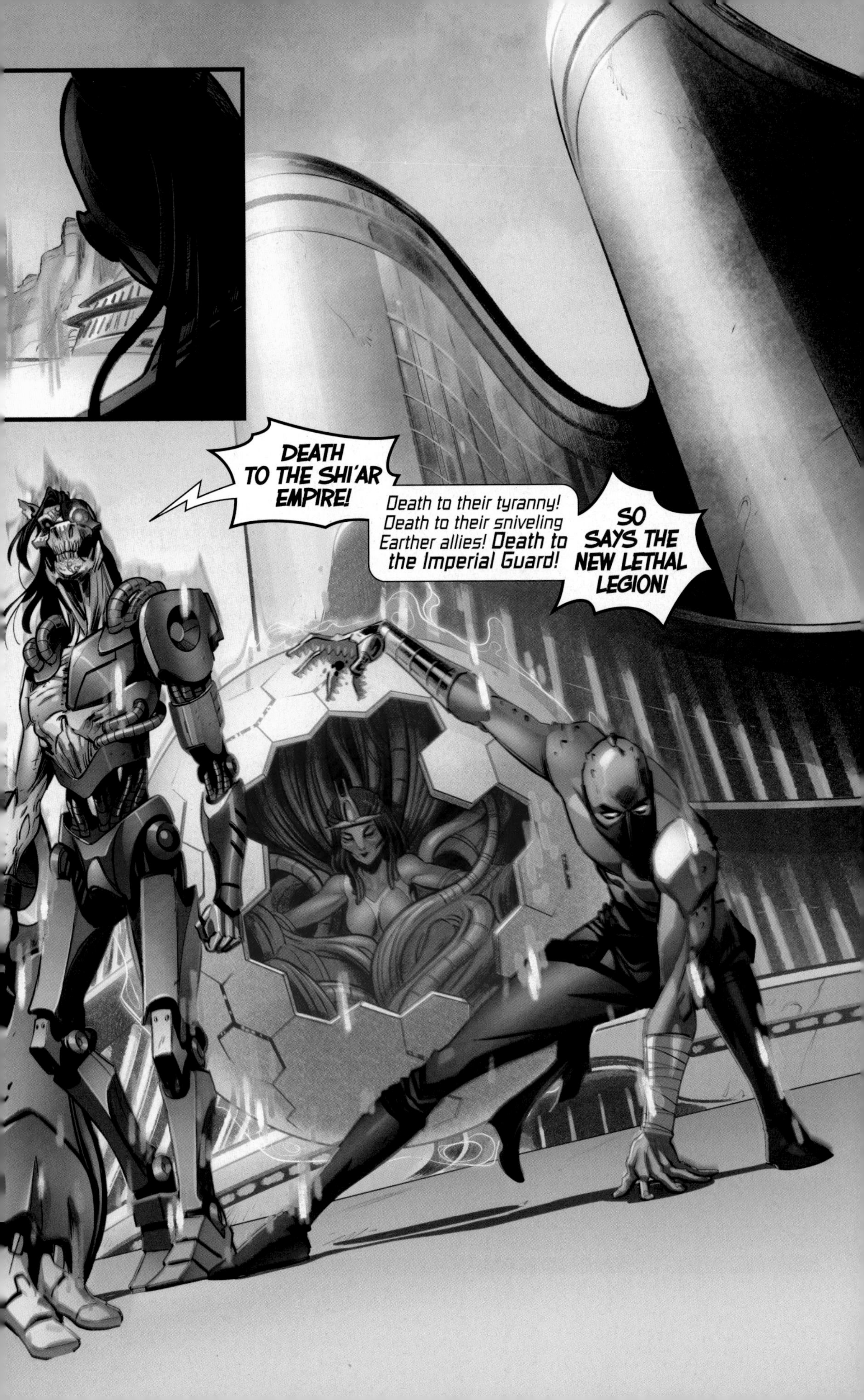
DEATH TO THE SHI'AR EMPIRE!
Death to their tyranny! Death to their sniveling Earther allies! Death to the Imperial Guard!
SO SAYS THE NEW LETHAL LEGION!

# OS017-SERIES ENHANCILE CATALOGUE :: "THE LETHAL LEGION"

Armed with the latest psychic warfare technology -- as well as some fan-favorite weaponry from previous years -- our latest enhanciles are our most powerful yet. Each can be utilized individually or combined seamlessly into the perfect five-being terror cell -- so whether you want to take full credit for their atrocities, or use them to throw suspicion off your larger goals, the OS017-Series "Lethal Legion" is here to meet your every need.

| OS017-001 ::<br>FIRST VARIETY ::<br><br>*"HALF-BOT"* |  | All the functionality of the OS016 Tactical Combat Droid you know and love, more efficient than ever -- and now with an additional organic component to induce psychological horror in any foe. Please specify planetary origin of corpse when ordering. |
|---|---|---|
| OS017-002 ::<br>SECOND VARIETY ::<br><br>*"MR. ELOQUENT"* |  | Augmented for melee combat -- with the return of OS015's award-winning "atomic chain saw" -- 017-002 comes media-ready with one of five winning personality types, each with a believable pre-programmed backstory for those vital to-camera monologues. |
| OS017-003 ::<br>THIRD VARIETY ::<br><br>*"THE ELECTRIC HEAD"* |  | For years, we were told that the problem with vat-grown telepathic super-brains was getting them out of the vat. So we brought the vat to us, built into a fully functional OS016 Bipedal Tank Unit. Just the thing to crush your enemies... physically and emotionally. |
| OS017-004 ::<br>FOURTH VARIETY ::<br><br>*"ORBIS EXTREMIS"* |  | Sometimes evolution needs a little help -- like the raw power of an "Orbis Stellaris" brand organo-mechanical fusion shell, routed through the brain of an Alpha-class psychic sensitive. That means laser-focused control of any element on the battlefield... or in the boardroom. |
| OS017-005 ::<br>FIFTH VARIETY ::<br><br>*"DEATH GRIP"* |  | OS017's emphasis on psychic combat doesn't mean we've forgotten the traditional pleasures of biological warfare. 017-005 combines next-gen necrotic bacteria with uploads of Kree, Xandarian and Centaurian unarmed combat styles for the perfect "one-touch" kill. |

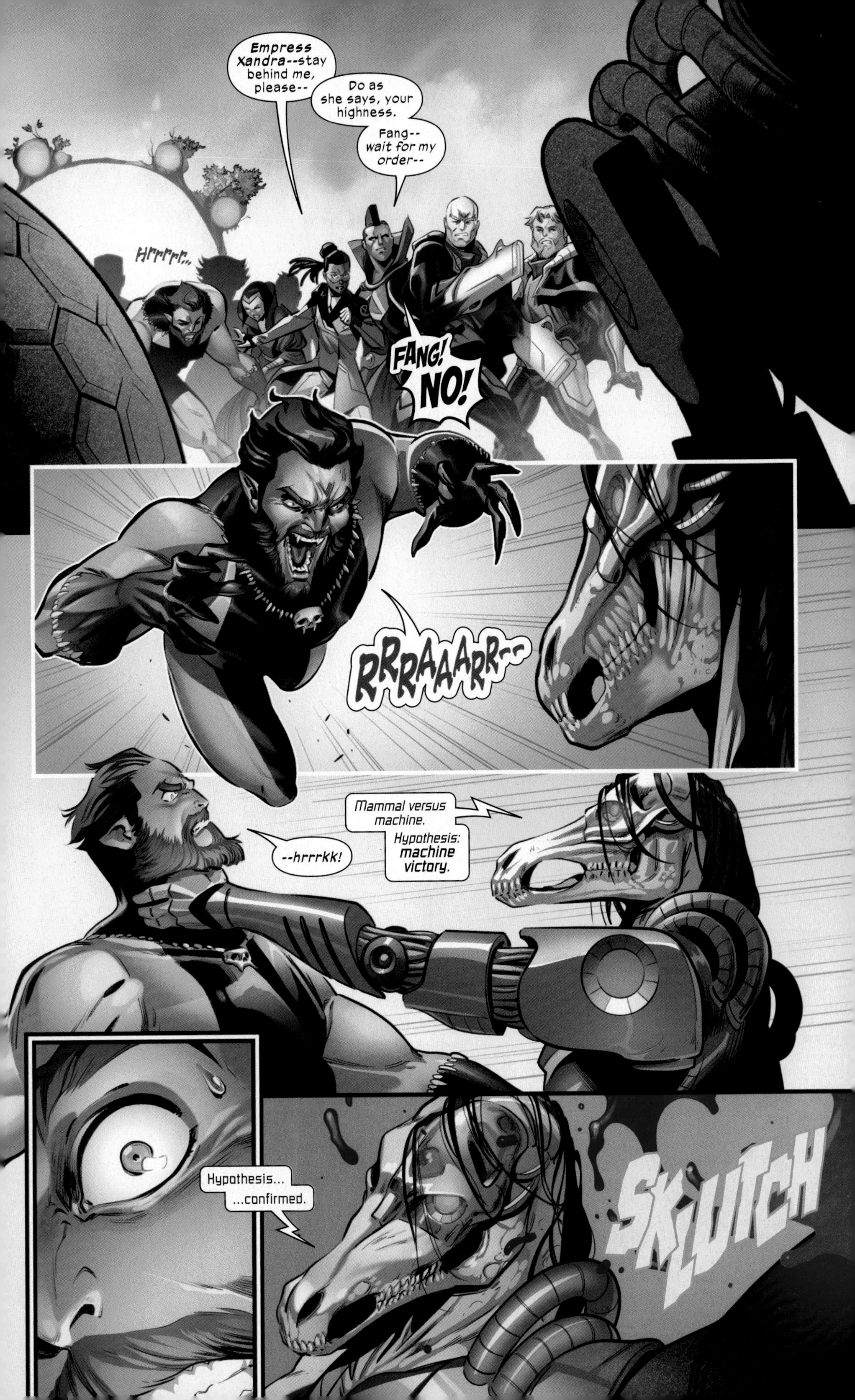
Empress Xandra--stay behind me, please--
Do as she says, your highness.
Fang--wait for my order--
Hrrrrr...
FANG! NO!
RRRAAARR--
--hrrrkk!
Mammal versus machine.
Hypothesis: machine victory.
Hypothesis...
...confirmed.
SKLUTCH

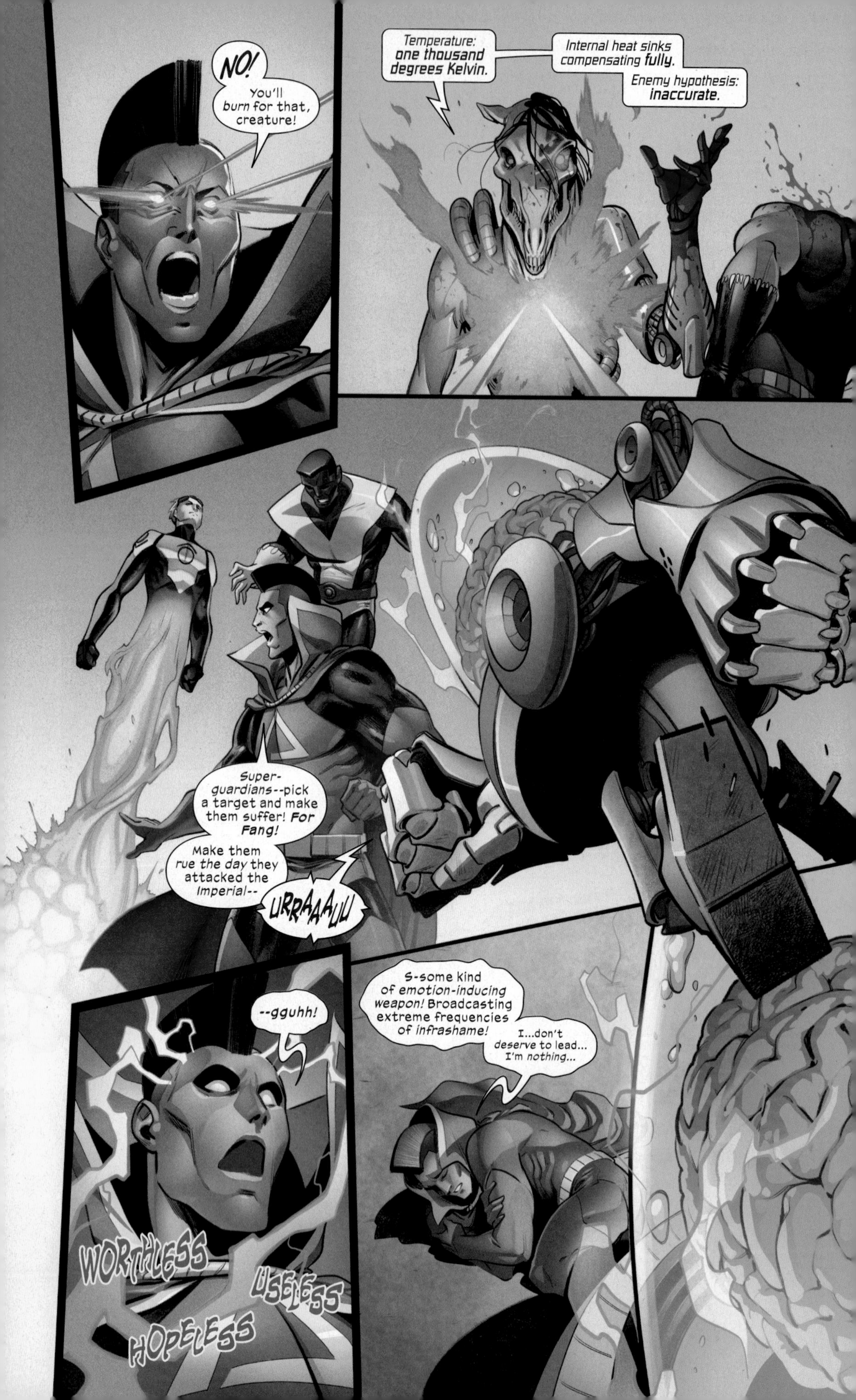
NO! You'll burn for that, creature!
Temperature: one thousand degrees Kelvin.
Internal heat sinks compensating fully.
Enemy hypothesis: inaccurate.
Super-guardians--pick a target and make them suffer! For Fang!
Make them rue the day they attacked the Imperial--
URRAAAUU
--gguhh!
S-some kind of emotion-inducing weapon! Broadcasting extreme frequencies of infrashame!
I...don't deserve to lead... I'm nothing...
WORTHLESS
USELESS
HOPELESS

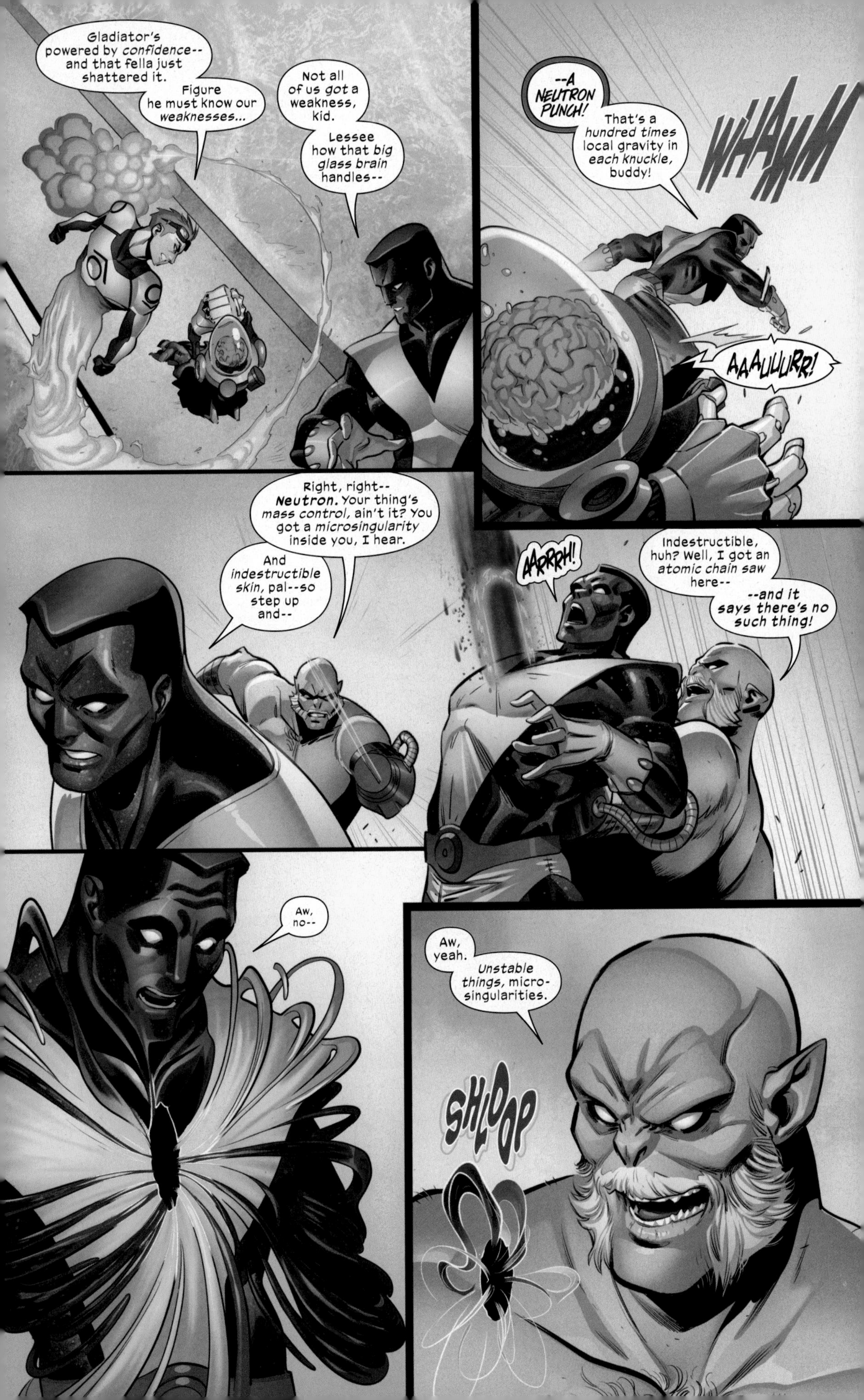

Gladiator's powered by *confidence*-- and that fella just shattered it.
Figure he must know our *weaknesses*...
Not all of us *got* a weakness, kid.
Lessee how that *big glass brain* handles--
--A NEUTRON PUNCH!
That's a *hundred times* local gravity in *each knuckle*, buddy!
WHAMM
AAAUUURR!
Right, right-- **Neutron.** Your thing's *mass control*, ain't it? You got a *microsingularity* inside you, I hear.
And *indestructible* skin, pal--so step up and--
AARRRH!
Indestructible, huh? Well, I got an *atomic chain saw* here--
--and it says there's no such thing!
Aw, no--
Aw, yeah.
*Unstable* things, micro-singularities.
SHLOOP

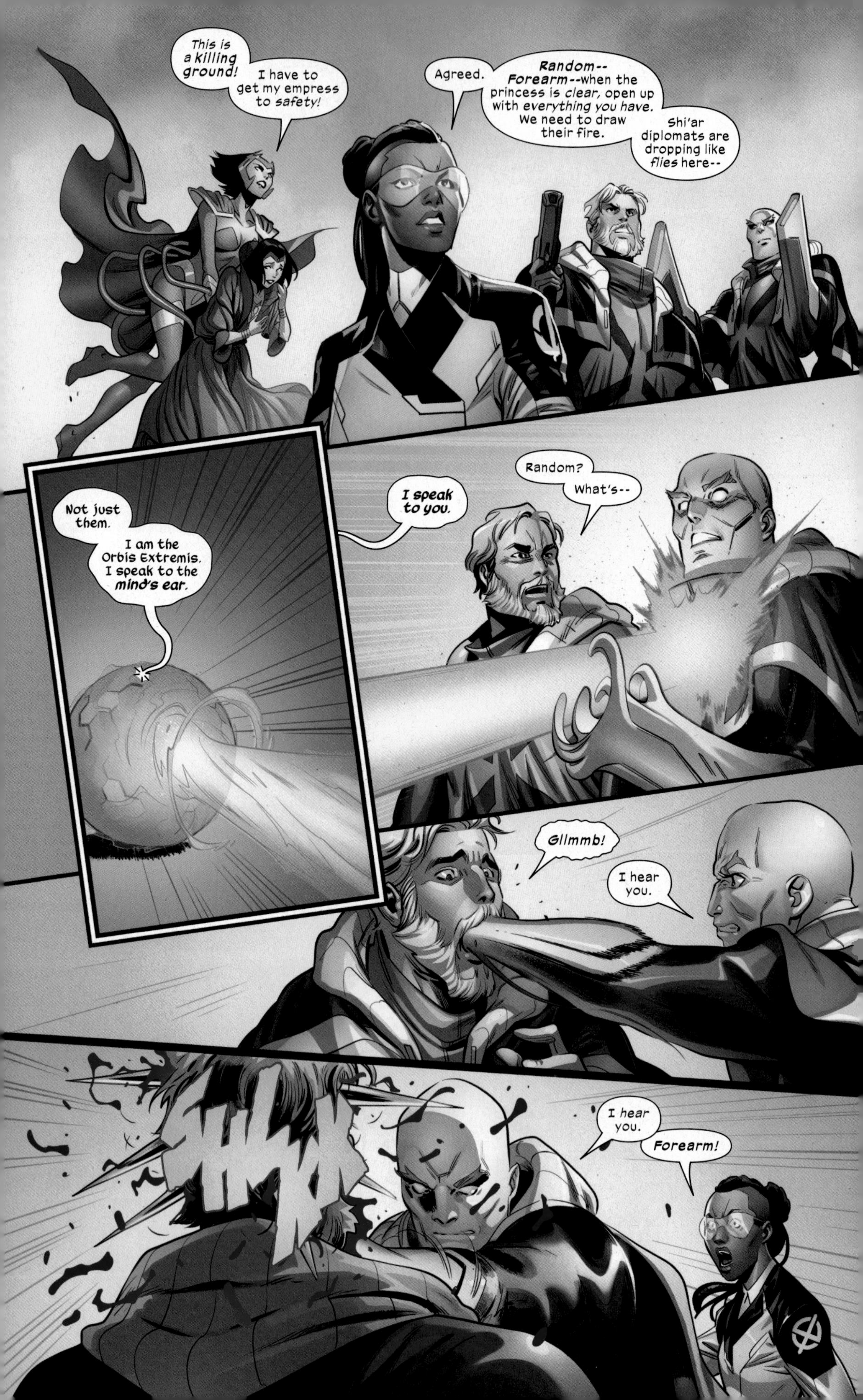
This is a killing ground!
I have to get my empress to safety!
Agreed.
Random-- Forearm--when the princess is clear, open up with everything you have. We need to draw their fire.
Shi'ar diplomats are dropping like flies here--
Not just them.
I am the Orbis Extremis. I speak to the mind's ear.
I speak to you.
Random?
What's--
Gllmmb!
I hear you.
I hear you.
Forearm!

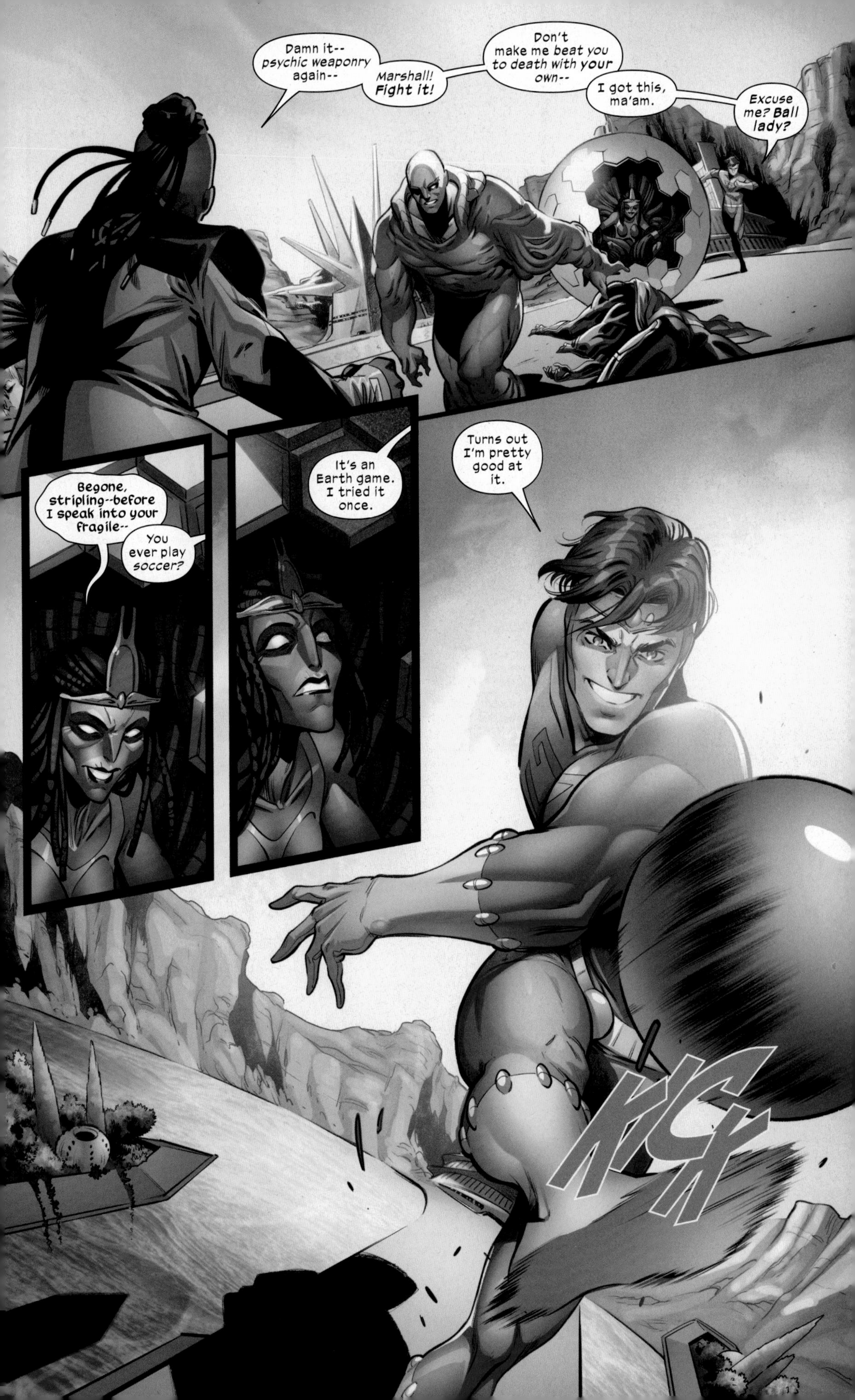

Damn it--
psychic weaponry
again--
Marshall!
Fight it!
Don't
make me beat you
to death with your
own--
I got this,
ma'am.
Excuse
me? Ball
lady?
Begone,
stripling--before
I speak into your
fragile--
You
ever play
soccer?
It's an
Earth game.
I tried it
once.
Turns out
I'm pretty
good at
it.
KIC

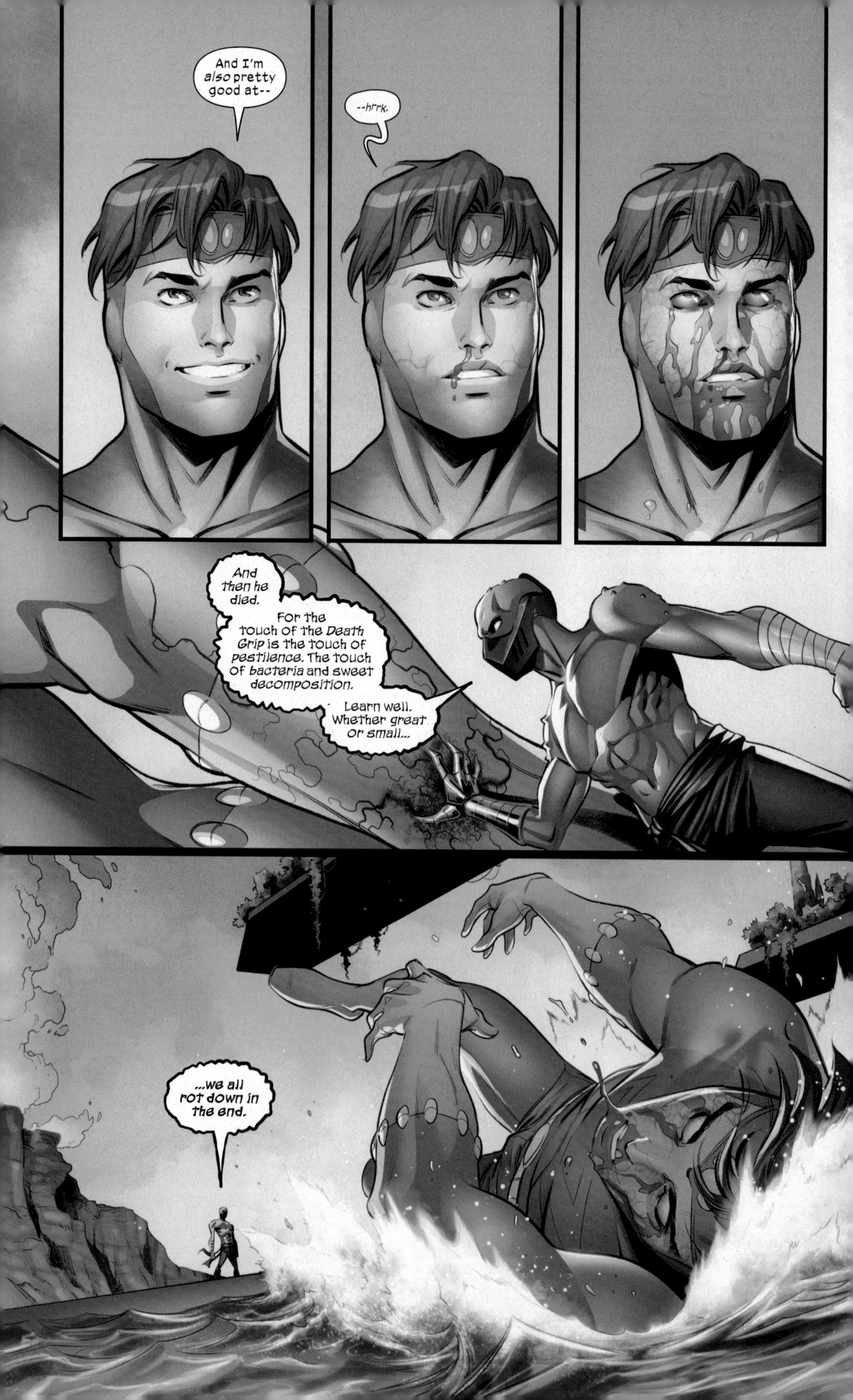

And I'm also pretty good at--
--hrrk.
And then he died.
For the touch of the Death Grip is the touch of pestilence. The touch of bacteria and sweet decomposition.
Learn well. Whether great or small...
...we all rot down in the end.

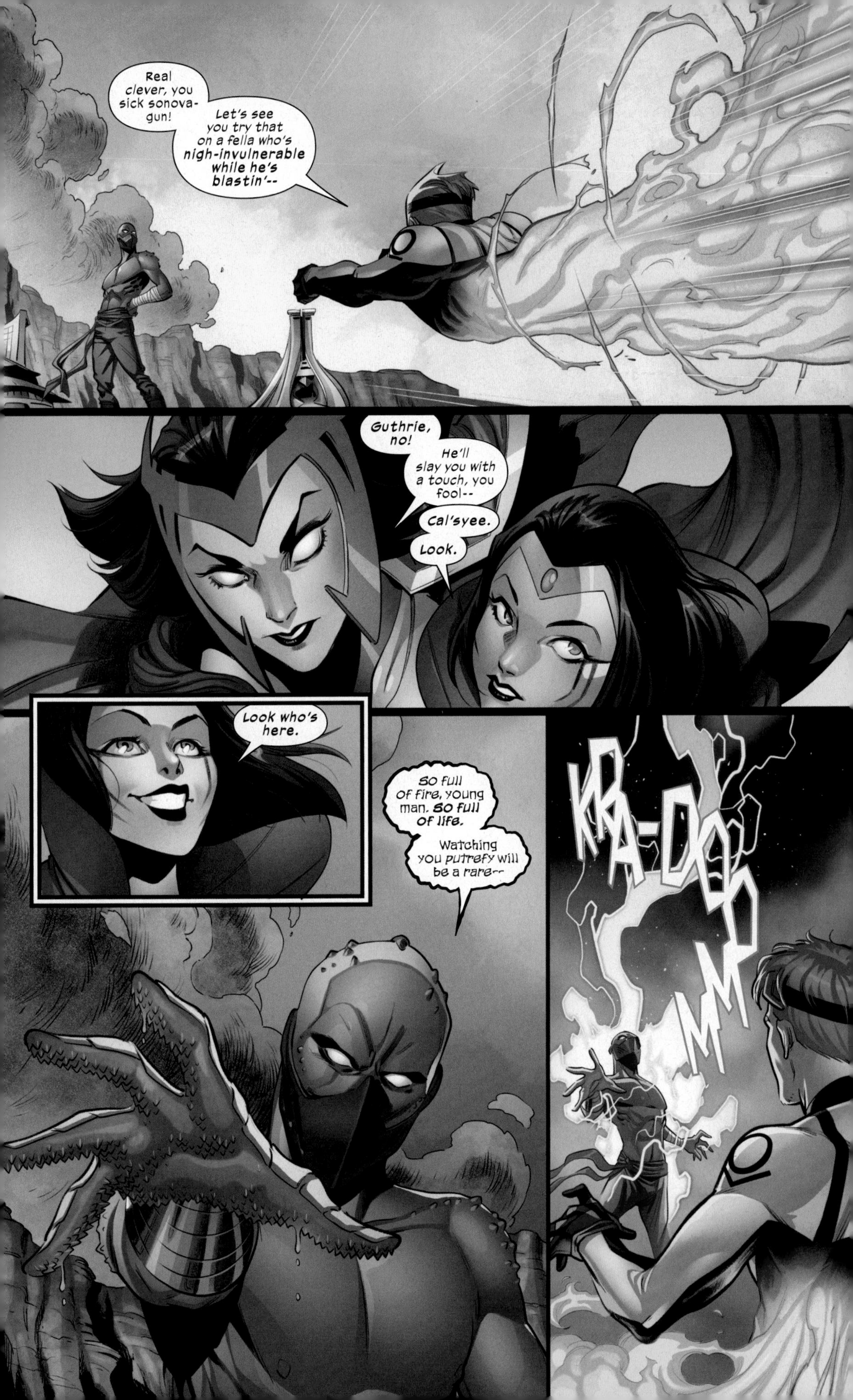
Real clever, you sick sonova-gun!
Let's see you try that on a fella who's nigh-invulnerable while he's blastin'--
Guthrie, no!
He'll slay you with a touch, you fool--
Cal'syee.
Look.
Look who's here.
So full of fire, young man. So full of life.
Watching you putrefy will be a rare--
KRA-DOOOMM

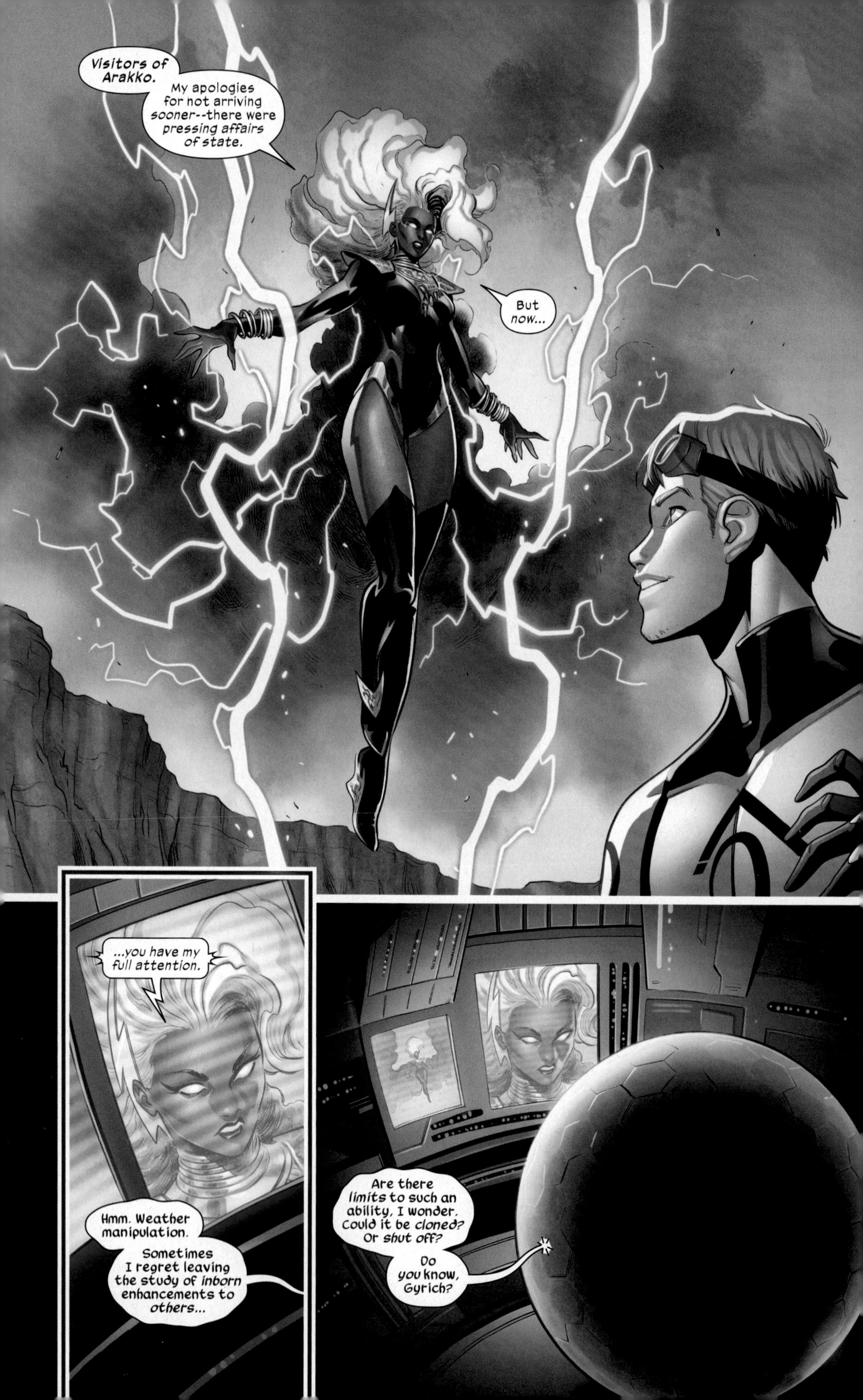
Visitors of Arakko.
My apologies for not arriving sooner--there were pressing affairs of state.
But now...
...you have my full attention.
Hmm. Weather manipulation.
Sometimes I regret leaving the study of inborn enhancements to others...
Are there limits to such an ability, I wonder. Could it be cloned? Or shut off?
Do you know, Gyrich?

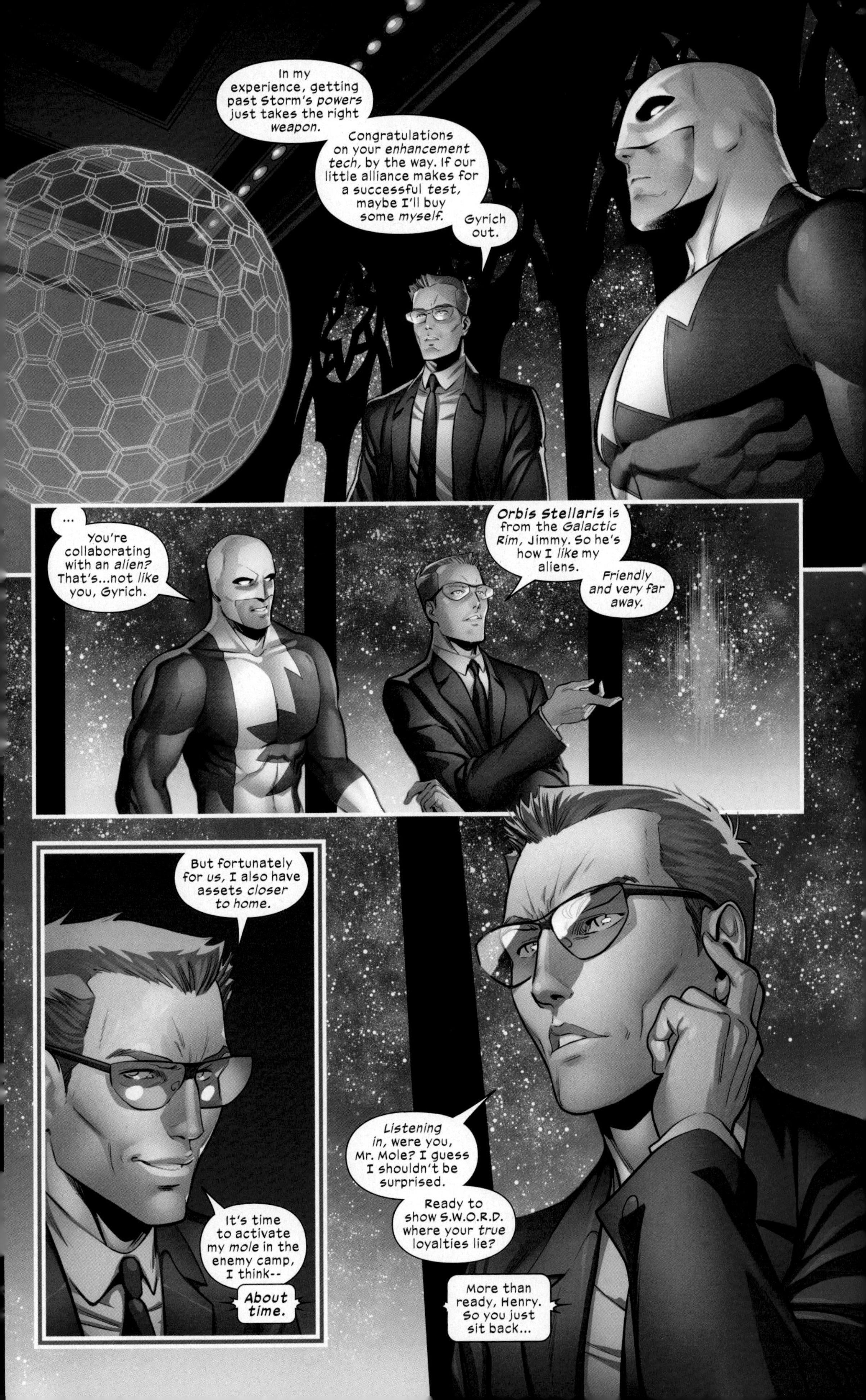
In my experience, getting past Storm's powers just takes the right weapon.
Congratulations on your enhancement tech, by the way. If our little alliance makes for a successful test, maybe I'll buy some myself.
Gyrich out.
...
You're collaborating with an alien? That's...not like you, Gyrich.
Orbis Stellaris is from the Galactic Rim, Jimmy. So he's how I like my aliens.
Friendly and very far away.
But fortunately for us, I also have assets closer to home.
It's time to activate my mole in the enemy camp, I think--
About time.
Listening in, were you, Mr. Mole? I guess I shouldn't be surprised.
Ready to show S.W.O.R.D. where your true loyalties lie?
More than ready, Henry. So you just sit back...

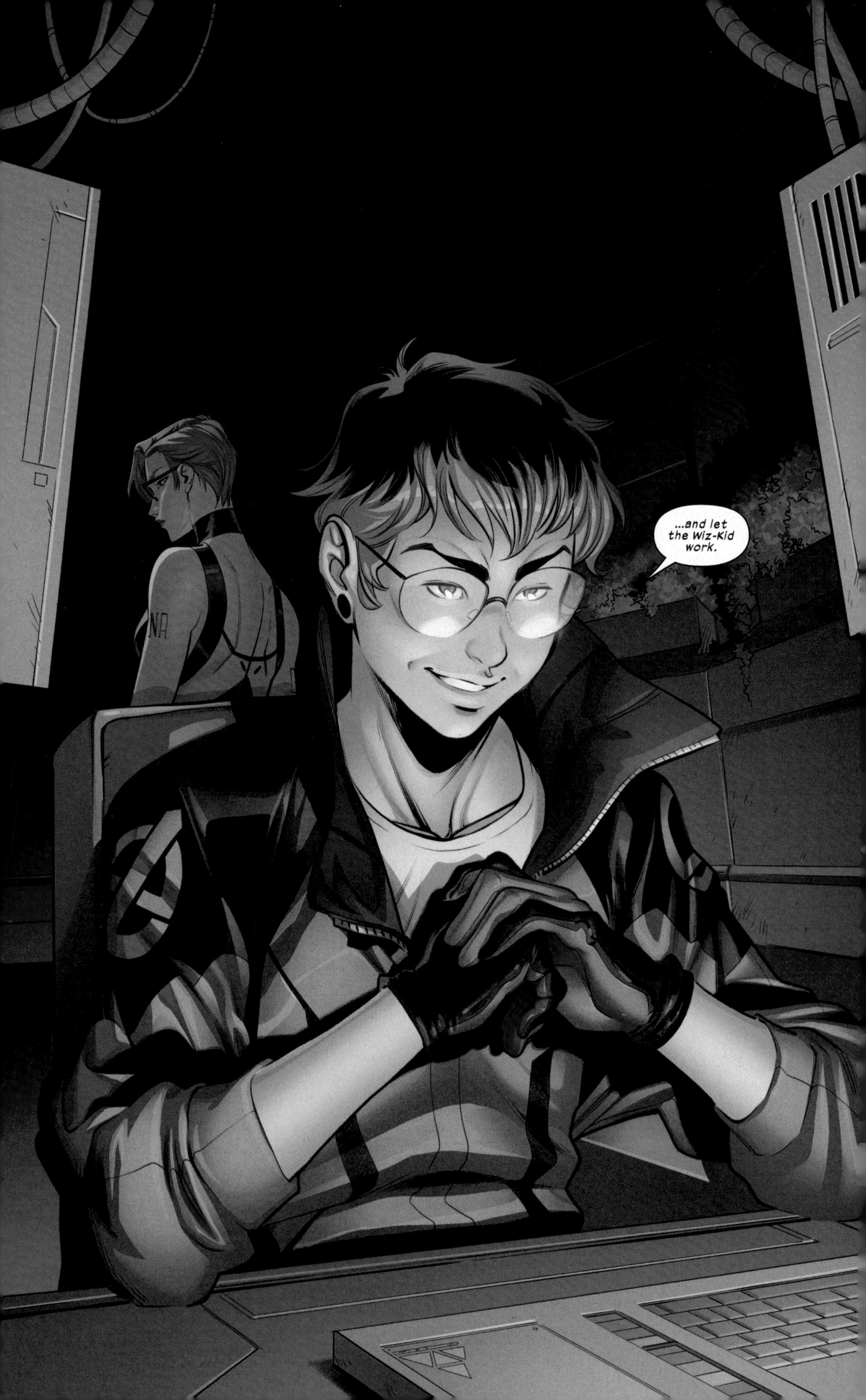
...and let the Wiz-Kid work.

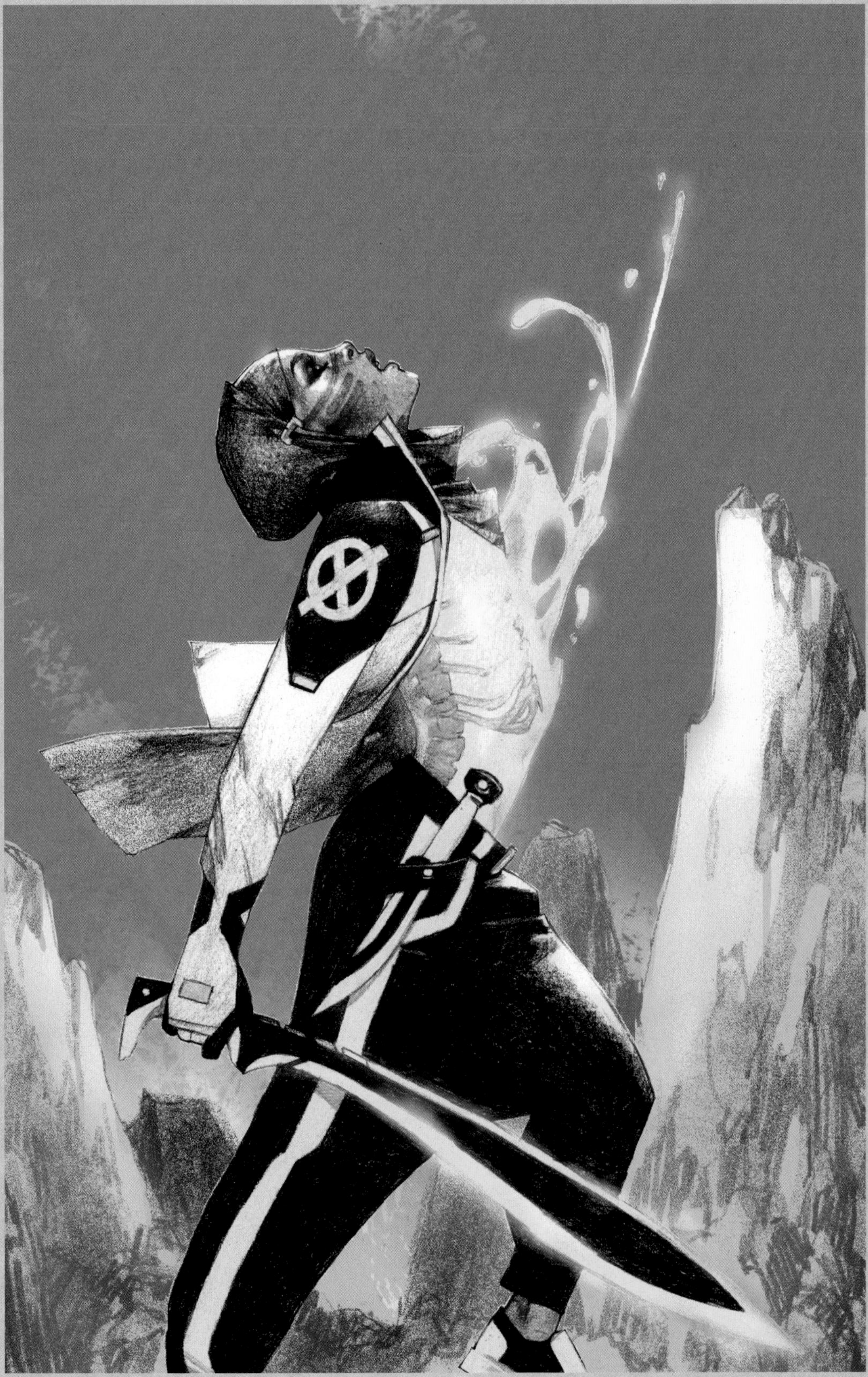

**S.W.O.R.D. #9 Variant** by Davi Go

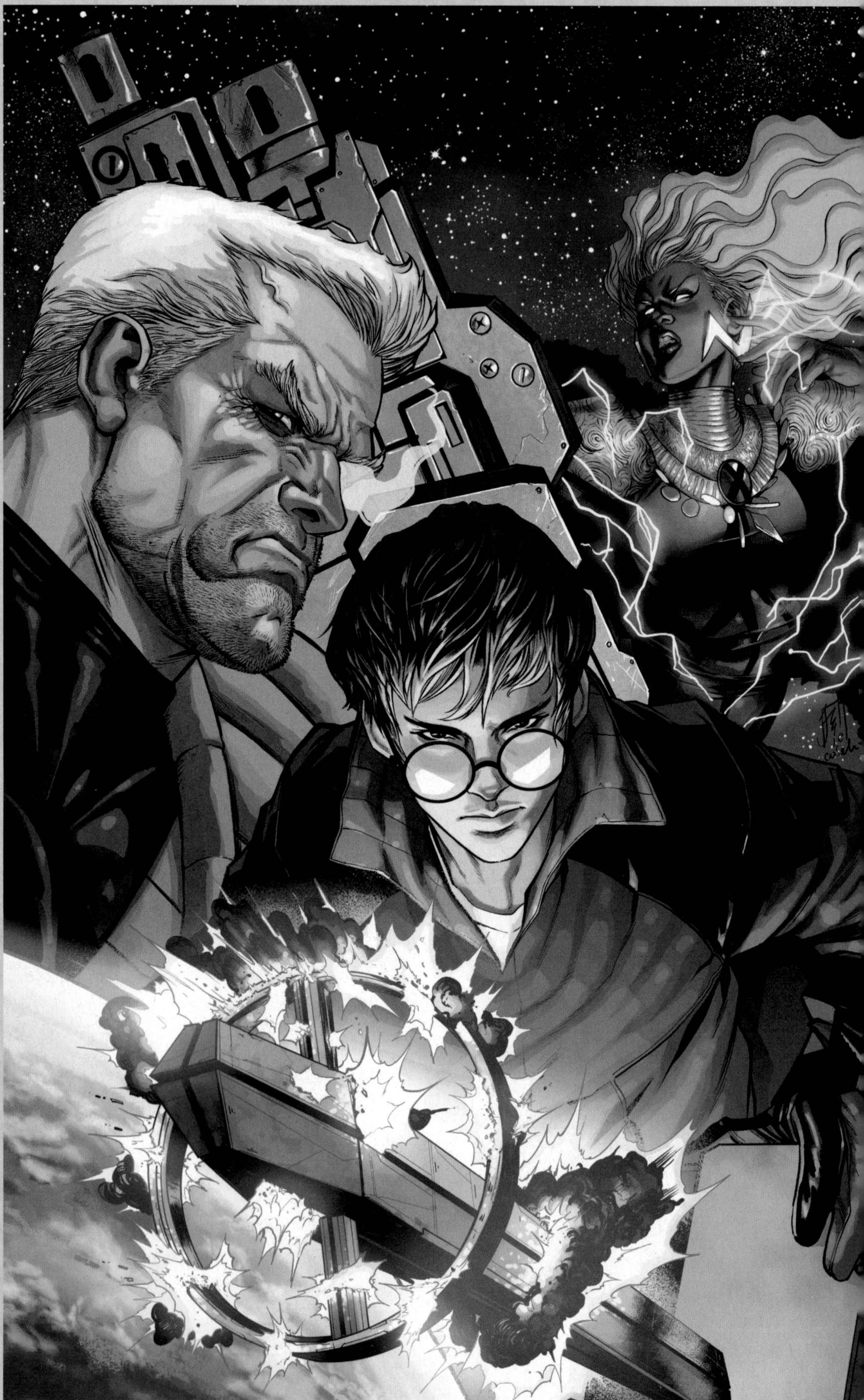

Triple Threat

# 10

[reign_of_x]

[mutants_of_X]
[the_world__X]

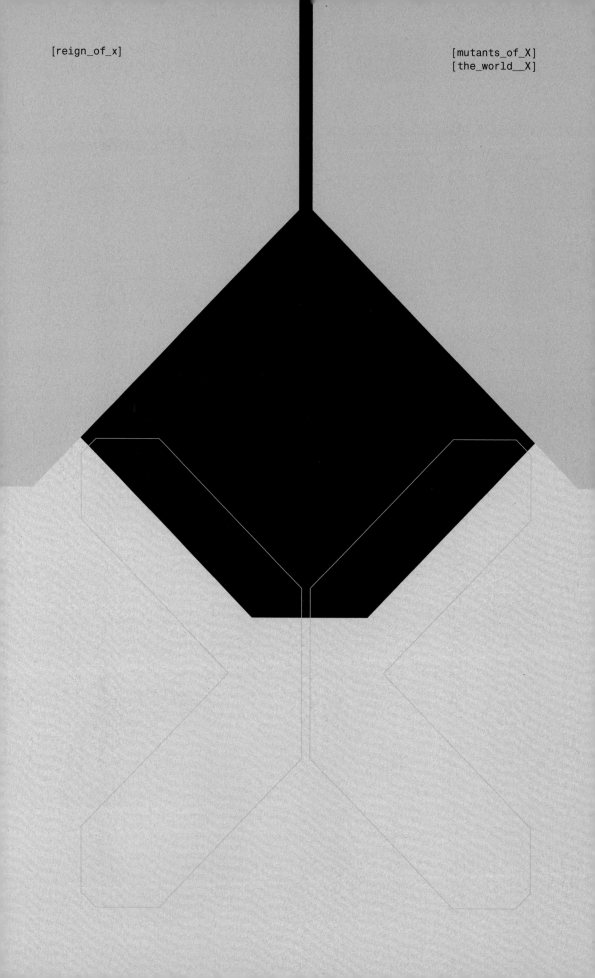

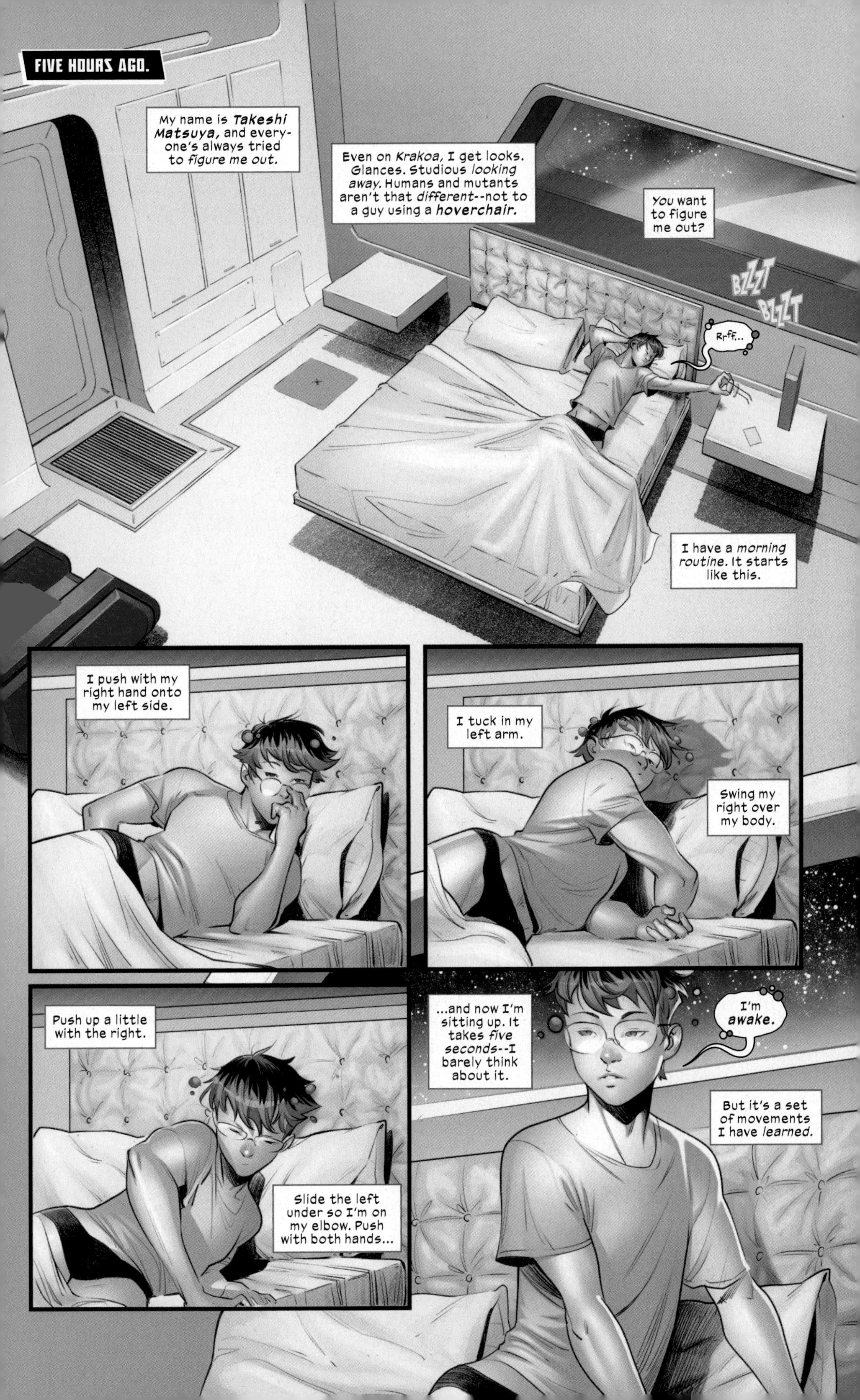
FIVE HOURS AGO.
My name is Takeshi Matsuya, and everyone's always tried to figure me out.
Even on Krakoa, I get looks. Glances. Studious looking away. Humans and mutants aren't that different--not to a guy using a hoverchair.
You want to figure me out?
BZZZT BZZZT
Rrff...
I have a morning routine. It starts like this.
I push with my right hand onto my left side.
I tuck in my left arm.
Swing my right over my body.
Push up a little with the right.
Slide the left under so I'm on my elbow. Push with both hands...
...and now I'm sitting up. It takes five seconds--I barely think about it.
I'm awake.
But it's a set of movements I have learned.

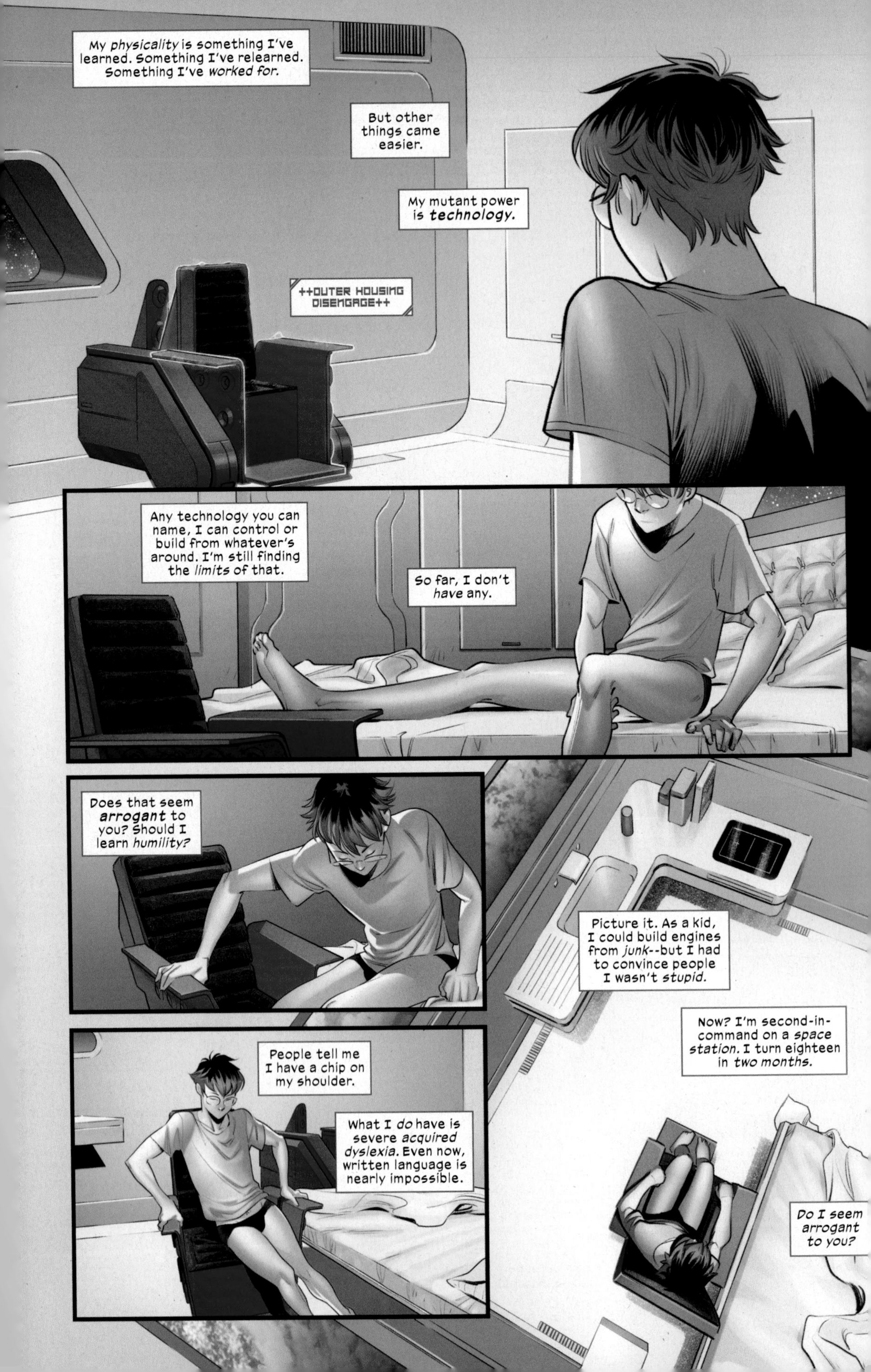

My *physicality* is something I've learned. Something I've relearned. Something I've *worked for.*
But other things came easier.
My mutant power is ***technology.***
++OUTER HOUSING DISENGAGE++
Any technology you can name, I can control or build from whatever's around. I'm still finding the *limits* of that.
So far, I don't *have* any.
Does that seem ***arrogant*** to you? Should I learn *humility?*
Picture it. As a kid, I could build engines from *junk*--but I had to convince people I wasn't *stupid.*
Now? I'm second-in-command on a *space station.* I turn eighteen in *two months.*
People tell me I have a chip on my shoulder.
What I *do* have is severe *acquired dyslexia.* Even now, written language is nearly impossible.
*Do I seem arrogant to you?*

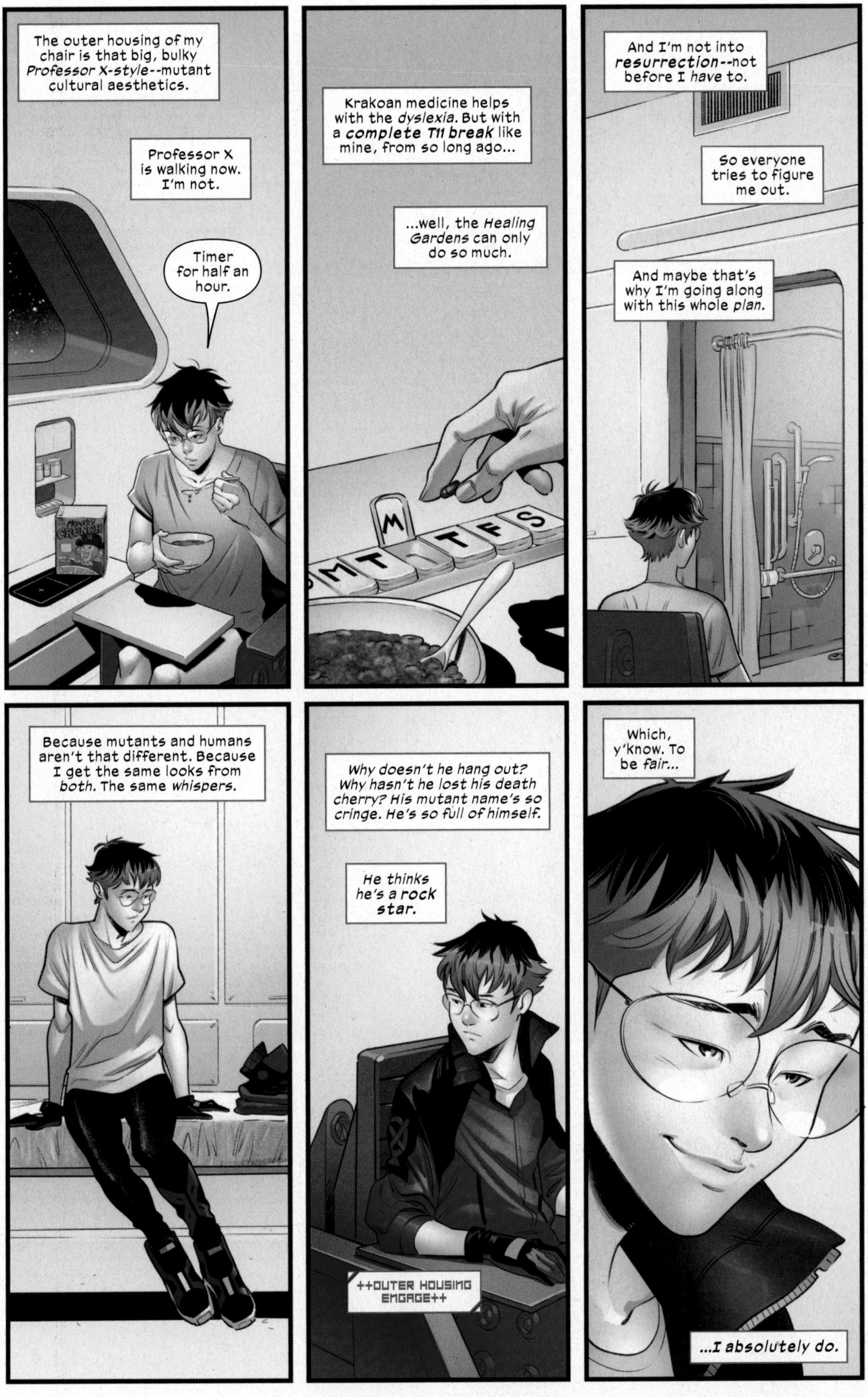
The outer housing of my chair is that big, bulky *Professor X-style*--mutant cultural aesthetics.
Professor X is walking now. I'm not.
Timer for half an hour.
MONKEY CRUNCH
Krakoan medicine helps with the *dyslexia*. But with a **complete T11 break** like mine, from so long ago...
...well, the *Healing Gardens* can only do so much.
M T W T F S
And I'm not into **resurrection**--not before I *have* to.
So everyone tries to figure me out.
And maybe that's why I'm going along with this whole *plan*.
Because mutants and humans aren't that different. Because I get the same looks from *both*. The same *whispers*.
*Why doesn't he hang out? Why hasn't he lost his death cherry? His mutant name's so cringe. He's so full of himself.*
*He thinks he's a* ***rock star.***
++OUTER HOUSING ENGAGE++
Which, y'know. To be *fair*...
*...I absolutely do.*

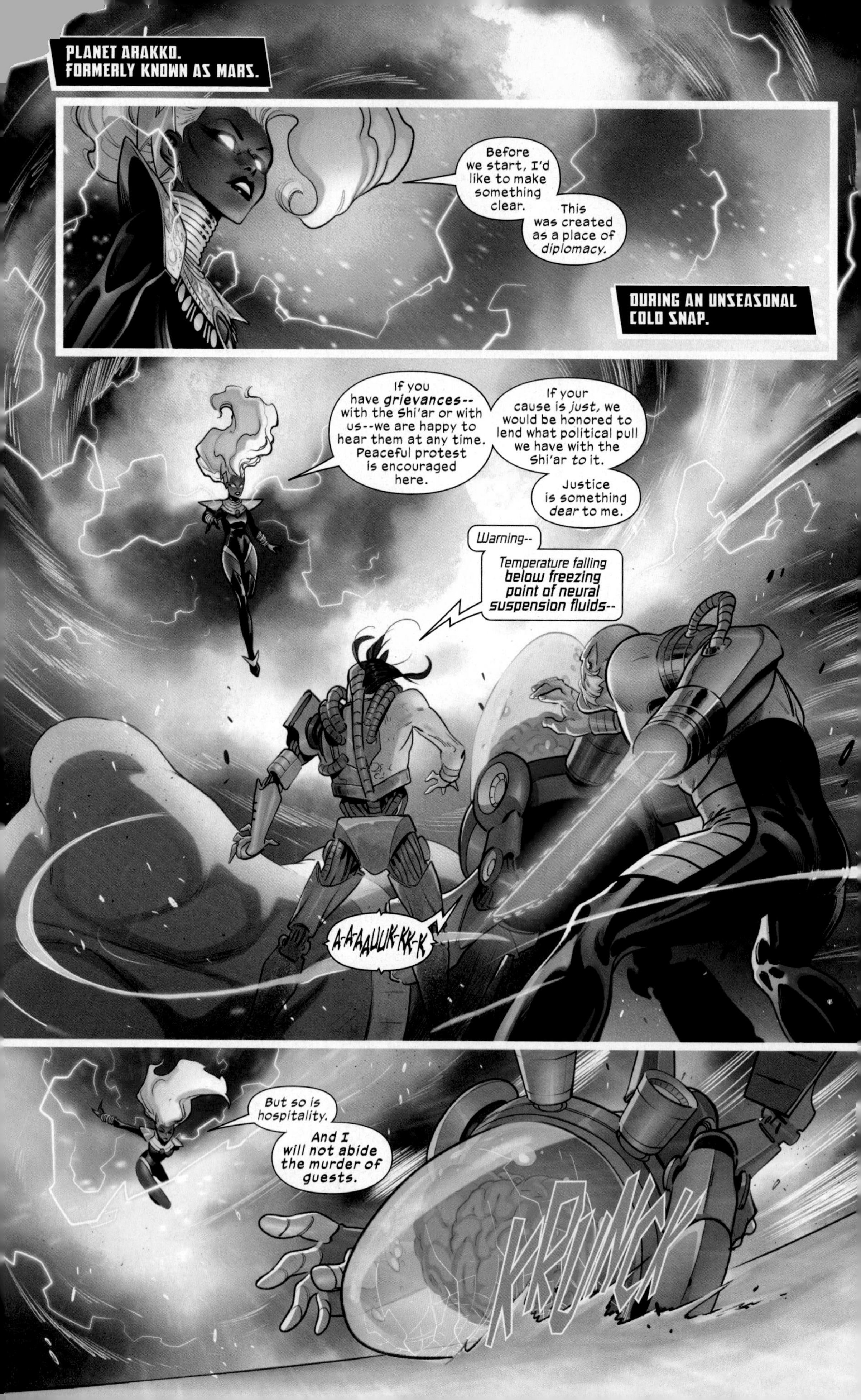
PLANET ARAKKO. FORMERLY KNOWN AS MARS.
Before we start, I'd like to make something clear.
This was created as a place of *diplomacy*.
DURING AN UNSEASONAL COLD SNAP.
If you have **grievances--** with the Shi'ar or with us--we are happy to hear them at any time. Peaceful protest is encouraged here.
If your cause is *just,* we would be honored to lend what political pull we have with the Shi'ar to it.
Justice is something *dear* to me.
Warning--
Temperature falling **below freezing point of neural** suspension fluids--
A-A-AAUUK-KK-K
But so is hospitality.
And I will not abide the murder of guests.
KRONCH

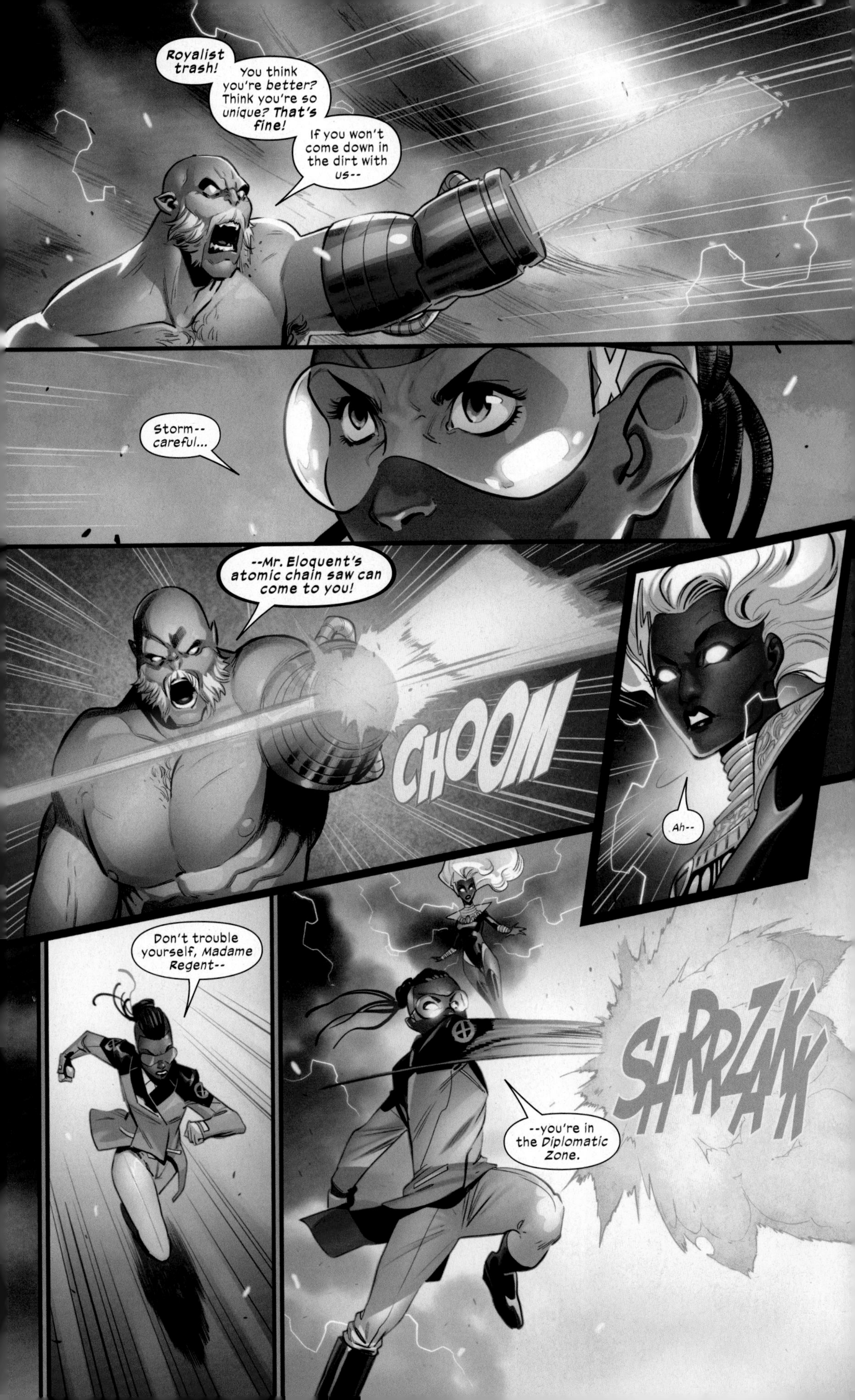

Royalist trash!
You think you're better? Think you're so unique? That's fine!
If you won't come down in the dirt with us--
Storm--careful...
--Mr. Eloquent's atomic chain saw can come to you!
CHOOM
Ah--
Don't trouble yourself, Madame Regent--
SHRRZAKK
--you're in the Diplomatic Zone.

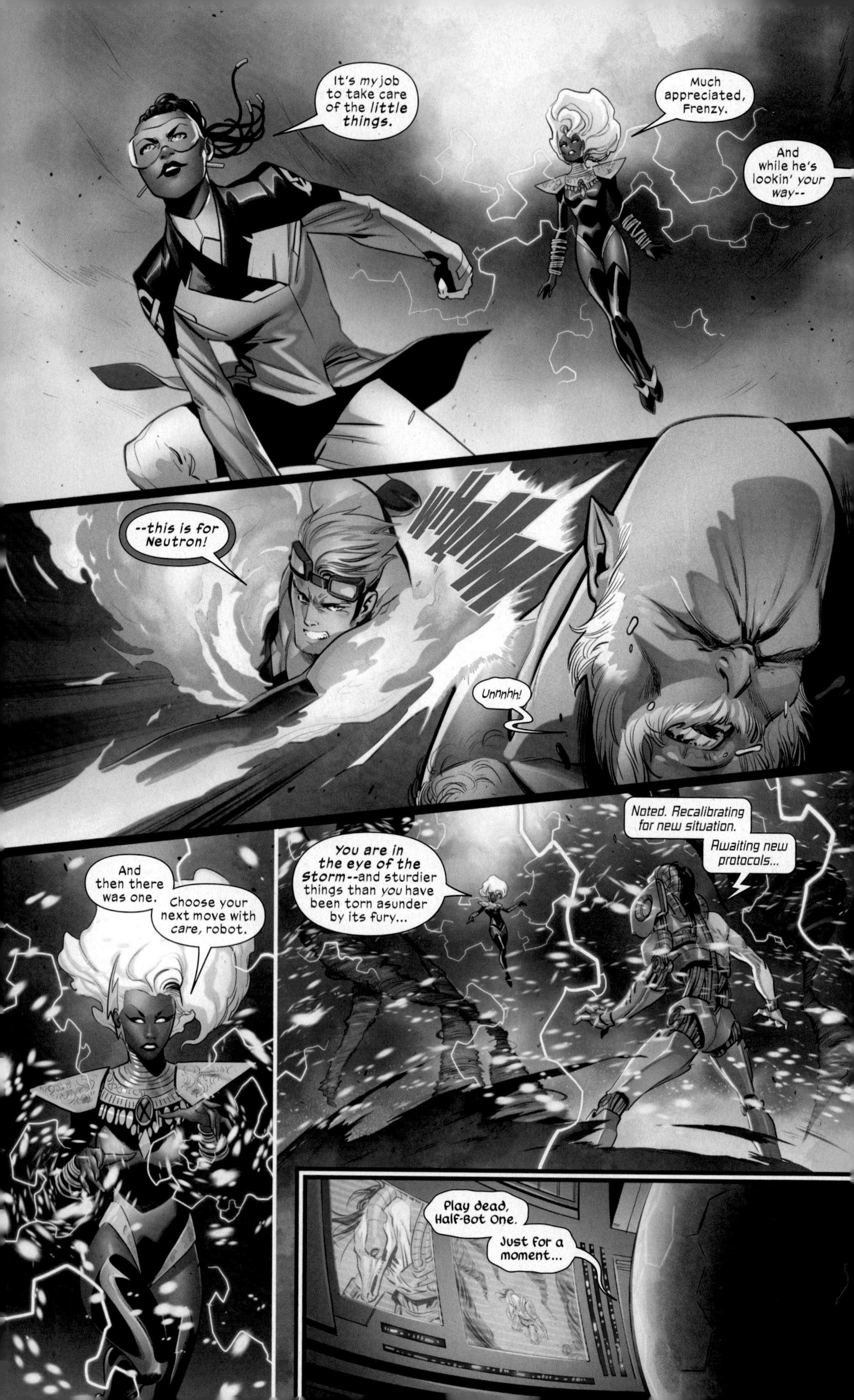
It's *my* job to take care of the *little things.*
Much appreciated, Frenzy.
And while he's lookin' *your* way--
--this is for Neutron!
WHHMM
Unnnhh!
And then there was one.
Choose your next move with *care,* robot.
You are in the eye of the Storm--and sturdier things than *you* have been torn asunder by its fury...
Noted. Recalibrating for new situation.
Awaiting new protocols...
Play dead, Half-Bot One.
Just for a moment...

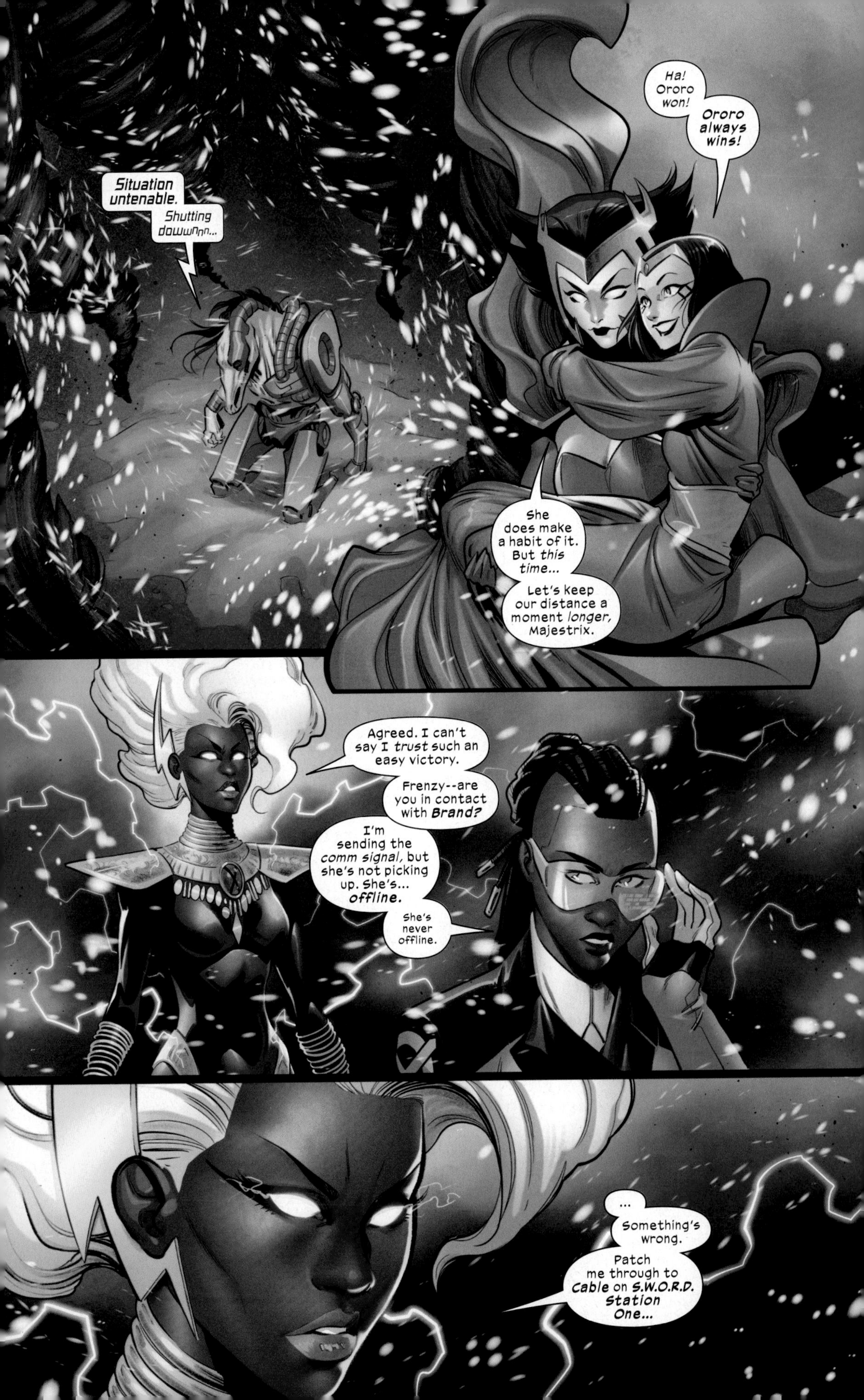
Situation untenable.
Shutting dowwnnn...
Ha! Ororo won!
Ororo always wins!
She does make a habit of it. But this time...
Let's keep our distance a moment longer, Majestrix.
Agreed. I can't say I trust such an easy victory.
Frenzy--are you in contact with Brand?
I'm sending the comm signal, but she's not picking up. She's... offline.
She's never offline.
...
Something's wrong.
Patch me through to Cable on S.W.O.R.D. Station One...

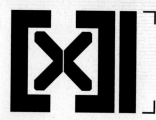

# PERSONNEL FILE :: "ABIGAIL" / BRAND :: UNRESTRICTED
## S.W.O.R.D. PERSONNEL SYSTEM :: Z-2-11 10/15 :: GSTC 0960

**"COMMANDER ABIGAIL BRAND" :: LOGGED MOVEMENTS :: UTC 1600 / GSTC 0960**

**0500 UTC / 0300 GSTC / Quarters**
Wake-up call scheduled, received

**0530 UTC / 0330 GSTC / Mess Hall 1**
Commander consumes Standard Breakfast 7a
*{-hash brown +egg +coffee +coffee +coffee}*

**0545 UTC / 0345 GSTC / Jump Suite 1**
Commander ready for transfer to Station 2
["The Keep"]

**0546 UTC / 0346 GSTC / Jump Suite 2**
Commander arrives on Station 2

**0600 UTC / 0360 GSTC / Command Deck 2**
Six-hour Command Shift begins

**0730 UTC / 0450 GSTC / Command Deck 2**
Comm link established with Gym 1
[Nathan Summers/Cable]

**0820 UTC / 0500 GSTC / Command Deck 2**
Comm link established with Shi'ar Empire/
Chandilar [Kallark]
*Gate Protocols confirmed*

**0945 UTC / 0585 GSTC / Command Deck 2**
Eden Fesi/Manifold on deck

**1000 UTC / 0600 GSTC / Command Deck 2**
Shi'ar Delegation arrive in Diplomatic Zone

**1003 UTC / 0604 GSTC / Command Deck 2**
Comm link established with Command Deck 1
[Nathan Summers/Cable]

**1004 UTC / 0604 GTSC / Command Deck 2**
Enemy incursion begins ["Lethal Legion"]

**1010 UTC / 0610 GTSC / Command Deck 2**
Commander moves to Tech Suite 2

**1015 UTC / 0615 GTSC / Tech Suite 2**
Commander arrives

**1017 UTC / 0617 GTSC / Tech Suite 2**
Discussion with Takeshi Matsuya/Wiz-Kid
*details unlogged at this time*

**1#18 UT# / 061# GT#C / #ech Su#te 2**
*St#tic dis#uption -- err#r -- sy#tem mal#u#ction*

**1019 UTC / 0619 GTSC / Unknown**
System restored -- Commander whereabouts
unknown

**1020 UTC / 0620 GTSC / Unknown**
Whereabouts unknown

**1030 UTC / 0630 GTSC / Unknown**
Whereabouts unknown

**1040 UTC / 0640 GTSC / Unknown**
Whereabouts unknown

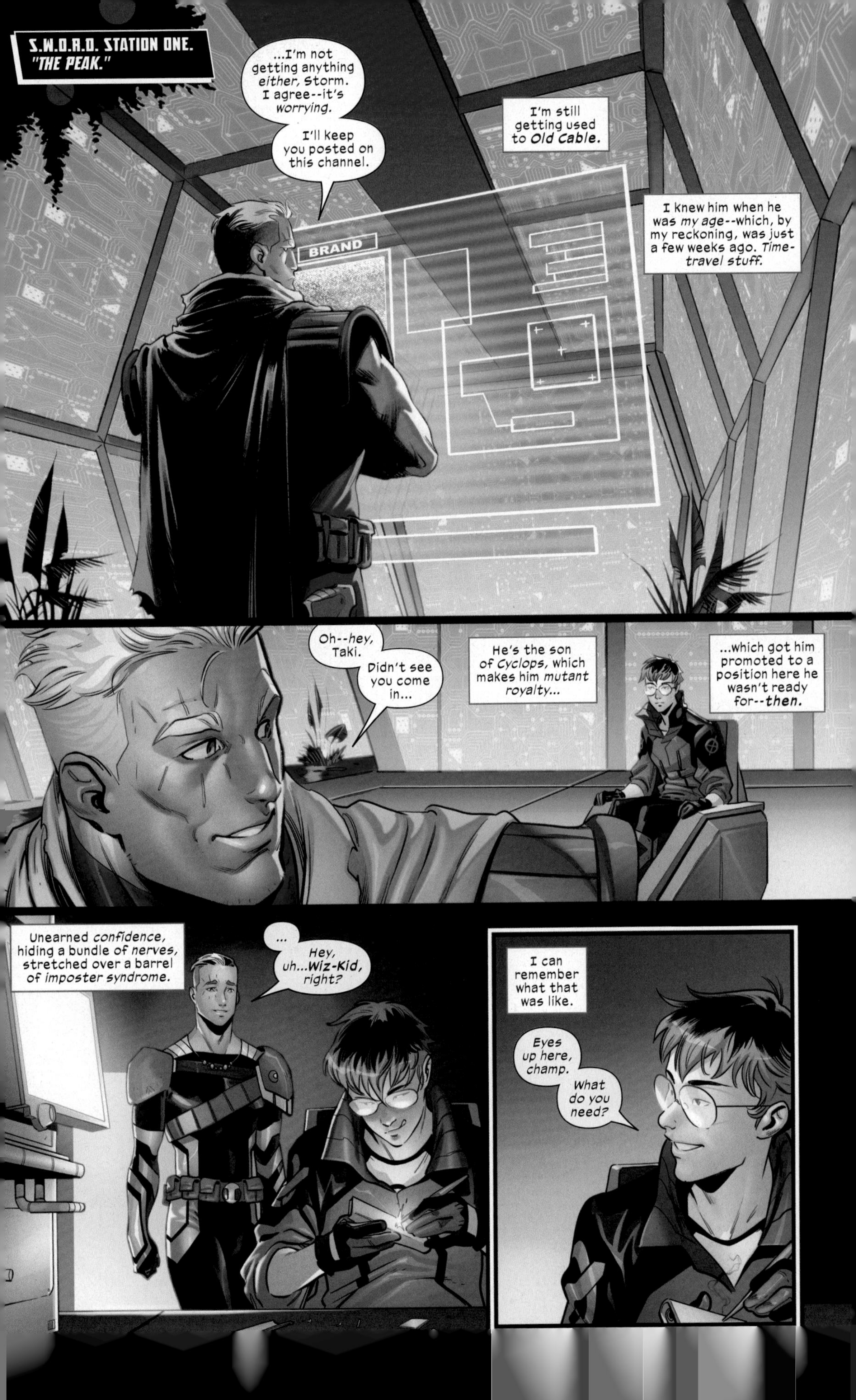

S.W.O.R.D. STATION ONE. "THE PEAK."
...I'm not getting anything either, Storm. I agree--it's worrying.
I'll keep you posted on this channel.
I'm still getting used to Old Cable.
I knew him when he was my age--which, by my reckoning, was just a few weeks ago. Time-travel stuff.
BRAND
Oh--hey, Taki.
Didn't see you come in...
He's the son of Cyclops, which makes him mutant royalty...
...which got him promoted to a position here he wasn't ready for--then.
Unearned confidence, hiding a bundle of nerves, stretched over a barrel of imposter syndrome.
...
Hey, uh...Wiz-Kid, right?
I can remember what that was like.
Eyes up here, champ.
What do you need?

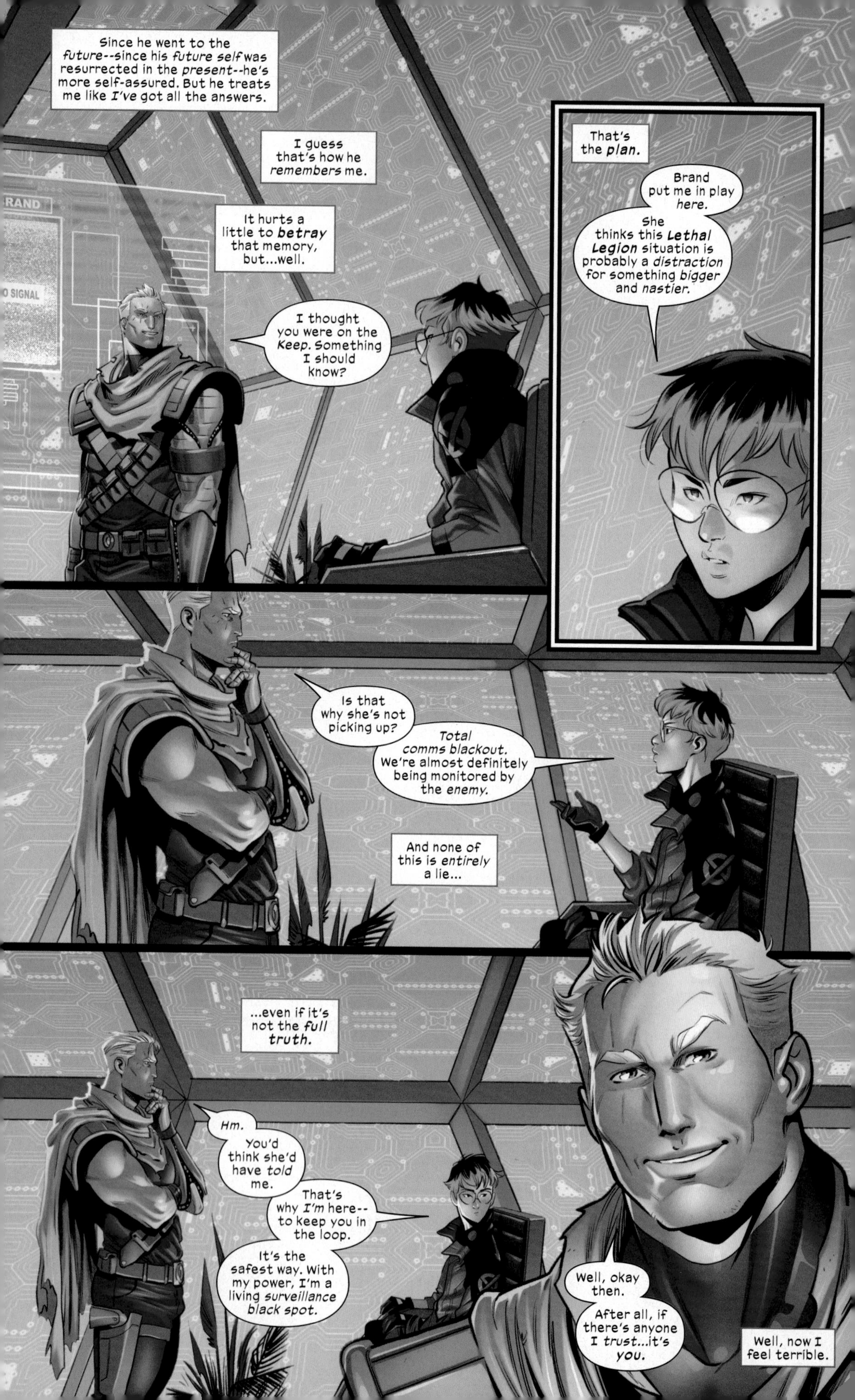

Since he went to the *future*--since his *future self* was resurrected in the *present*--he's more self-assured. But he treats me like *I've* got all the answers.
I guess that's how he *remembers* me.
It hurts a little to **betray** that memory, but...well.
BRAND
NO SIGNAL
I thought you were on the *Keep*. Something I should know?
That's the **plan.**
Brand put me in play *here.*
She thinks this **Lethal Legion** situation is probably a *distraction* for something *bigger* and *nastier.*
Is that why she's not picking up?
*Total comms blackout.* We're almost definitely being monitored by the *enemy.*
And none of this is *entirely* a lie...
...even if it's not the *full* **truth.**
*Hm.*
You'd think she'd have *told* me.
That's why *I'm* here--to keep you in the loop.
It's the safest way. With my power, I'm a living *surveillance black spot.*
Well, okay then.
After all, if there's anyone I *trust*...it's *you.*
Well, now I feel terrible.

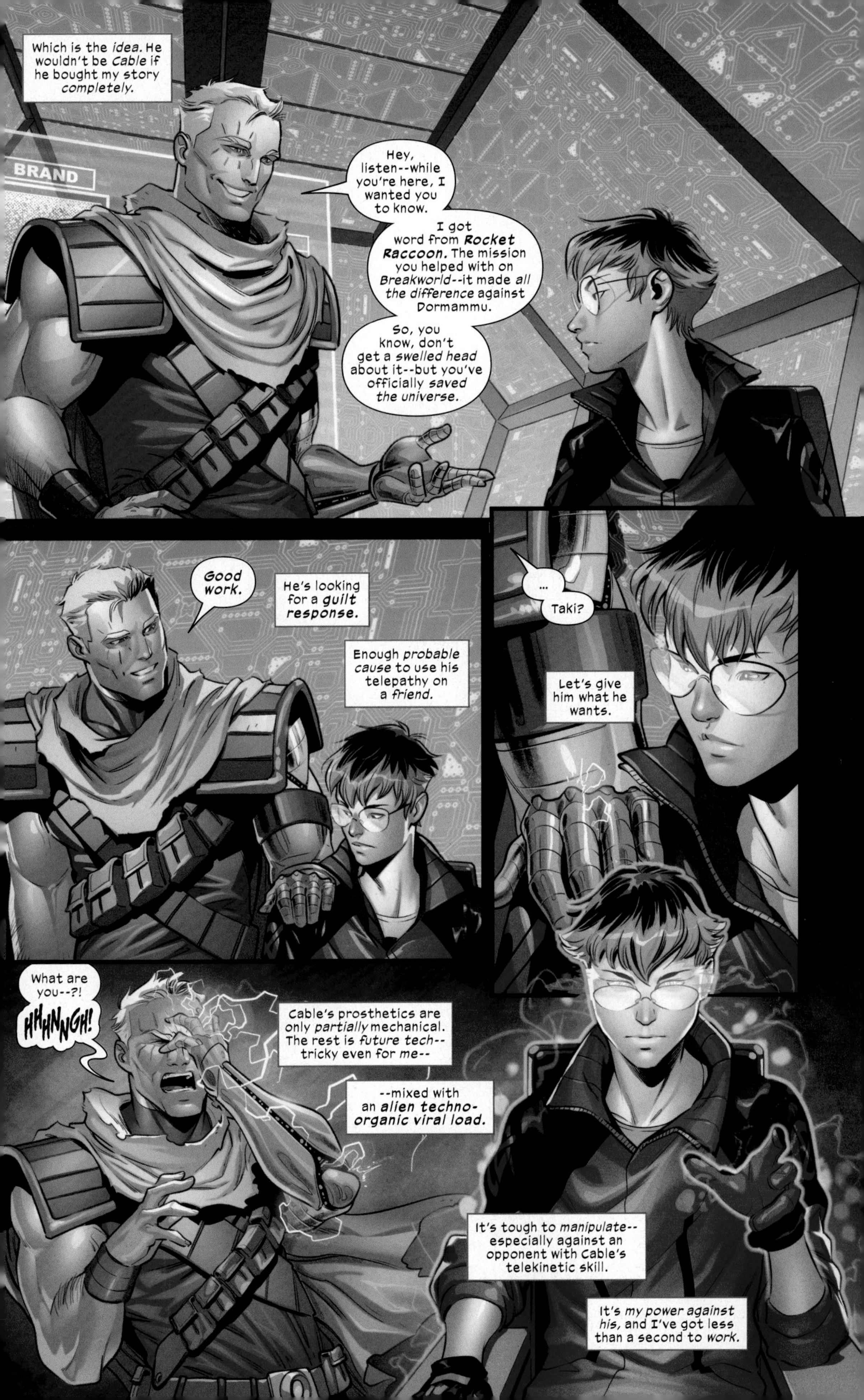

Which is the *idea.* He wouldn't be *Cable* if he bought my story *completely.*
BRAND
Hey, listen--while you're here, I wanted you to know.
I got word from **Rocket Raccoon.** The mission you helped with on *Breakworld*--it made *all the difference* against Dormammu.
So, you know, don't get a *swelled head* about it--but you've officially *saved the universe.*
*Good work.*
He's looking for a ***guilt response.***
Enough *probable cause* to use his telepathy on a *friend.*
... Taki?
Let's give him what he wants.
What are you--?!
HHHNNGH!
Cable's prosthetics are only *partially* mechanical. The rest is *future tech*--tricky even for *me*--
--mixed with an ***alien techno-organic viral load.***
It's tough to *manipulate*--especially against an opponent with Cable's telekinetic skill.
It's *my power against his,* and I've got less than a second to *work.*

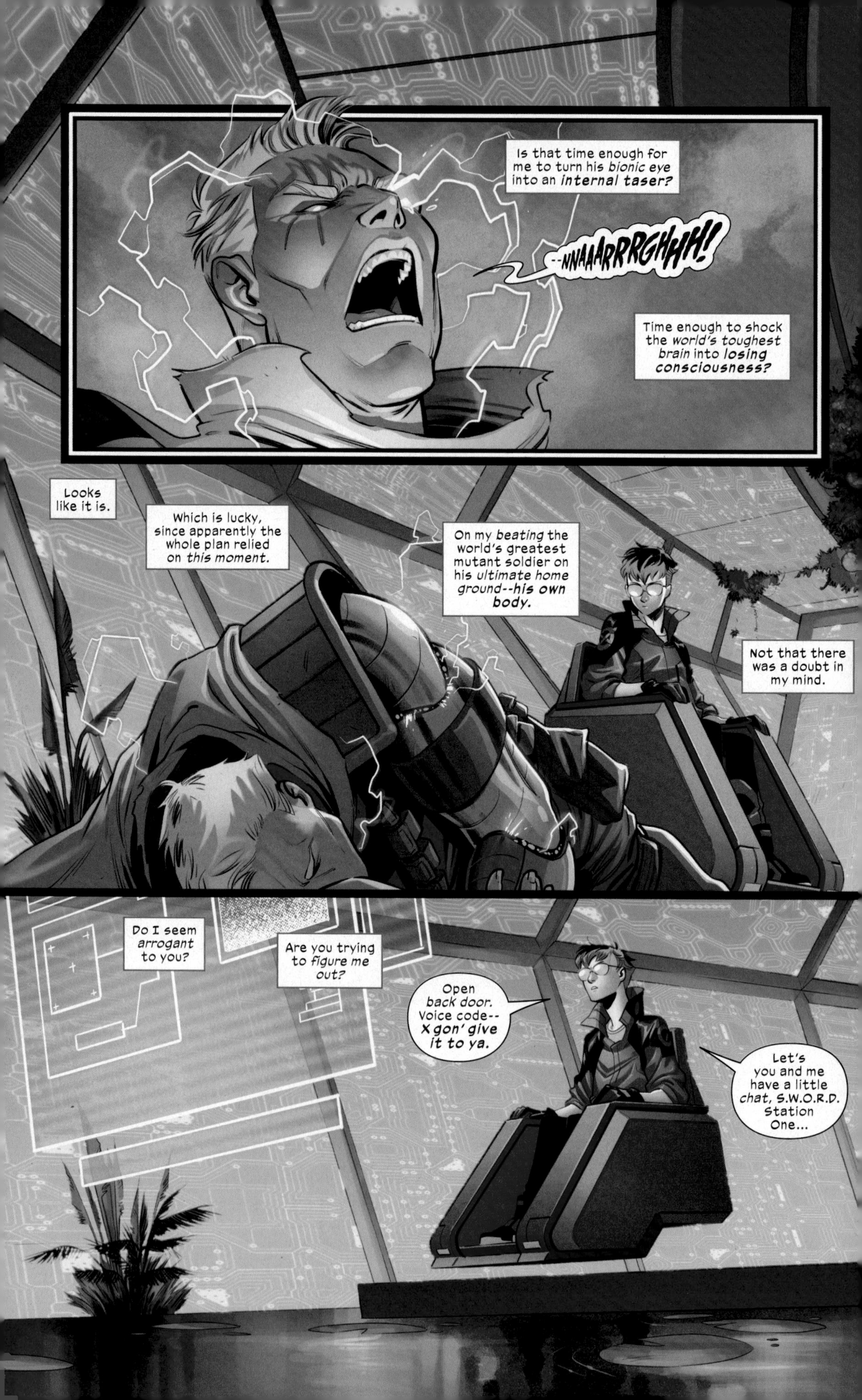
Is that time enough for me to turn his *bionic eye* into an ***internal taser?***
--NNAAARRRGHHH!
Time enough to shock the *world's toughest brain* into ***losing consciousness?***
Looks like it is.
Which is lucky, since apparently the whole plan relied on *this moment.*
On my *beating* the world's greatest mutant soldier on his *ultimate home ground*--**his own body.**
Not that there was a doubt in my mind.
Do I seem *arrogant* to you?
Are you trying to *figure* me out?
Open *back door.* Voice code-- ***X gon' give it to ya.***
Let's you and me have a little *chat,* S.W.O.R.D. Station One...

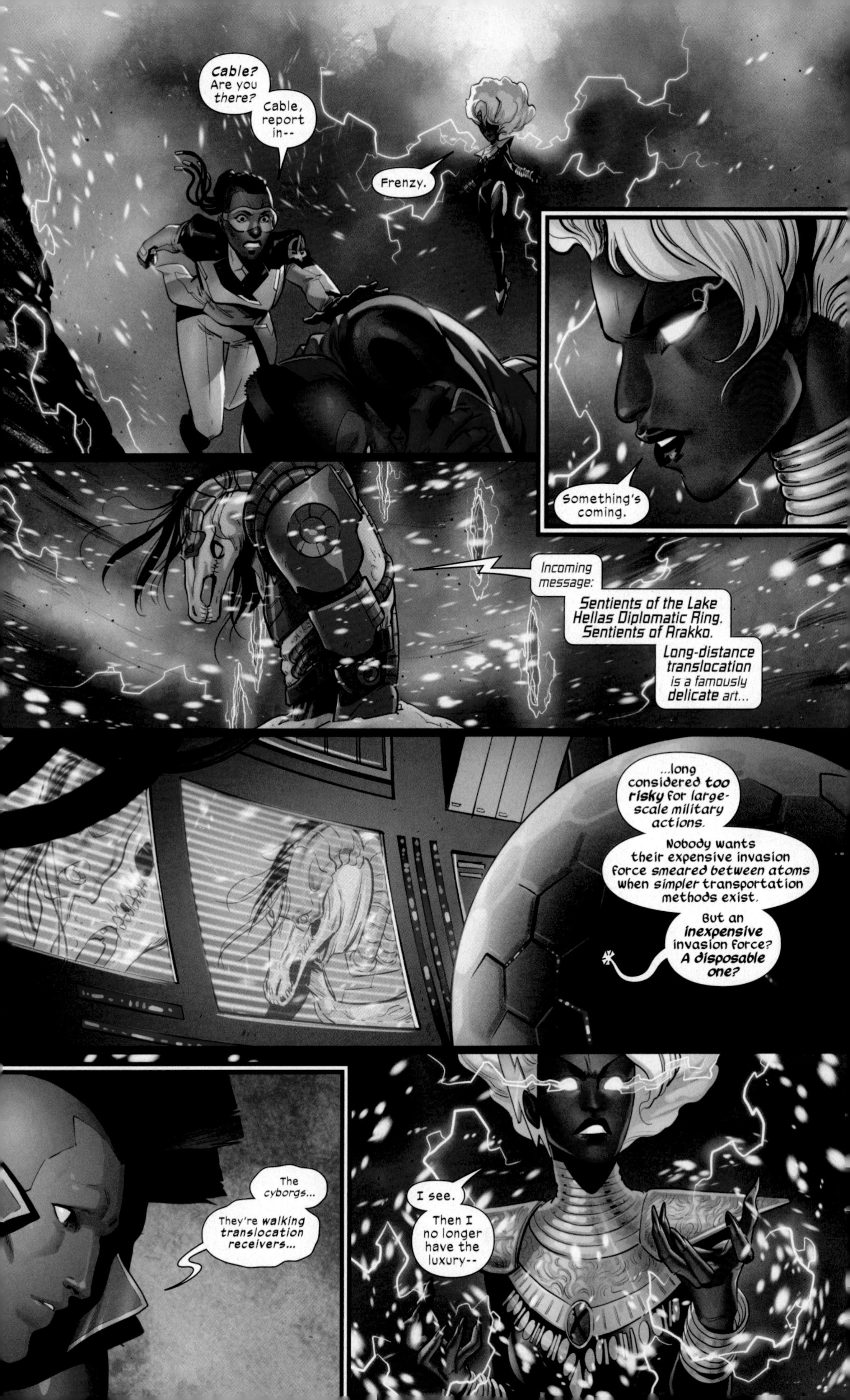
Cable? Are you there?
Cable, report in--
Frenzy.
Something's coming.
Incoming message:
Sentients of the Lake Hellas Diplomatic Ring. Sentients of Arakko.
Long-distance translocation is a famously delicate art...
...long considered too risky for large-scale military actions.
Nobody wants their expensive invasion force smeared between atoms when simpler transportation methods exist.
But an inexpensive invasion force? A disposable one?
The cyborgs...
They're walking translocation receivers...
I see.
Then I no longer have the luxury--

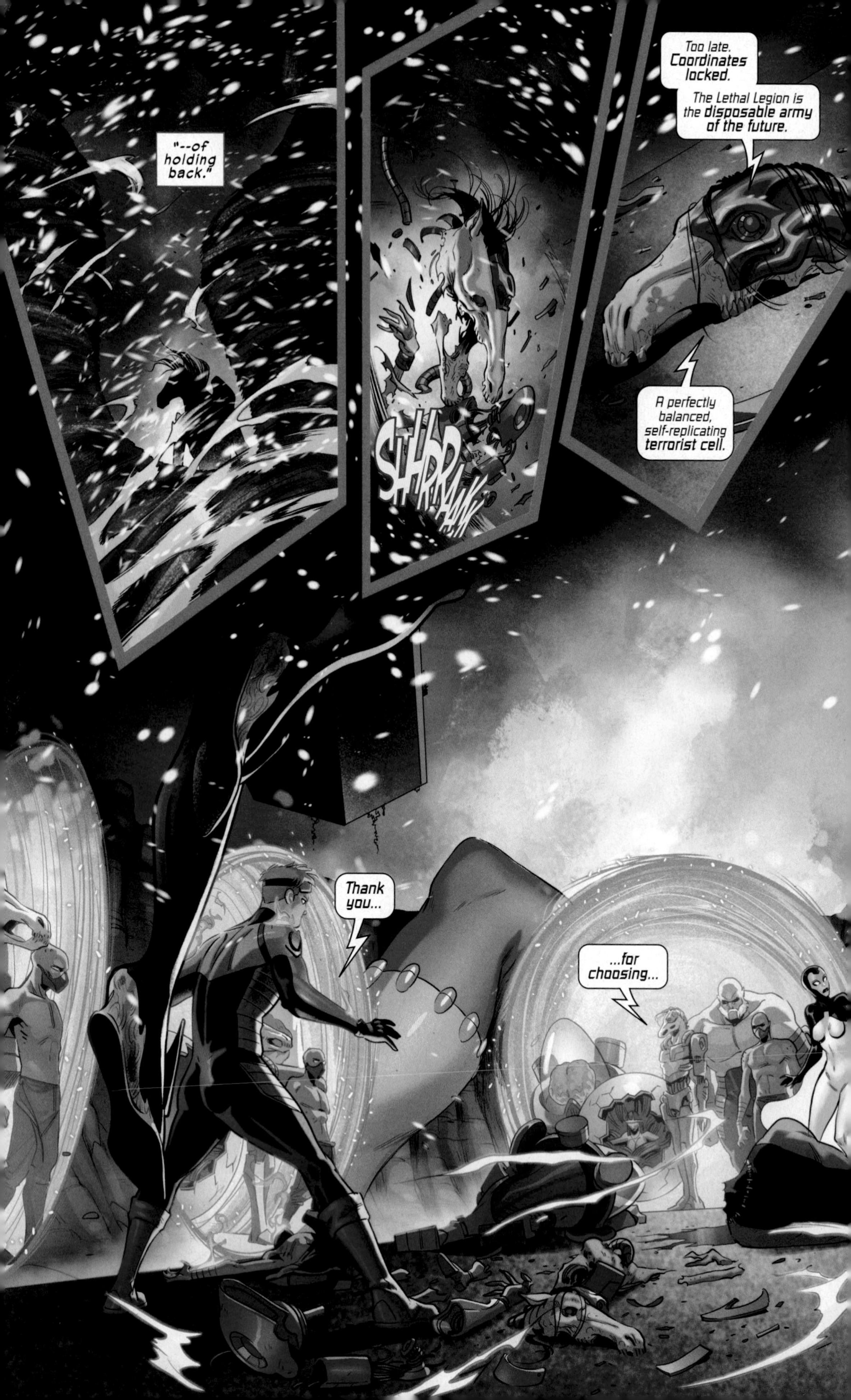
"--of holding back."
SHHRRAAK
Too late. Coordinates locked.
The Lethal Legion is the disposable army of the future.
A perfectly balanced, self-replicating terrorist cell.
Thank you...
...for choosing...

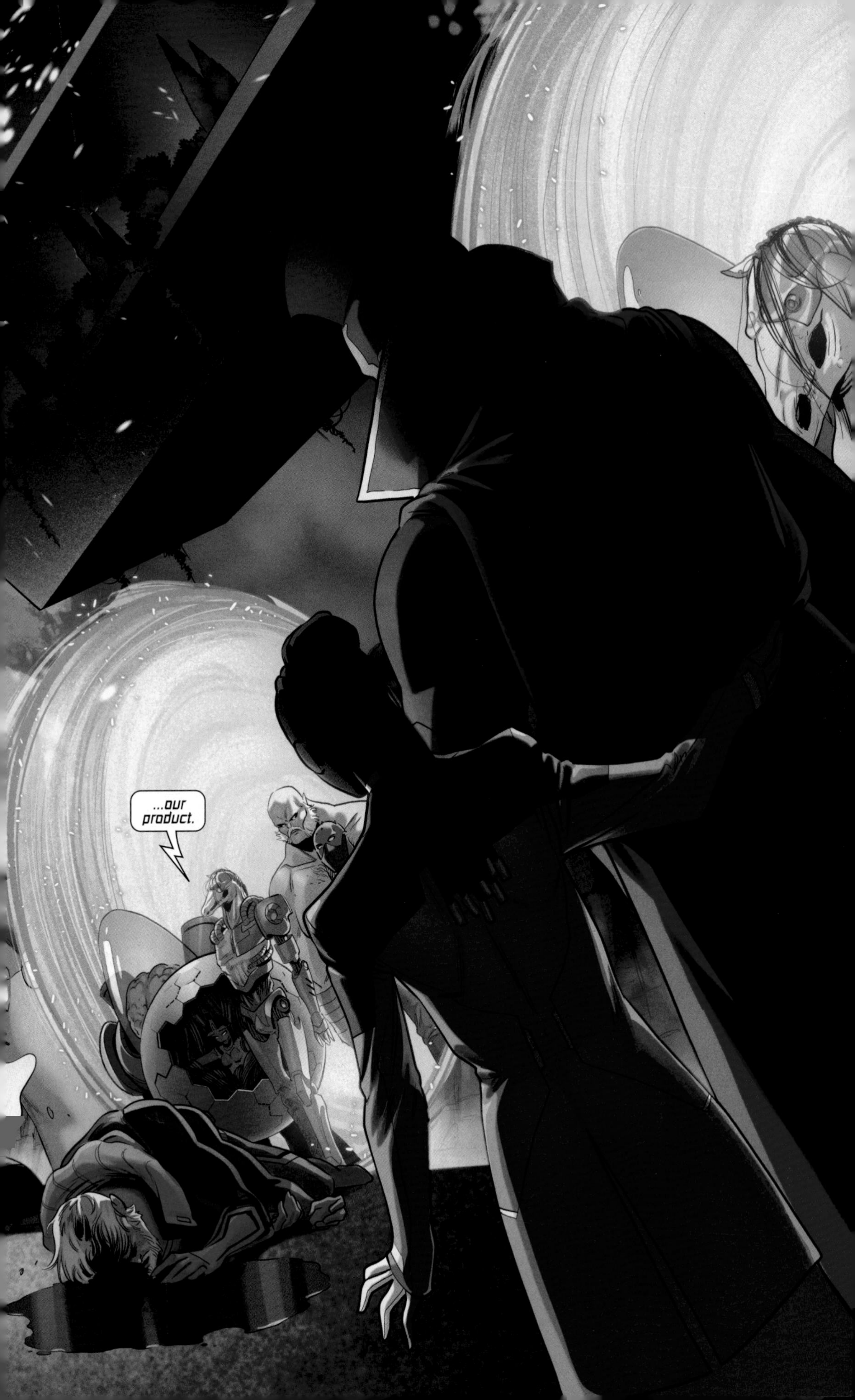
...our product.

## OS017-SERIES ENHANCILE CATALOG :: "THE LETHAL LEGION"

Meanwhile, for repeat (and discreet) customers, we can offer *33.3% off* our Premiere Gold service.  What do you get at the Premiere Gold level? We're so glad you asked!

At the Premiere Gold level, for every three OS017-Series Enhancile Packages you purchase, we will deliver a fourth at no further cost -- fresh from our cloning facilities and tailored entirely to your specifications.

*So Premiere Gold customers **already** have 25% off on medium-scale orders -- and with a further 1/3 off, you get four Enhancile Packages for every two you buy. In Standard Galactic, the word for that is -- **HALF PRICE!***

And do you want to go bigger? *Premiere Gold scales as big as your needs.* Do you need four hundred units? Four thousand? Four million? *The cost is still halved -- and we can clone and outfit our enhanciles as many times as you can imagine.*

The "Lethal Legion" is not just a simple terrorist cell.

It's the terrorist army of tomorrow -- *at a price you can afford today.*

### *You're welcome.*

## *We Make Friends.*

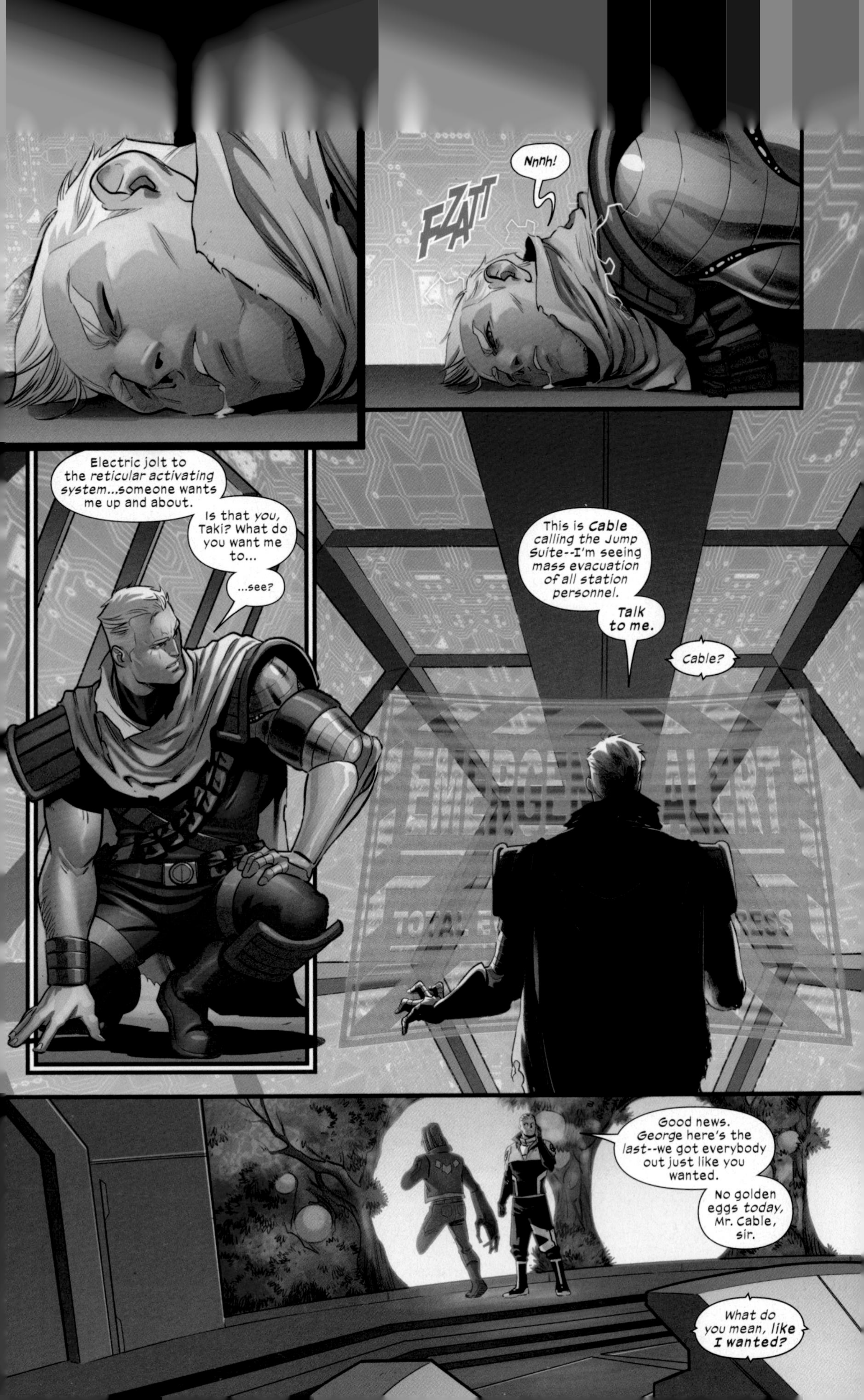
FZATT
Nnnh!
Electric jolt to the reticular activating system...someone wants me up and about.
Is that you, Taki? What do you want me to...
...see?
This is Cable calling the Jump Suite--I'm seeing mass evacuation of all station personnel.
Talk to me.
Cable?
EMERGENCY ALERT
Good news. George here's the last--we got everybody out just like you wanted.
No golden eggs today, Mr. Cable, sir.
What do you mean, like I wanted?

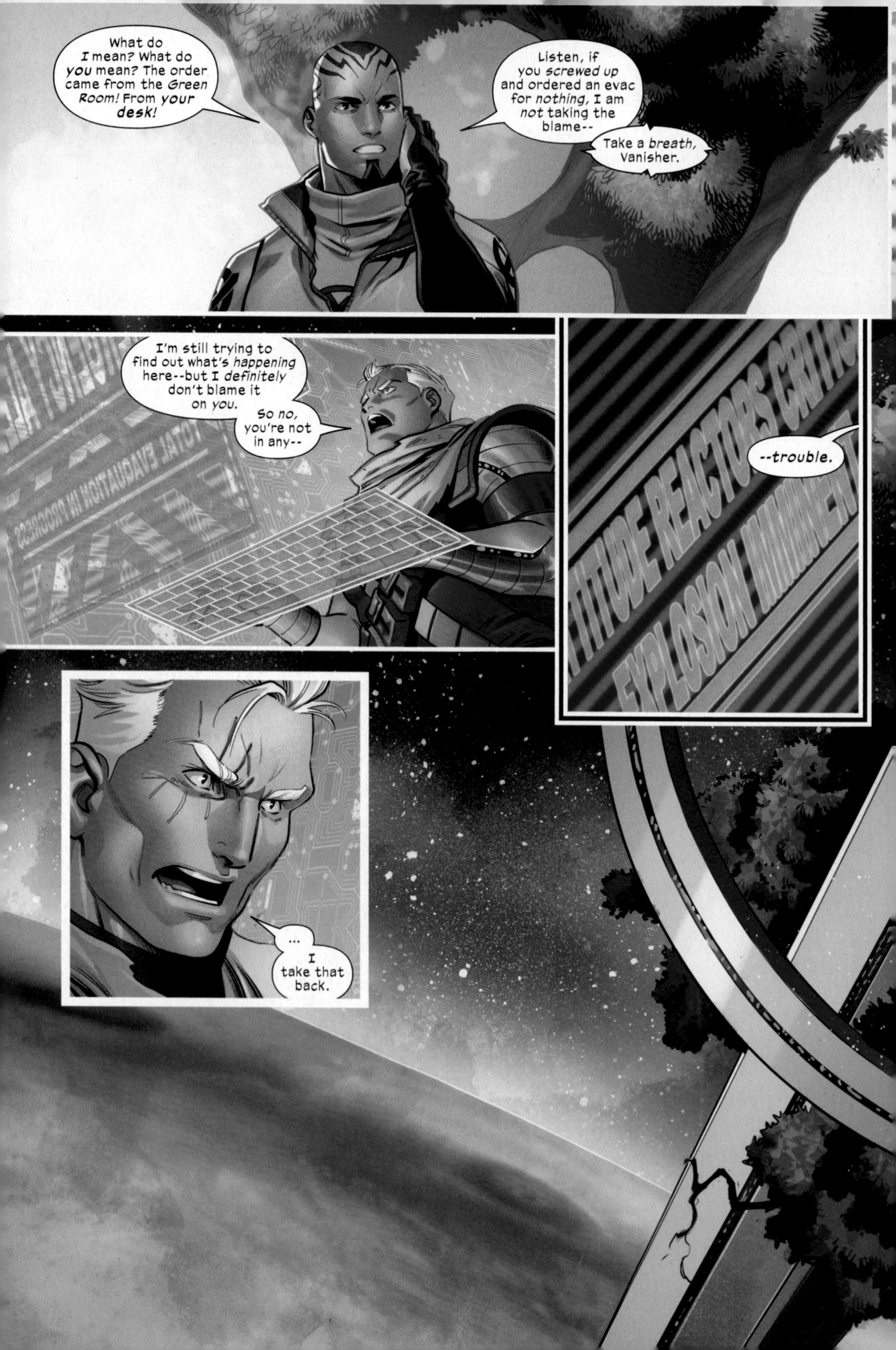

What do I mean? What do you mean? The order came from the Green Room! From your desk!
Listen, if you screwed up and ordered an evac for nothing, I am not taking the blame--
Take a breath, Vanisher.
I'm still trying to find out what's happening here--but I definitely don't blame it on you.
So no, you're not in any--
TOTAL EVACUATION IN PROGRESS
--trouble.
TITUDE REACTORS CRITIC
EXPLOSION IMMINENT
... I take that back.

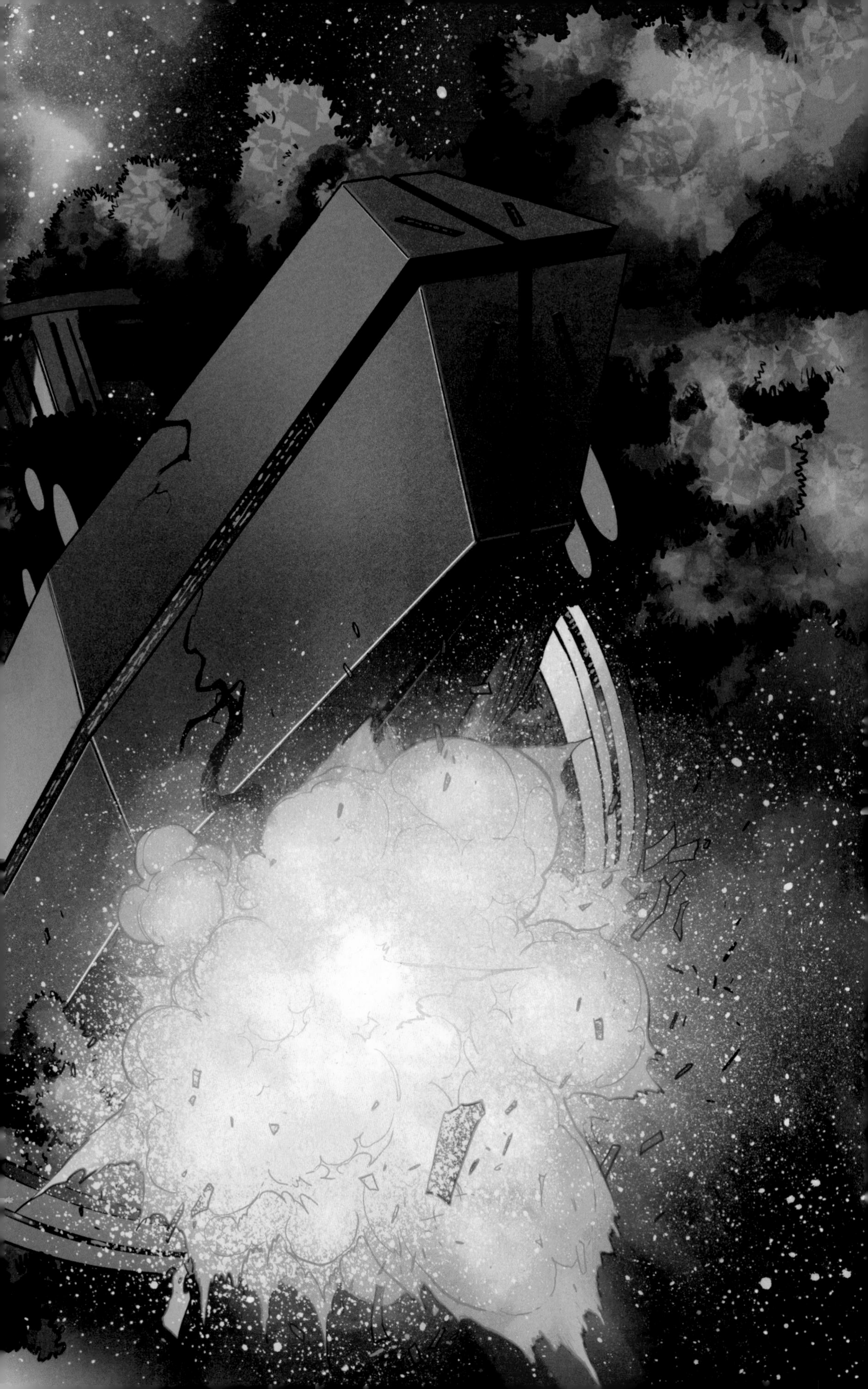

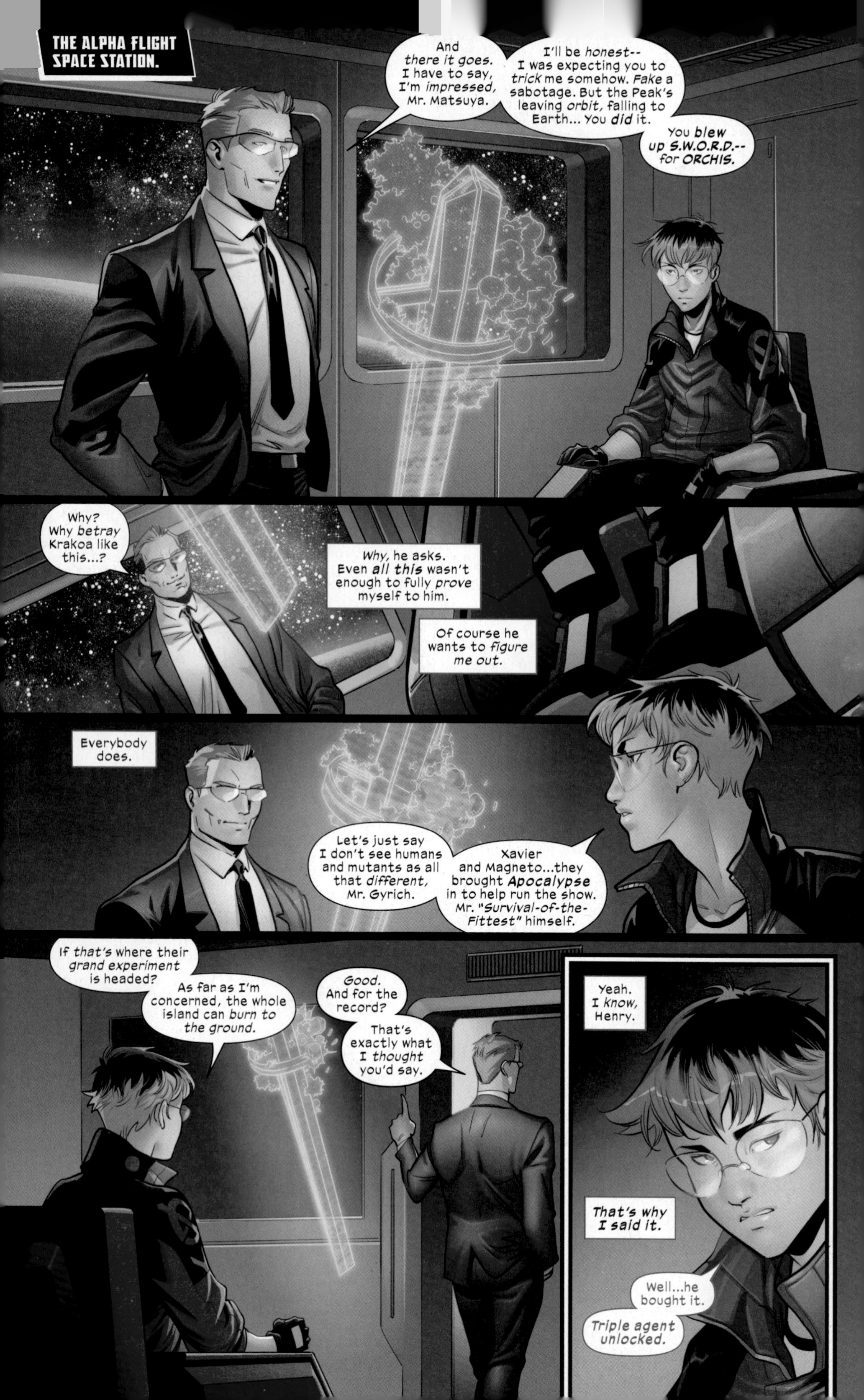
THE ALPHA FLIGHT SPACE STATION.
And there it goes. I have to say, I'm impressed, Mr. Matsuya.
I'll be honest-- I was expecting you to trick me somehow. Fake a sabotage. But the Peak's leaving orbit, falling to Earth... You did it.
You blew up S.W.O.R.D.-- for ORCHIS.
Why? Why betray Krakoa like this...?
Why, he asks. Even all this wasn't enough to fully prove myself to him.
Of course he wants to figure me out.
Everybody does.
Let's just say I don't see humans and mutants as all that different, Mr. Gyrich.
Xavier and Magneto...they brought Apocalypse in to help run the show. Mr. "Survival-of-the-Fittest" himself.
If that's where their grand experiment is headed?
As far as I'm concerned, the whole island can burn to the ground.
Good. And for the record?
That's exactly what I thought you'd say.
Yeah. I know, Henry.
That's why I said it.
Well...he bought it.
Triple agent unlocked.

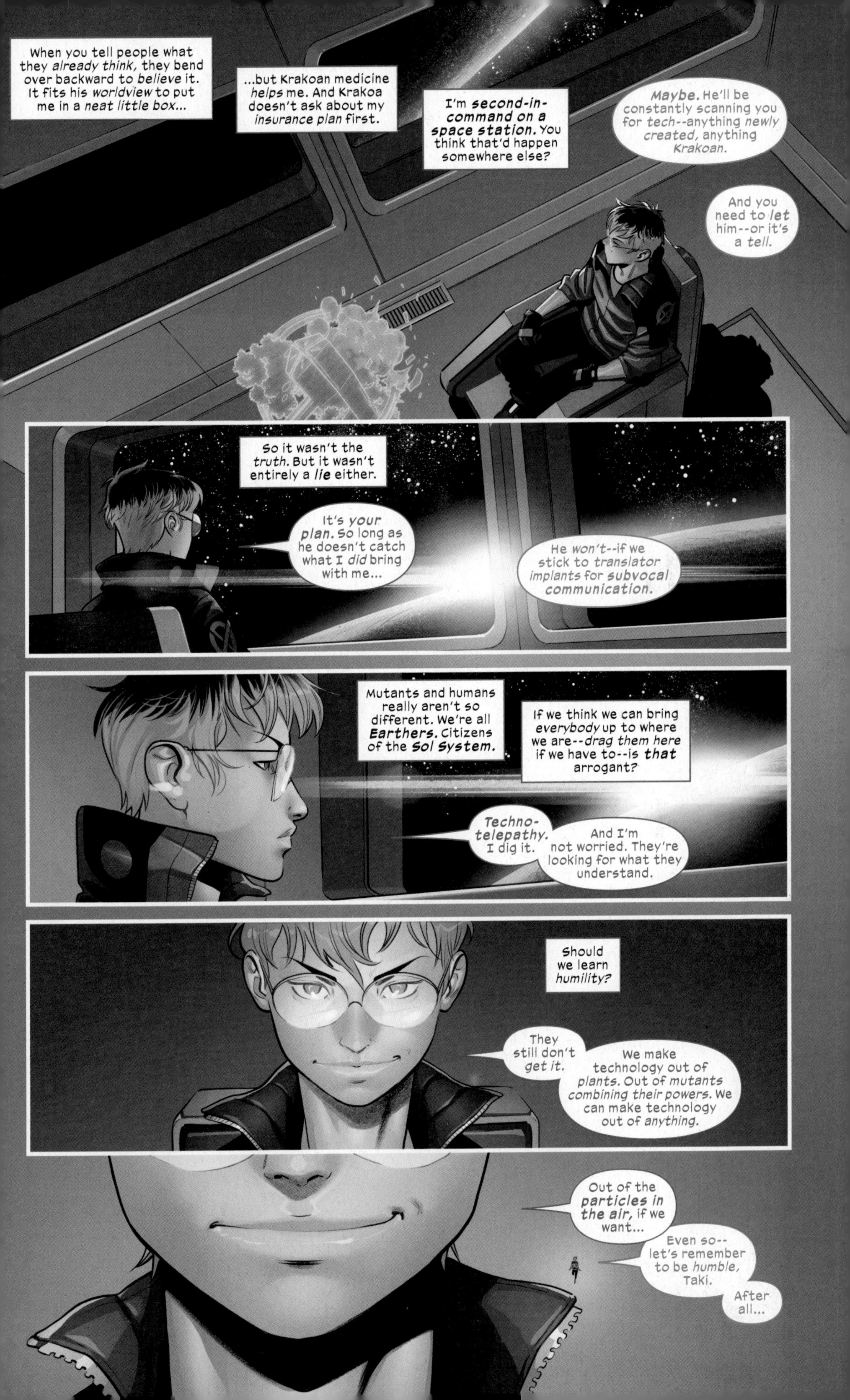
When you tell people what they already think, they bend over backward to believe it. It fits his worldview to put me in a neat little box...
...but Krakoan medicine helps me. And Krakoa doesn't ask about my insurance plan first.
I'm second-in-command on a space station. You think that'd happen somewhere else?
Maybe. He'll be constantly scanning you for tech--anything newly created, anything Krakoan.
And you need to let him--or it's a tell.
So it wasn't the truth. But it wasn't entirely a lie either.
It's your plan. So long as he doesn't catch what I did bring with me...
He won't--if we stick to translator implants for subvocal communication.
Mutants and humans really aren't so different. We're all Earthers. Citizens of the Sol System.
If we think we can bring everybody up to where we are--drag them here if we have to--is that arrogant?
Techno-telepathy. I dig it.
And I'm not worried. They're looking for what they understand.
Should we learn humility?
They still don't get it.
We make technology out of plants. Out of mutants combining their powers. We can make technology out of anything.
Out of the particles in the air, if we want...
Even so--let's remember to be humble, Taki.
After all...

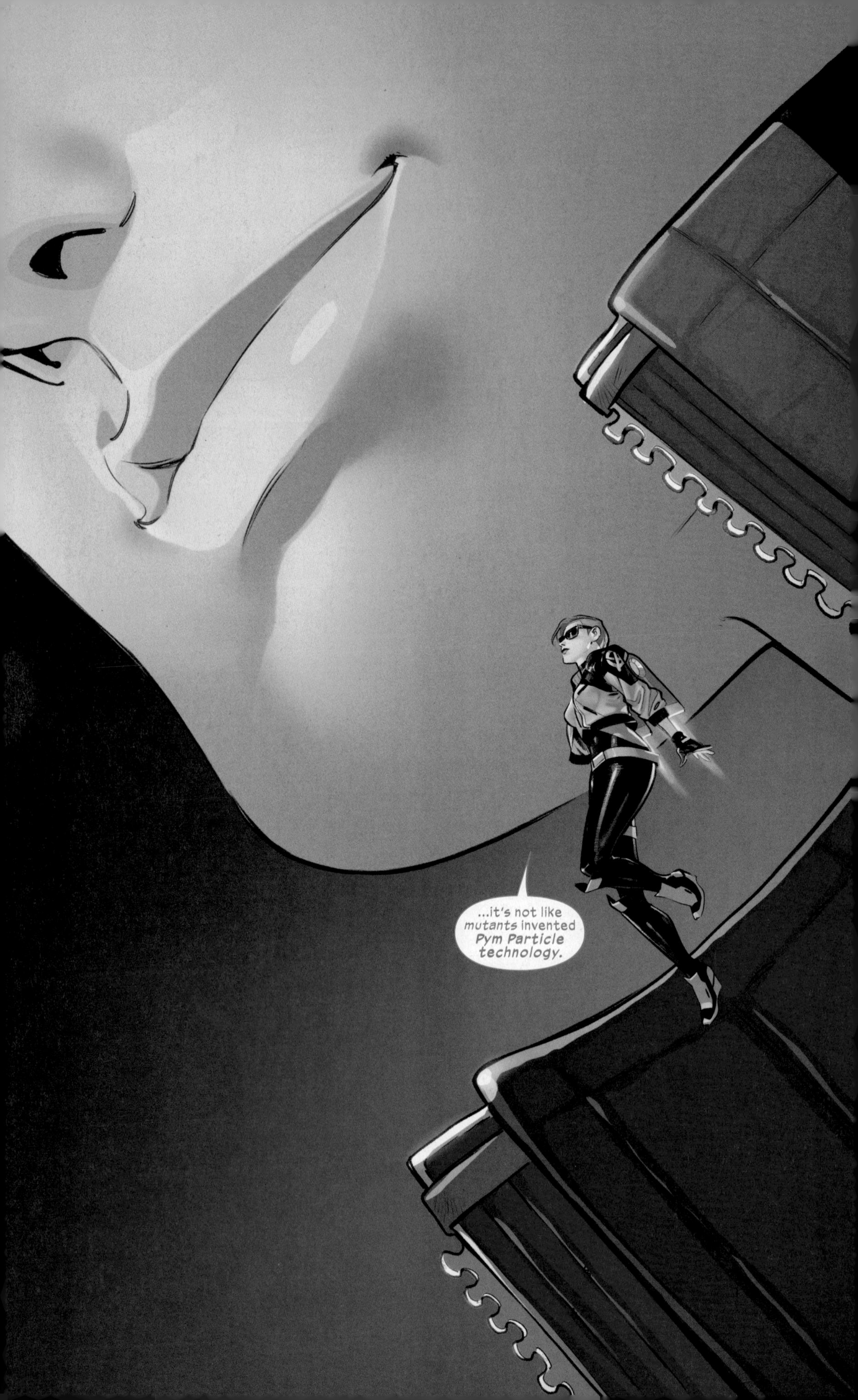
...it's not like mutants invented Pym Particle technology.

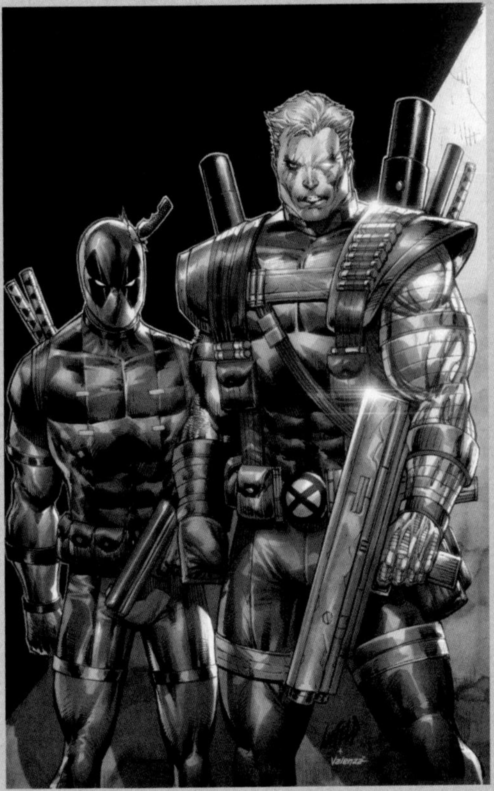

**Cable: Reloaded #1**
**Deapool 30th Anniversary Variant**
by Rob Liefeld

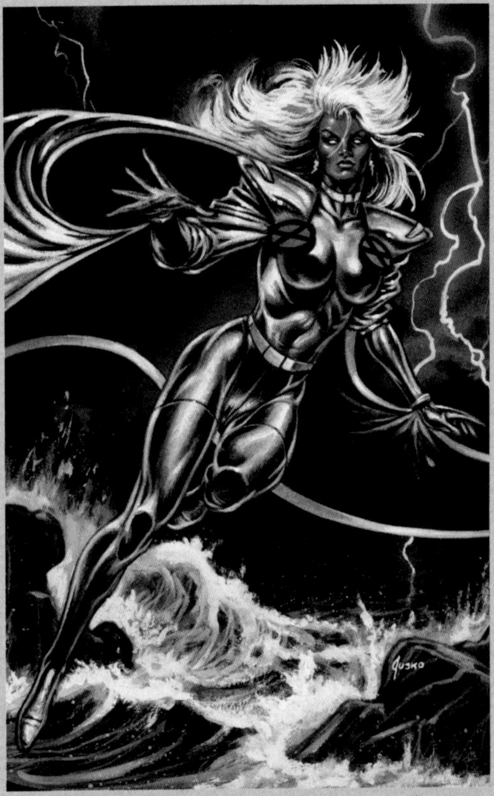

**S.W.O.R.D. #9 Marvel Masterpieces Variant**
by Joe Jusko

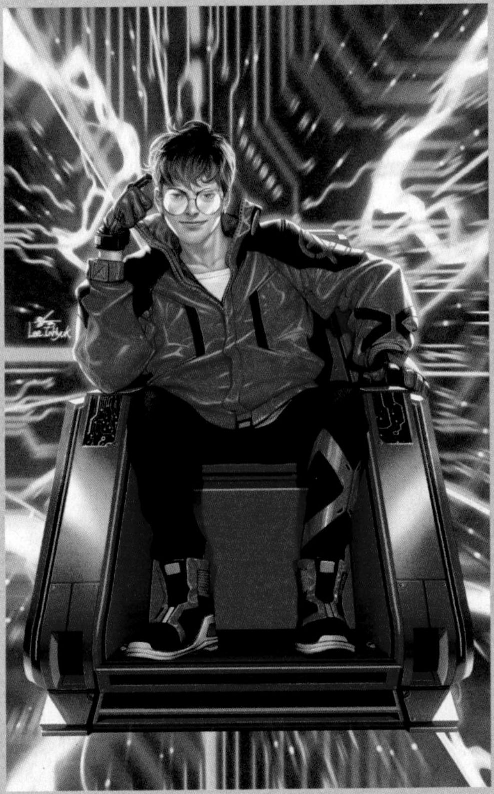

**S.W.O.R.D. #10 Variant**
by InHyuk Lee

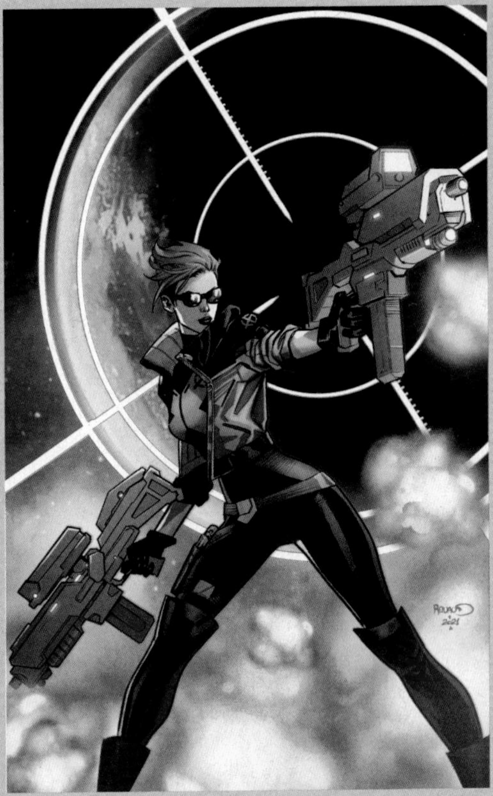

**S.W.O.R.D. #11 Variant**
by Paul Renaud

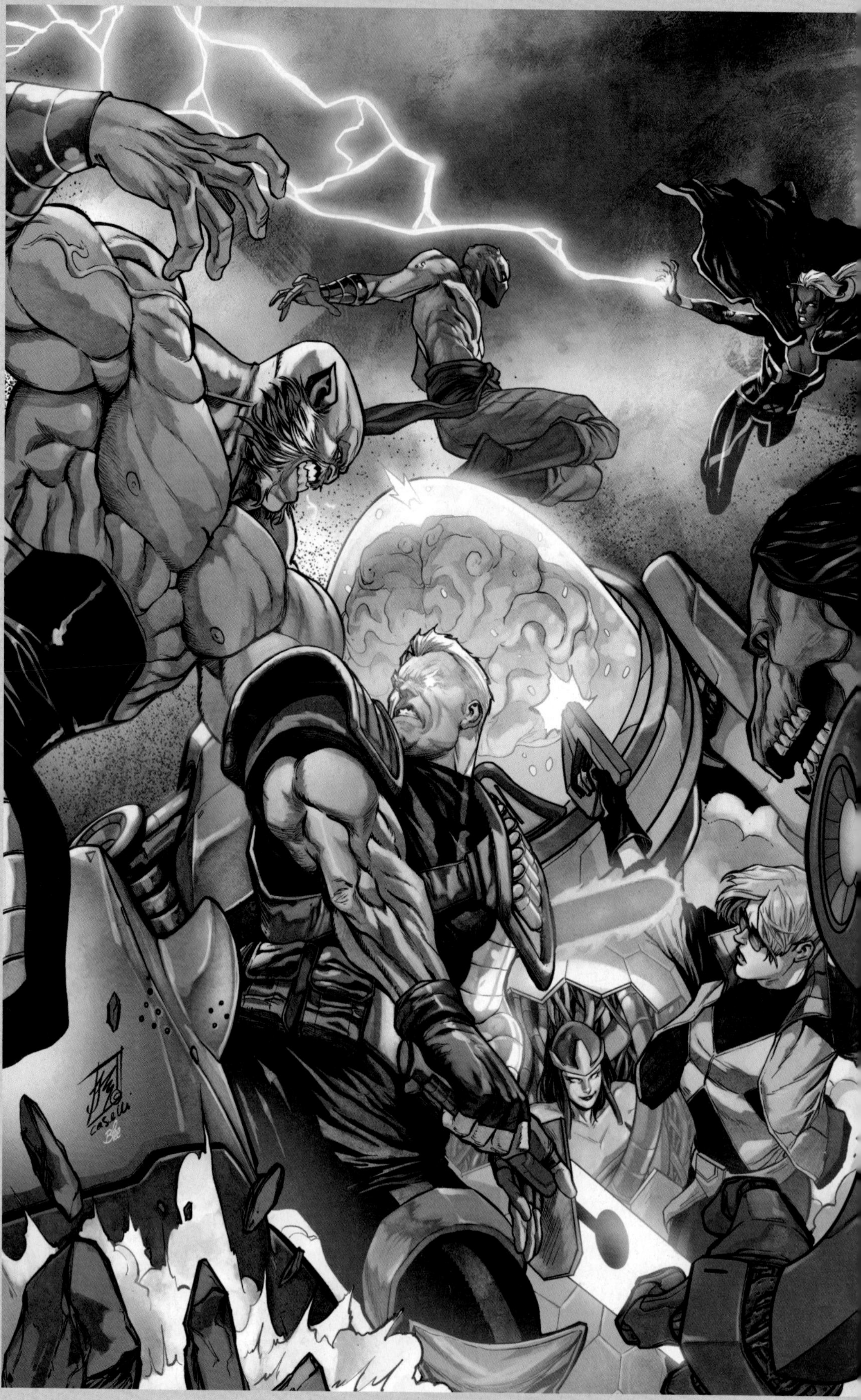

Final Frontier

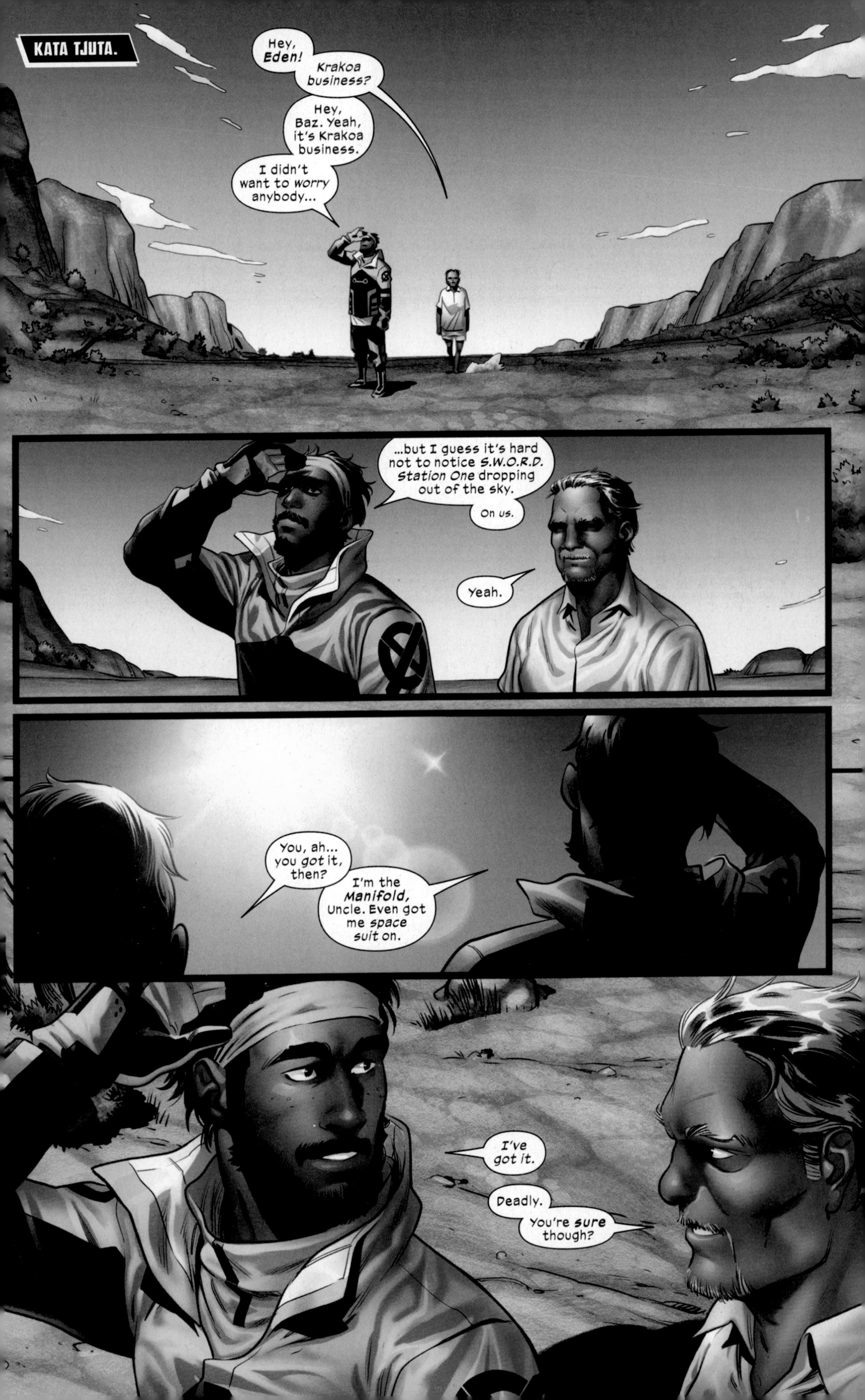
KATA TJUTA.
Hey, Eden! Krakoa business?
Hey, Baz. Yeah, it's Krakoa business.
I didn't want to worry anybody...
...but I guess it's hard not to notice S.W.O.R.D. Station One dropping out of the sky.
On us.
Yeah.
You, ah... you got it, then?
I'm the Manifold, Uncle. Even got me space suit on.
I've got it.
Deadly.
You're sure though?

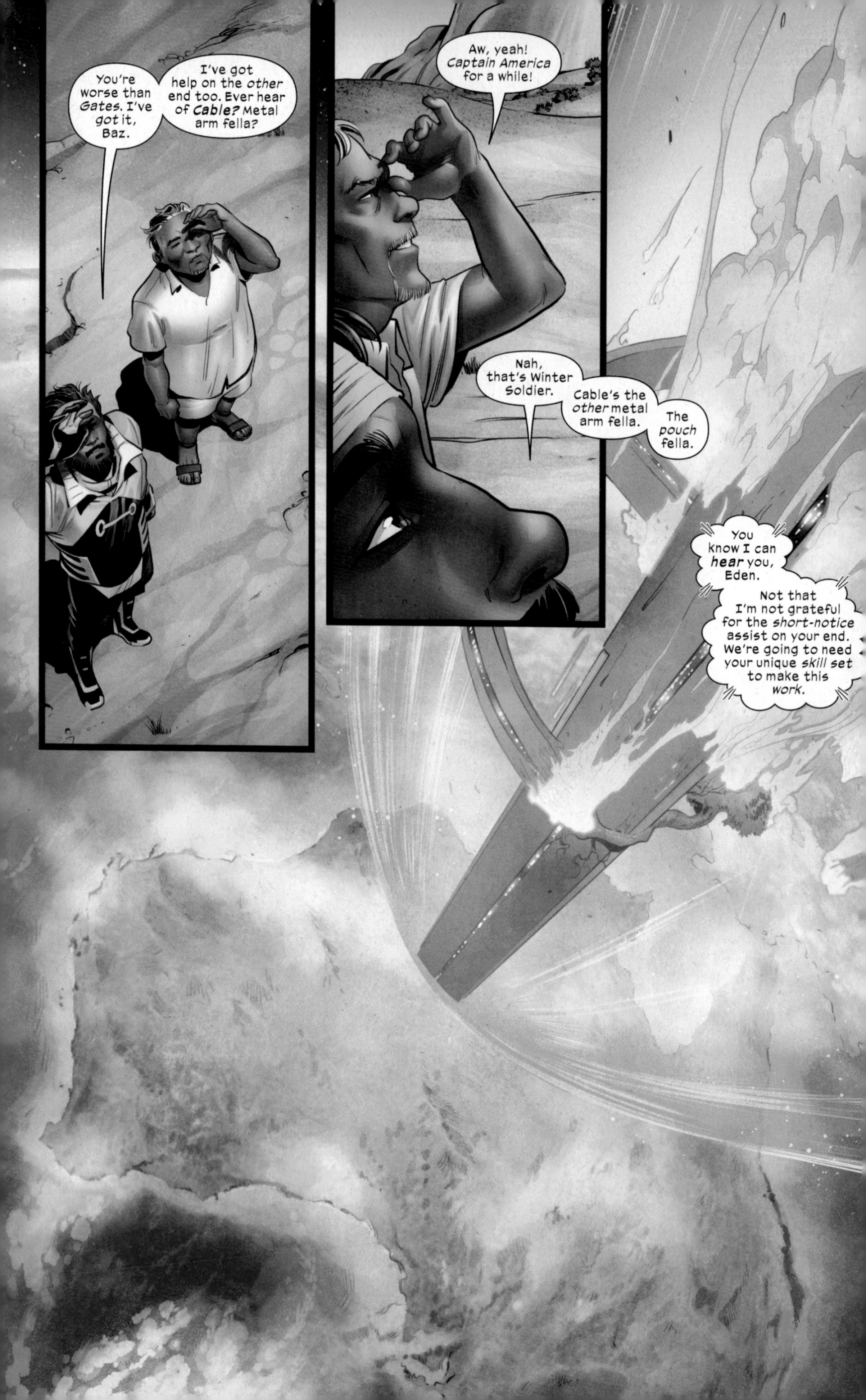
You're worse than Gates. I've got it, Baz.
I've got help on the other end too. Ever hear of Cable? Metal arm fella?
Aw, yeah! Captain America for a while!
Nah, that's Winter Soldier.
Cable's the other metal arm fella.
The pouch fella.
You know I can hear you, Eden.
Not that I'm not grateful for the short-notice assist on your end. We're going to need your unique skill set to make this work.

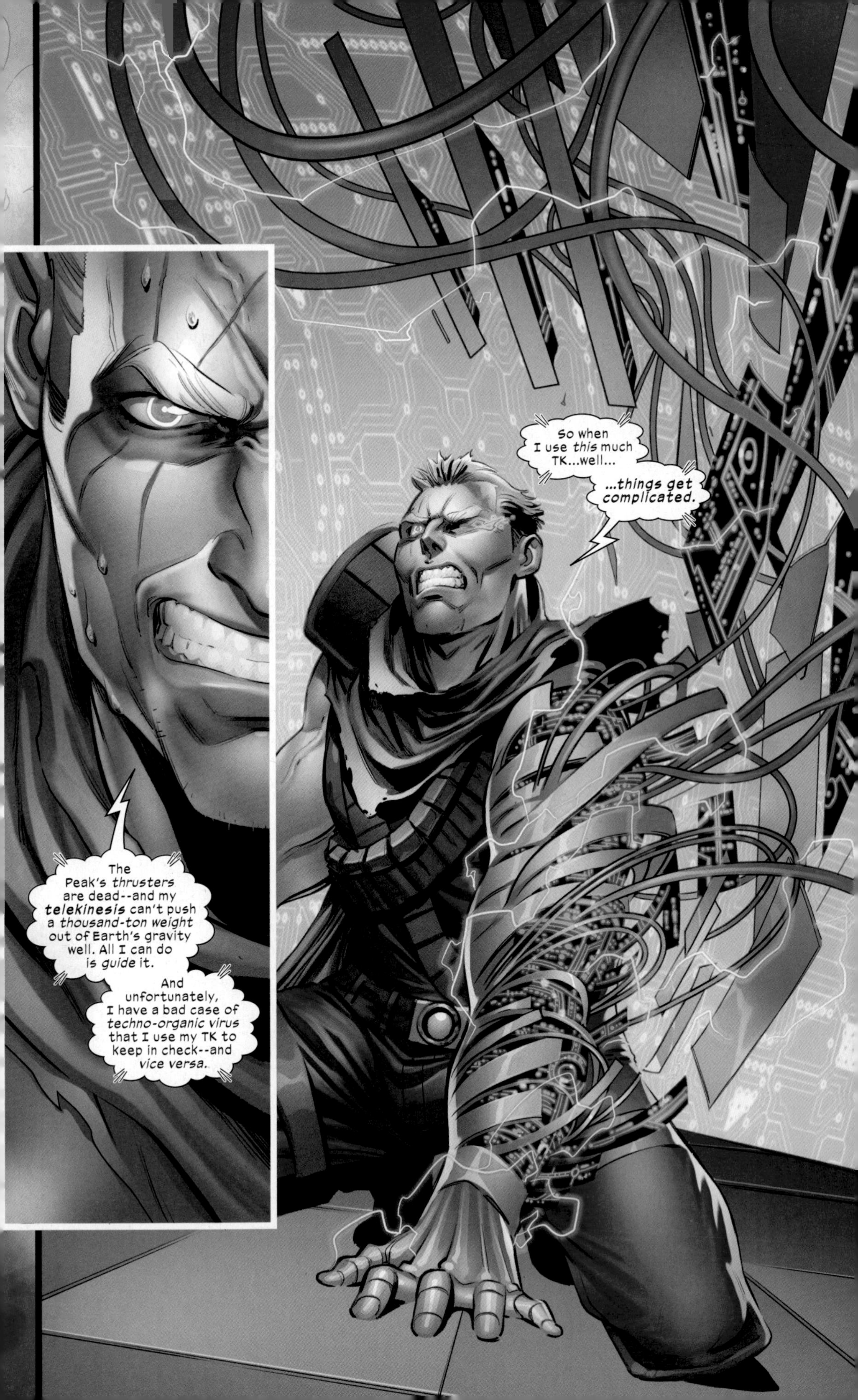
The Peak's *thrusters* are dead--and my **telekinesis** can't push a *thousand-ton weight* out of Earth's gravity well. All I can do is *guide* it.
And unfortunately, I have a bad case of *techno-organic virus* that I use my TK to keep in check--and *vice versa.*
So when I use *this* much TK...well...
*...things get complicated.*

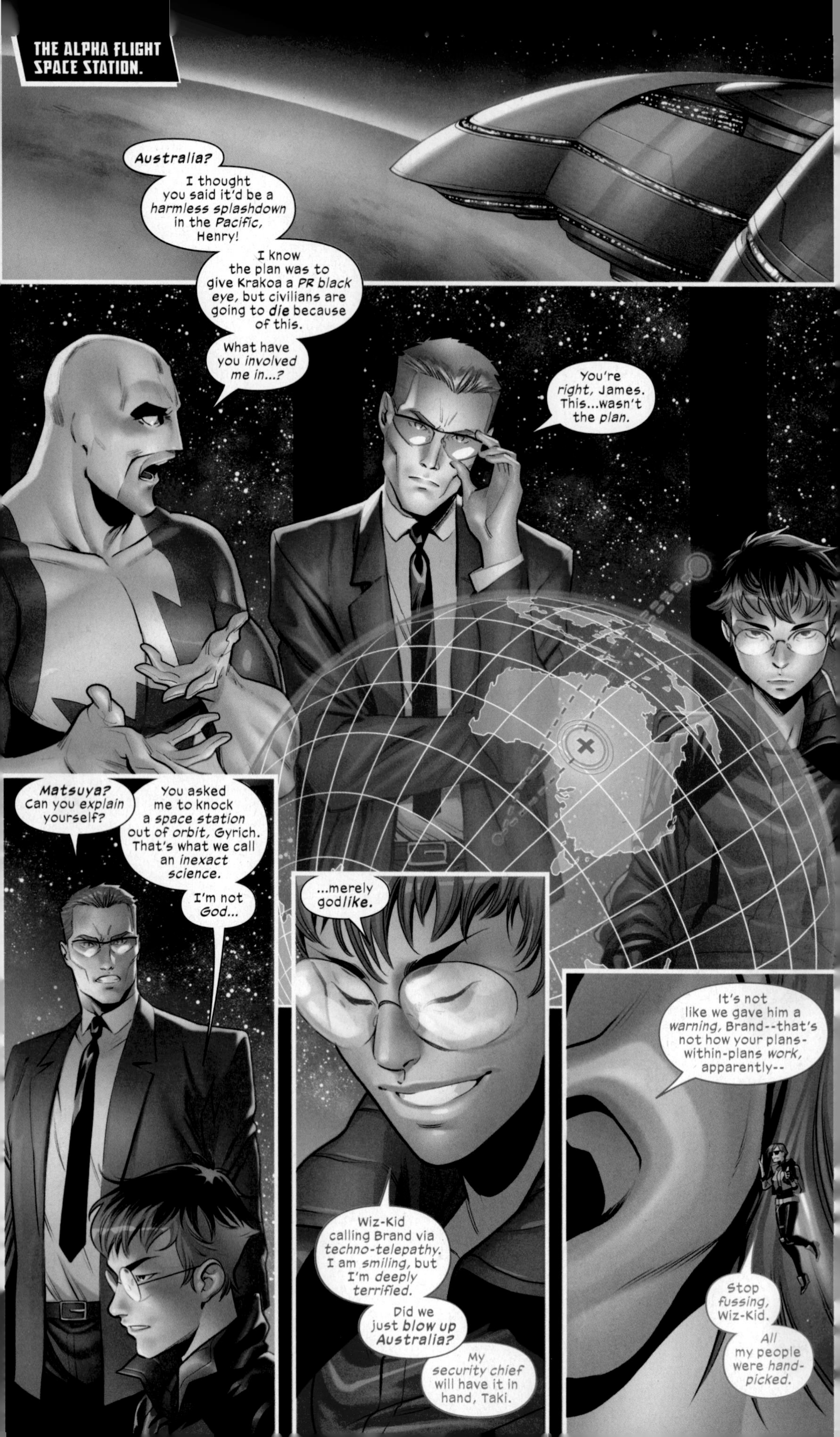
THE ALPHA FLIGHT SPACE STATION.
Australia?
I thought you said it'd be a harmless splashdown in the Pacific, Henry!
I know the plan was to give Krakoa a PR black eye, but civilians are going to die because of this.
What have you involved me in...?
You're right, James. This...wasn't the plan.
Matsuya? Can you explain yourself?
You asked me to knock a space station out of orbit, Gyrich. That's what we call an inexact science.
I'm not God...
...merely godlike.
Wiz-Kid calling Brand via techno-telepathy. I am smiling, but I'm deeply terrified.
Did we just blow up Australia?
My security chief will have it in hand, Taki.
It's not like we gave him a warning, Brand--that's not how your plans-within-plans work, apparently--
Stop fussing, Wiz-Kid.
All my people were hand-picked.

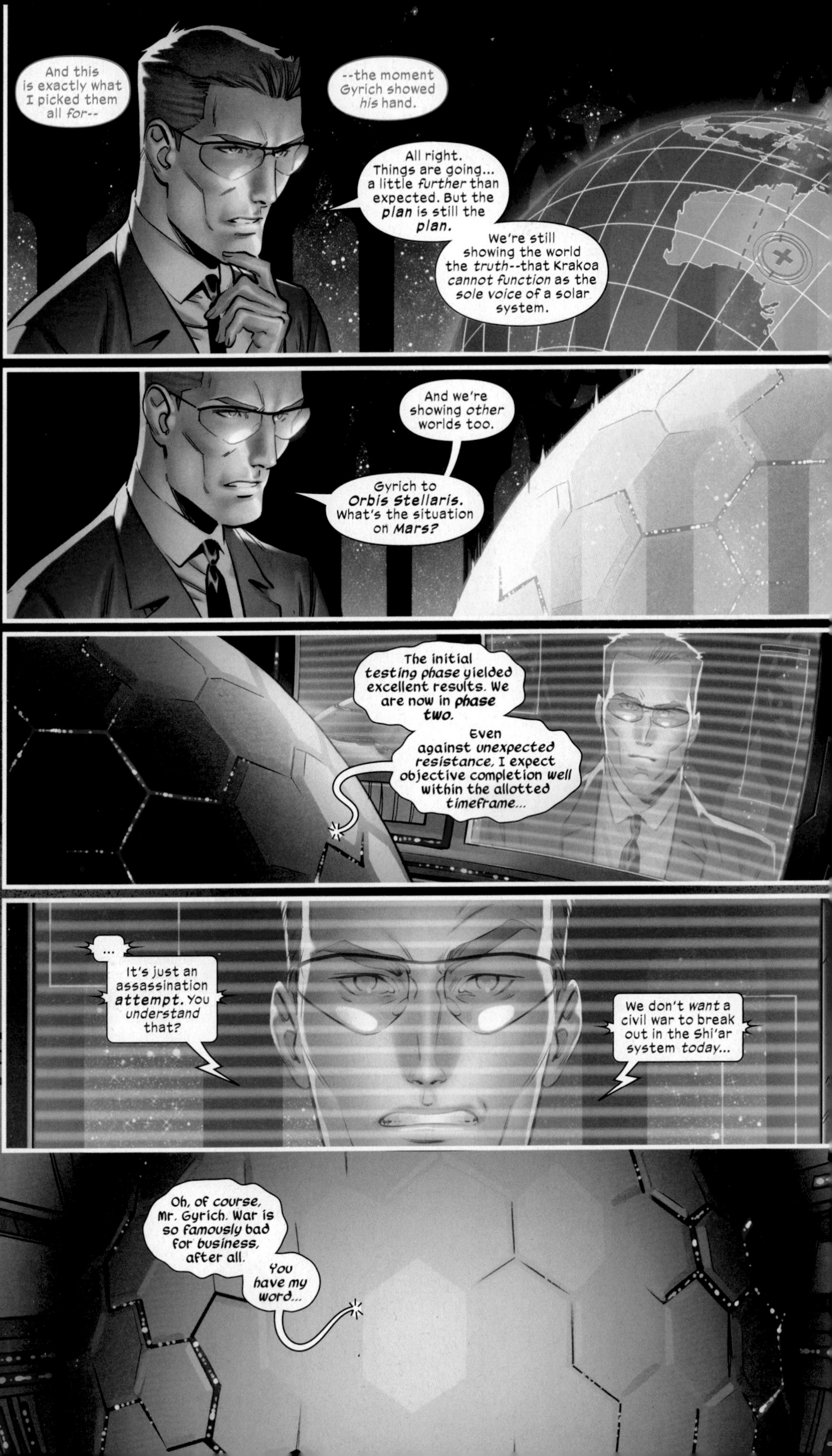

And this is exactly what I picked them all for--
--the moment Gyrich showed his hand.
All right. Things are going... a little further than expected. But the plan is still the plan.
We're still showing the world the truth--that Krakoa cannot function as the sole voice of a solar system.
And we're showing other worlds too.
Gyrich to Orbis Stellaris. What's the situation on Mars?
The initial testing phase yielded excellent results. We are now in phase two.
Even against unexpected resistance, I expect objective completion well within the allotted timeframe...
...
It's just an assassination attempt. You understand that?
We don't want a civil war to break out in the Shi'ar system today...
Oh, of course, Mr. Gyrich. War is so famously bad for business, after all.
You have my word...

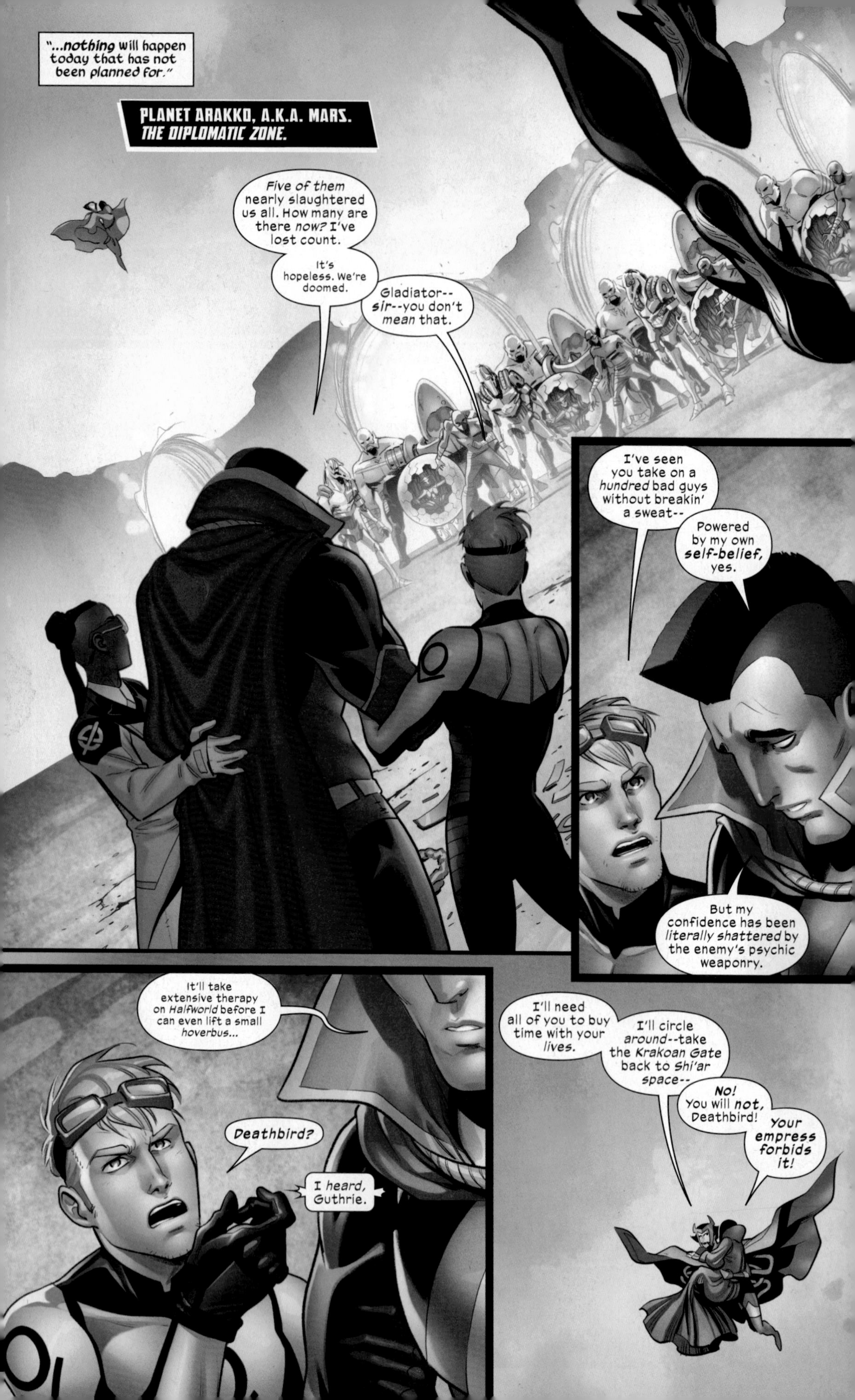
"...*nothing* will happen today that has not been planned for."
PLANET ARAKKO, A.K.A. MARS.
*THE DIPLOMATIC ZONE.*
*Five of them* nearly slaughtered us all. How many are there *now?* I've lost count.
It's hopeless. We're doomed.
Gladiator-- *sir*--you don't *mean* that.
I've seen you take on a *hundred* bad guys without breakin' a sweat--
Powered by my own **self-belief,** yes.
But my confidence has been *literally shattered* by the enemy's psychic weaponry.
It'll take extensive therapy on *Halfworld* before I can even lift a small *hoverbus...*
*Deathbird?*
*I heard,* Guthrie.
I'll need all of you to buy time with your *lives.*
I'll circle *around*--take the *Krakoan Gate* back to *Shi'ar space*--
*No!* You will *not,* Deathbird!
*Your empress forbids it!*

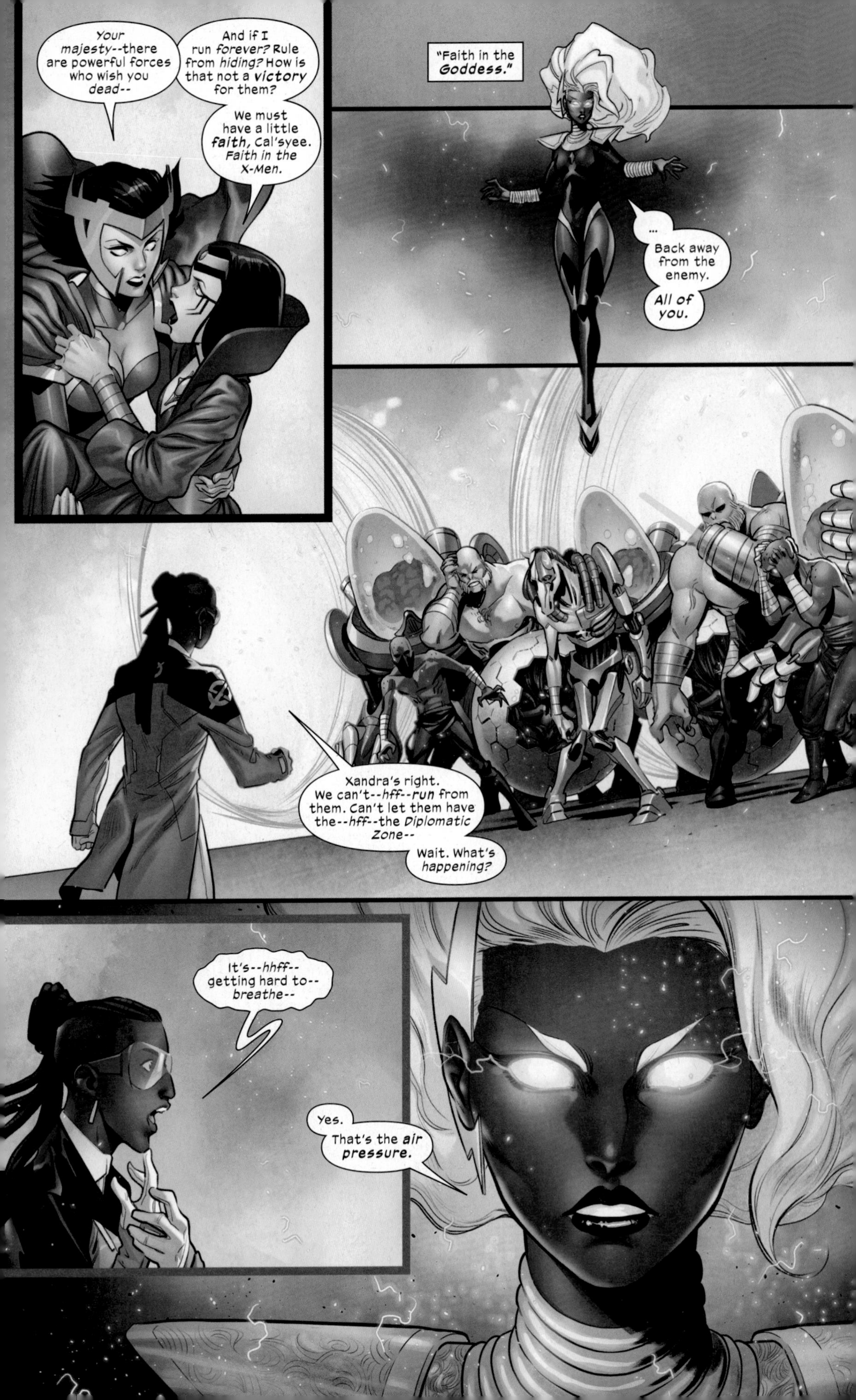

Your majesty--there are powerful forces who wish you dead--
And if I run forever? Rule from hiding? How is that not a victory for them?
We must have a little faith, Cal'syee. Faith in the X-Men.
"Faith in the Goddess."
... Back away from the enemy.
All of you.
Xandra's right. We can't--hff--run from them. Can't let them have the--hff--the Diplomatic Zone--
Wait. What's happening?
It's--hhff--getting hard to--breathe--
Yes.
That's the air pressure.

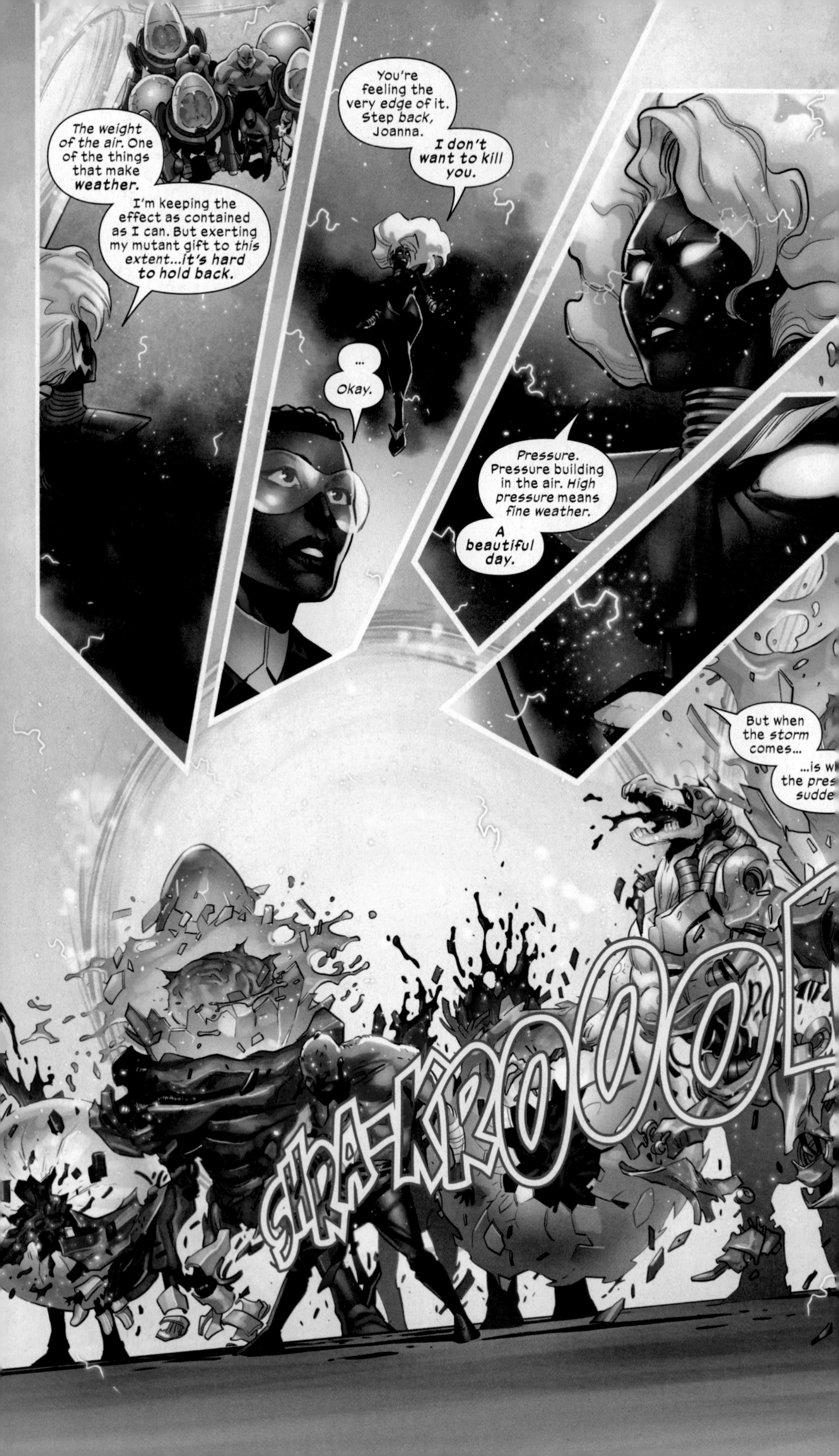

The weight of the air. One of the things that make weather.
I'm keeping the effect as contained as I can. But exerting my mutant gift to this extent...it's hard to hold back.
You're feeling the very edge of it. Step back, Joanna.
I don't want to kill you.
...
Okay.
Pressure. Pressure building in the air. High pressure means fine weather.
A beautiful day.
But when the storm comes...
SHA-KROOOO

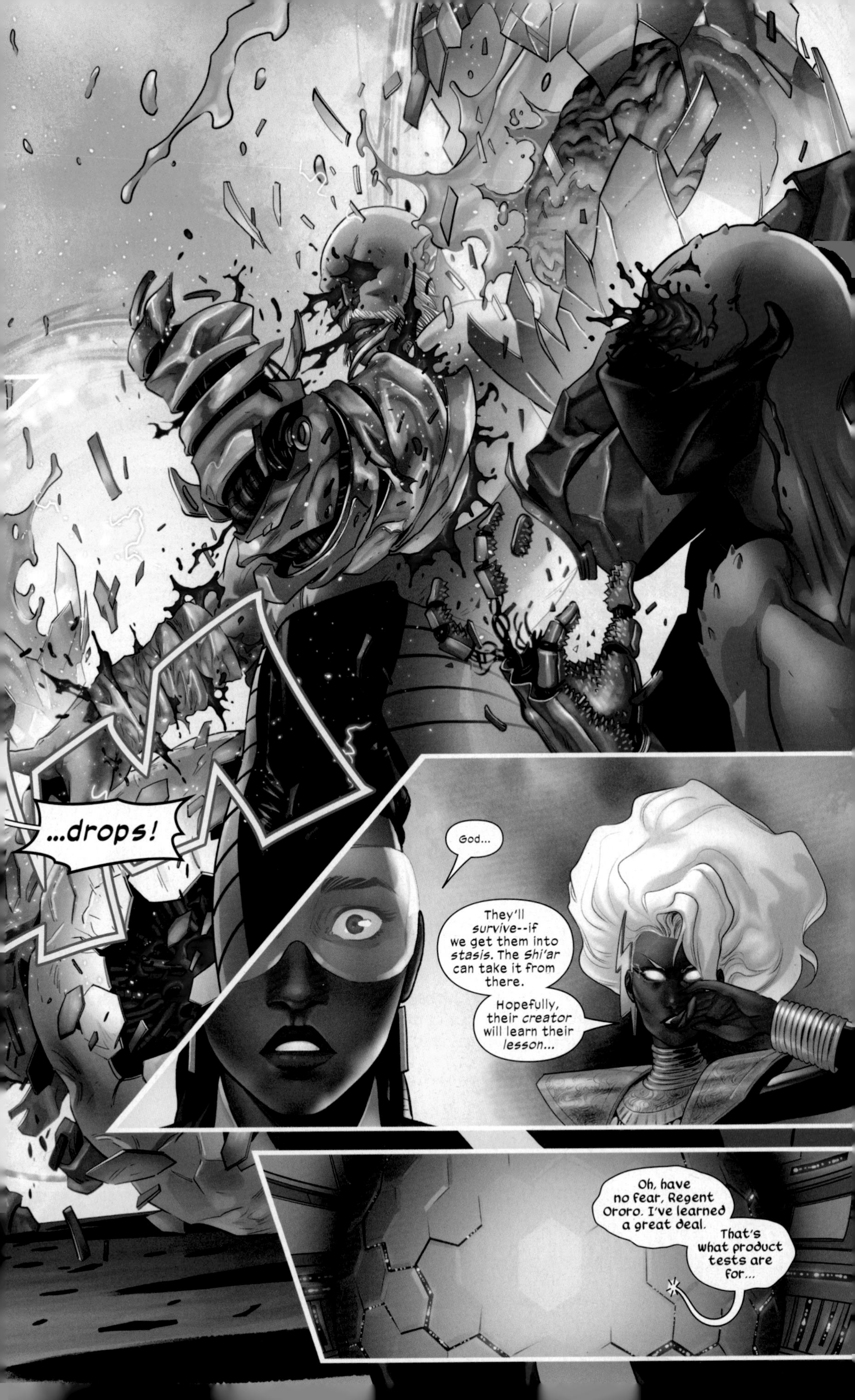
...drops!
God...
They'll survive--if we get them into stasis. The Shi'ar can take it from there.
Hopefully, their creator will learn their lesson...
Oh, have no fear, Regent Ororo. I've learned a great deal.
That's what product tests are for...

# STELLARIS ®
## MANUFACTURING

**////ORBIS STELLARIS AFTER-ACTION REPORT////**
**////STARDATE ZETA-TWO-ELEVENTY////REDACTED COPY////**

Field-testing of the OS-017 "Lethal Legion" went mostly better than expected.

Faced with an all but impossible task -- the assassination of the Shi'ar Empress -- the basic five-unit cell performed more than adequately. The major success, of course, is the new psychic weaponry, which was enough to remove Gladiator from the field of play. I'll instruct the ███████ Farm to accelerate production of the necessary materials -- I can see the Orbis Extremis model doing very well in Shi'ar space.

With Gladiator out of the picture, the basic cell was then able to eliminate three Superguardians, as well as two of the local enforcers. Needless to say, even in large numbers, the basic cell was incapable of holding out against an Omega-level mutant Earthling -- but even so, it's a surprising result that points to a growing weakness in Shi'ar superhuman defence.

I wonder if I'm being shortsighted. I can make money selling to anti-Shi'ar interests, but if I wanted to make *real* money... enough to fund, say, the ███████ Project... it might be worth letting the wider media know the finer details of this battle. If the current generation of Superguardians were past their prime...unable to stand against a simple cell of cyber-terrorists...who would be called on to replace them? Obviously, it'd have to be through a shell company rather than Stellaris itself. But I'm used to a certain level of disguise. Very few people know that I'm originally from Earth, after all.

But then...it could be anyone in here.

On to less exciting matters. The deal with Henry Peter Gyrich was, as expected, mostly useless. He brought nothing to the table beyond his permission to act, which I certainly did not require. If I want a silent partner in the Sol System, it's clear I'll have to look elsewhere.

Which I have done, of course -- but this has already drifted too far off topic.

I'll save the subject of my *new* alliance for the relevant file.

**/////////////ORBIS STELLARIS Z-2-11/////////////**

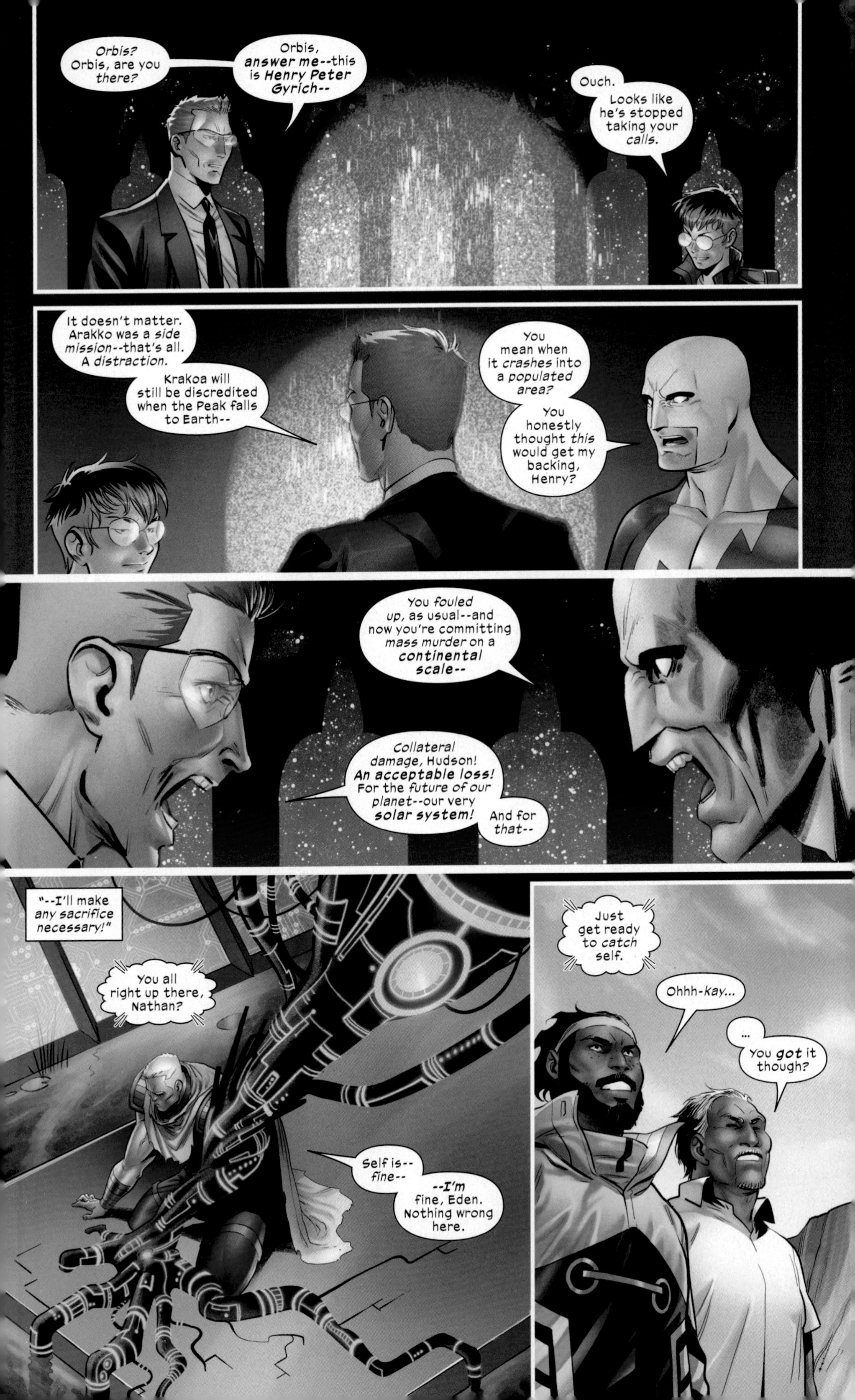
Orbis? Orbis, are you there?
Orbis, answer me--this is Henry Peter Gyrich--
Ouch.
Looks like he's stopped taking your calls.
It doesn't matter. Arakko was a side mission--that's all. A distraction.
Krakoa will still be discredited when the Peak falls to Earth--
You mean when it crashes into a populated area?
You honestly thought this would get my backing, Henry?
You fouled up, as usual--and now you're committing mass murder on a continental scale--
Collateral damage, Hudson! An acceptable loss! For the future of our planet--our very solar system!
And for that--
"--I'll make any sacrifice necessary!"
You all right up there, Nathan?
Self is-- fine--
--I'm fine, Eden. Nothing wrong here.
Just get ready to catch self.
Ohhh-kay...
... You got it though?

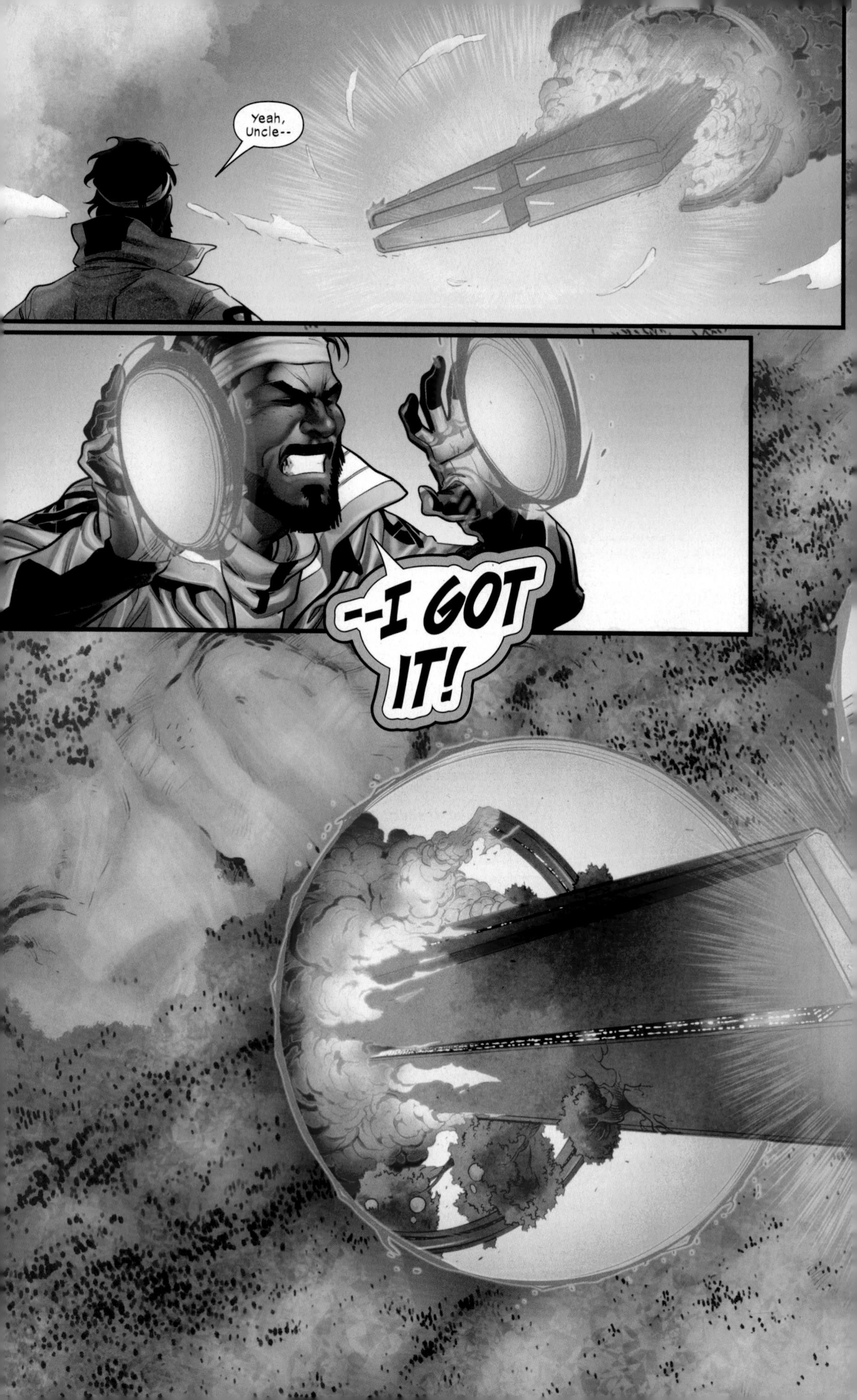
Yeah, Uncle--
--I GOT IT!

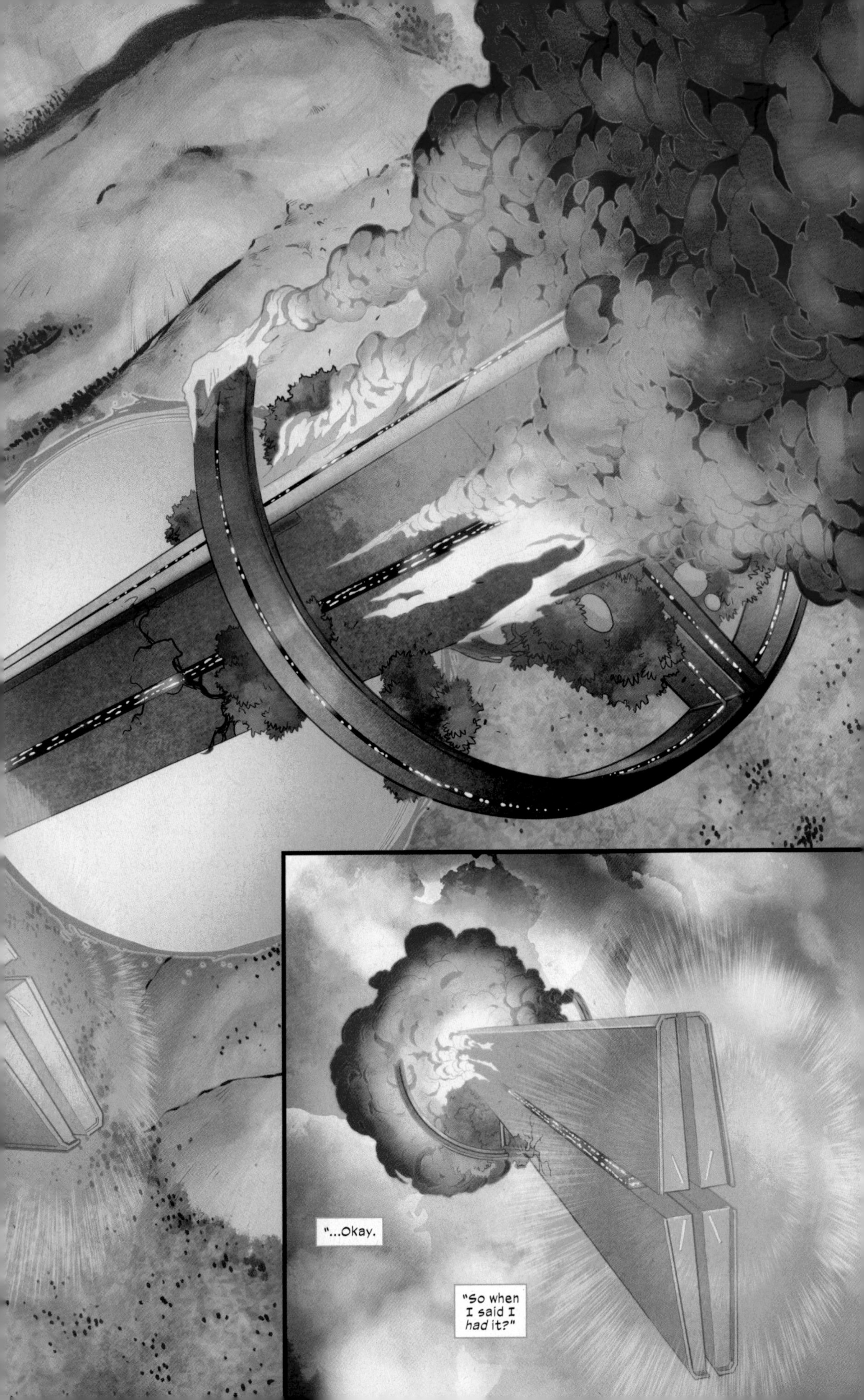
"...Okay.
"So when I said I *had* it?"

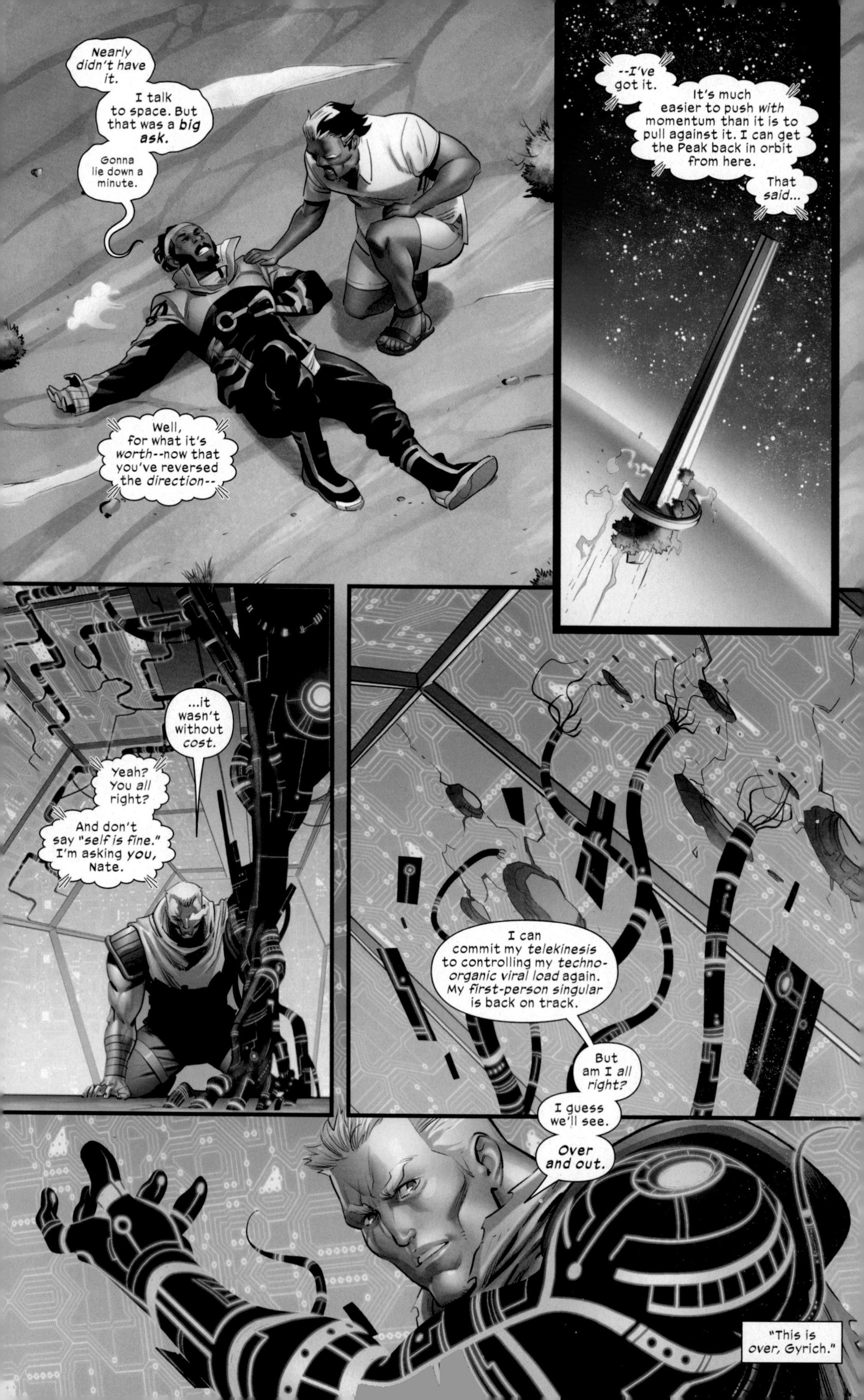
Nearly didn't have it.
I talk to space. But that was a *big* ***ask.***
Gonna lie down a minute.
Well, for what it's *worth*--now that you've reversed the *direction*--
*--I've* got it.
It's much easier to push *with* momentum than it is to pull against it. I can get the Peak back in orbit from here.
That *said...*
...it wasn't without *cost.*
Yeah? You *all* right?
And don't say "*self is fine.*" I'm asking *you,* Nate.
I can commit my *telekinesis* to controlling my *techno-organic viral load* again. My *first-person singular* is back on track.
But am I *all right?*
I guess we'll see.
***Over and out.***
"This is over, Gyrich."

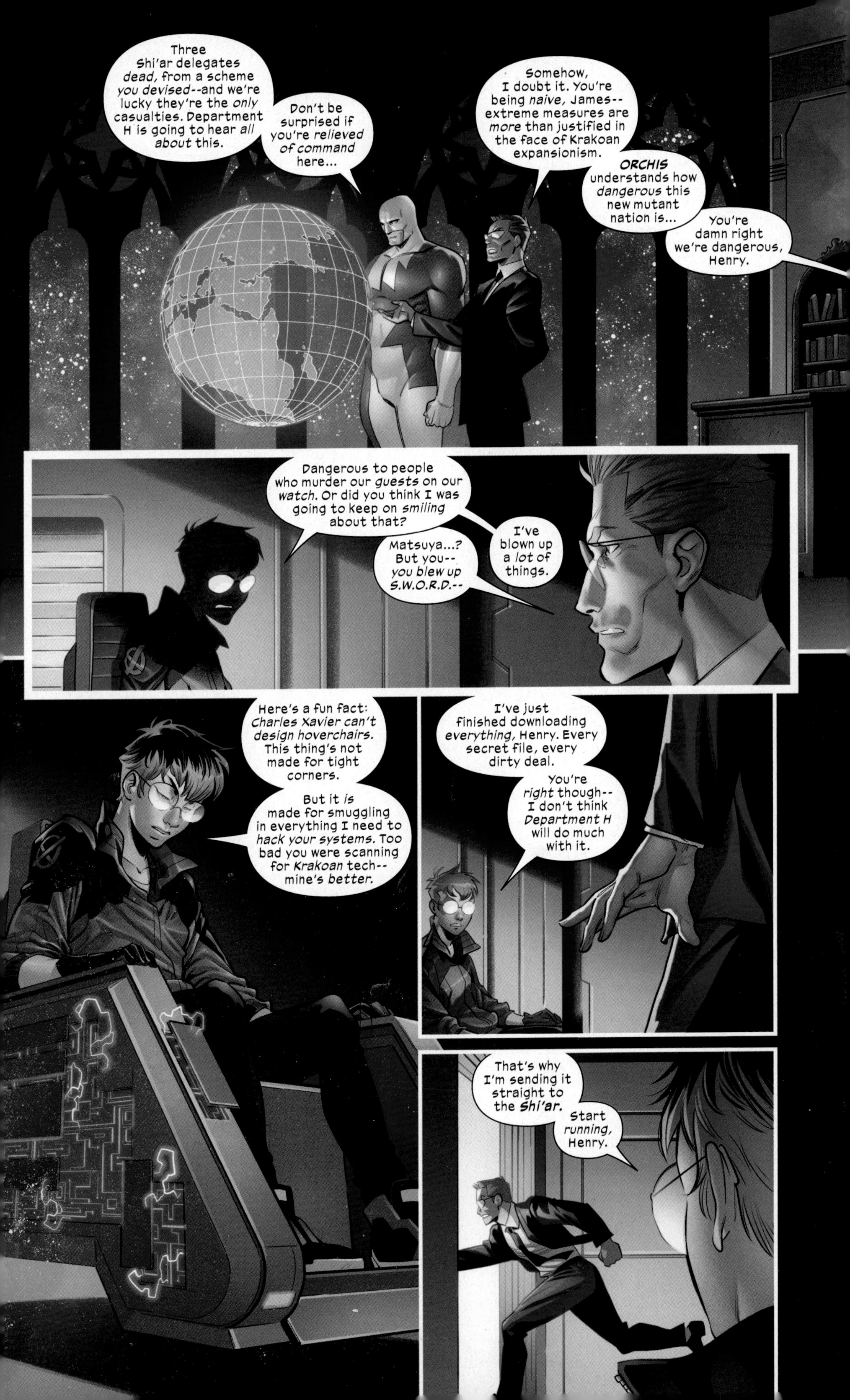
Three Shi'ar delegates dead, from a scheme you devised--and we're lucky they're the only casualties. Department H is going to hear all about this.
Don't be surprised if you're relieved of command here...
Somehow, I doubt it. You're being naive, James--extreme measures are more than justified in the face of Krakoan expansionism.
ORCHIS understands how dangerous this new mutant nation is...
You're damn right we're dangerous, Henry.
Dangerous to people who murder our guests on our watch. Or did you think I was going to keep on smiling about that?
Matsuya...? But you--you blew up S.W.O.R.D.--
I've blown up a lot of things.
Here's a fun fact: Charles Xavier can't design hoverchairs. This thing's not made for tight corners.
But it is made for smuggling in everything I need to hack your systems. Too bad you were scanning for Krakoan tech--mine's better.
I've just finished downloading everything, Henry. Every secret file, every dirty deal.
You're right though--I don't think Department H will do much with it.
That's why I'm sending it straight to the Shi'ar.
Start running, Henry.

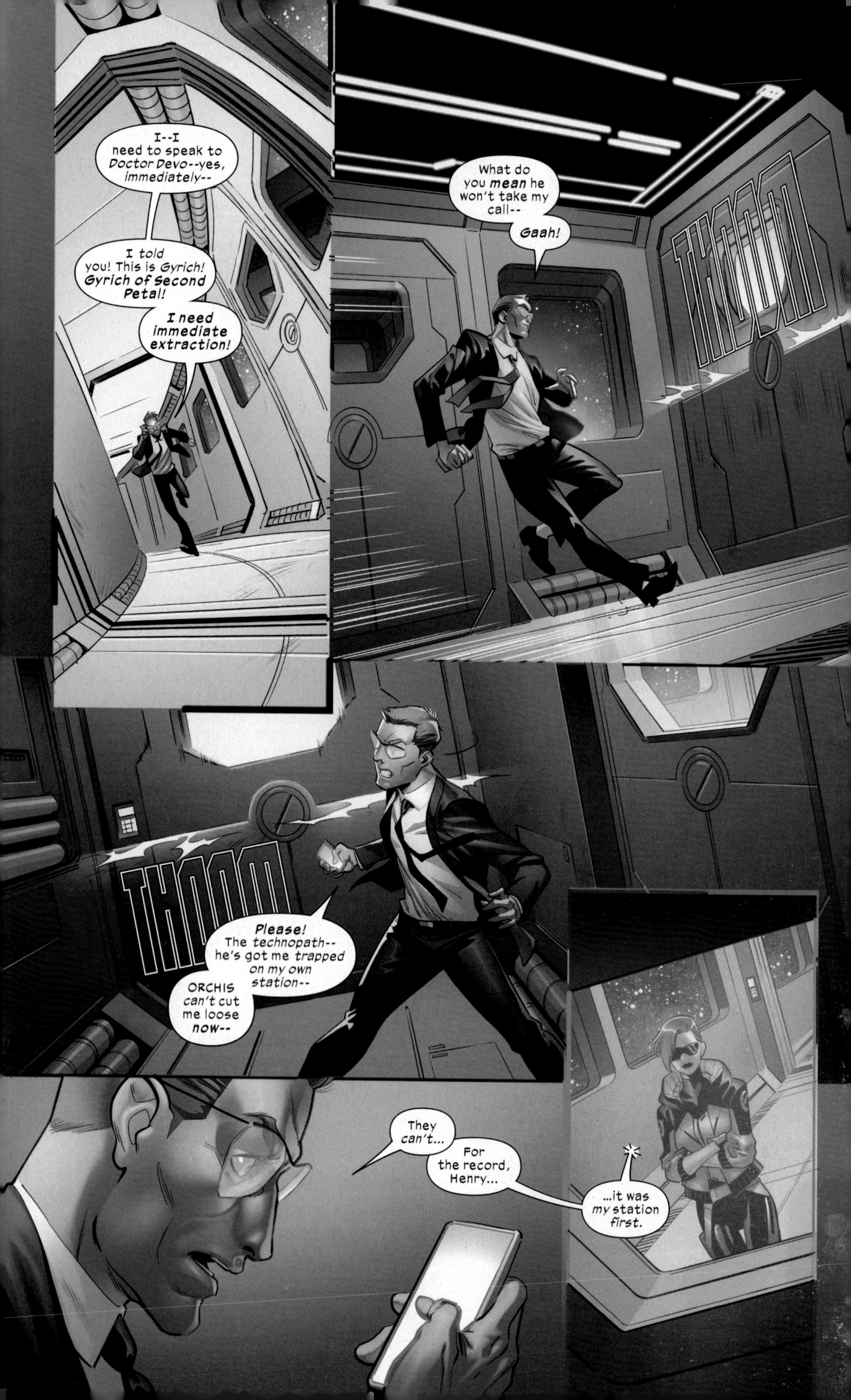
I--I need to speak to Doctor Devo--yes, immediately--
I told you! This is Gyrich! Gyrich of Second Petal!
I need immediate extraction!
What do you mean he won't take my call--
Gaah!
THOOM
THOOM
Please! The technopath--he's got me trapped on my own station--
ORCHIS can't cut me loose now--
They can't...
For the record, Henry...
...it was my station first.

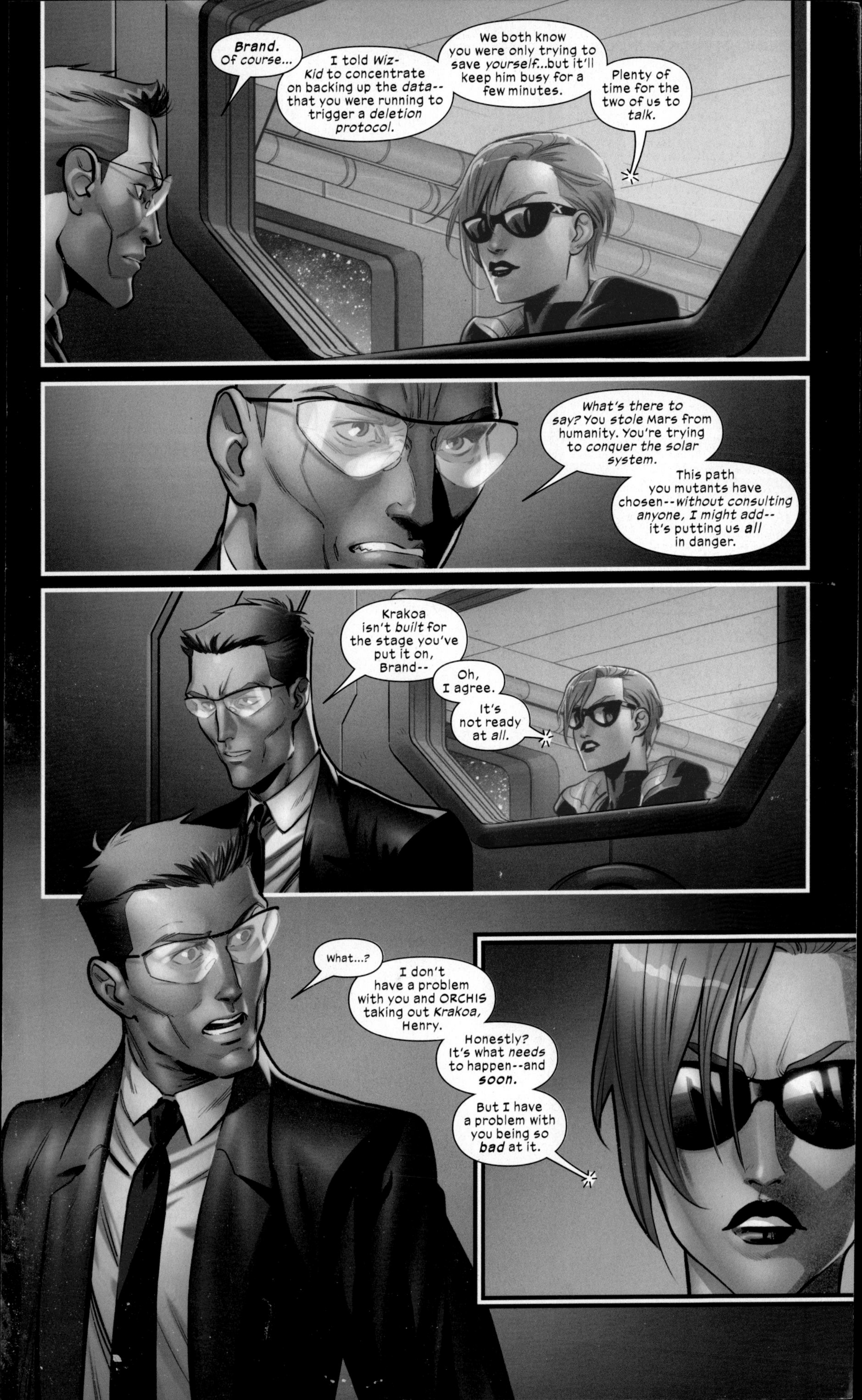
Brand. Of course...
I told Wiz-Kid to concentrate on backing up the data--that you were running to trigger a deletion protocol.
We both know you were only trying to save yourself...but it'll keep him busy for a few minutes.
Plenty of time for the two of us to talk.
What's there to say? You stole Mars from humanity. You're trying to conquer the solar system.
This path you mutants have chosen--without consulting anyone, I might add--it's putting us all in danger.
Krakoa isn't built for the stage you've put it on, Brand--
Oh, I agree.
It's not ready at all.
What...?
I don't have a problem with you and ORCHIS taking out Krakoa, Henry.
Honestly? It's what needs to happen--and soon.
But I have a problem with you being so bad at it.

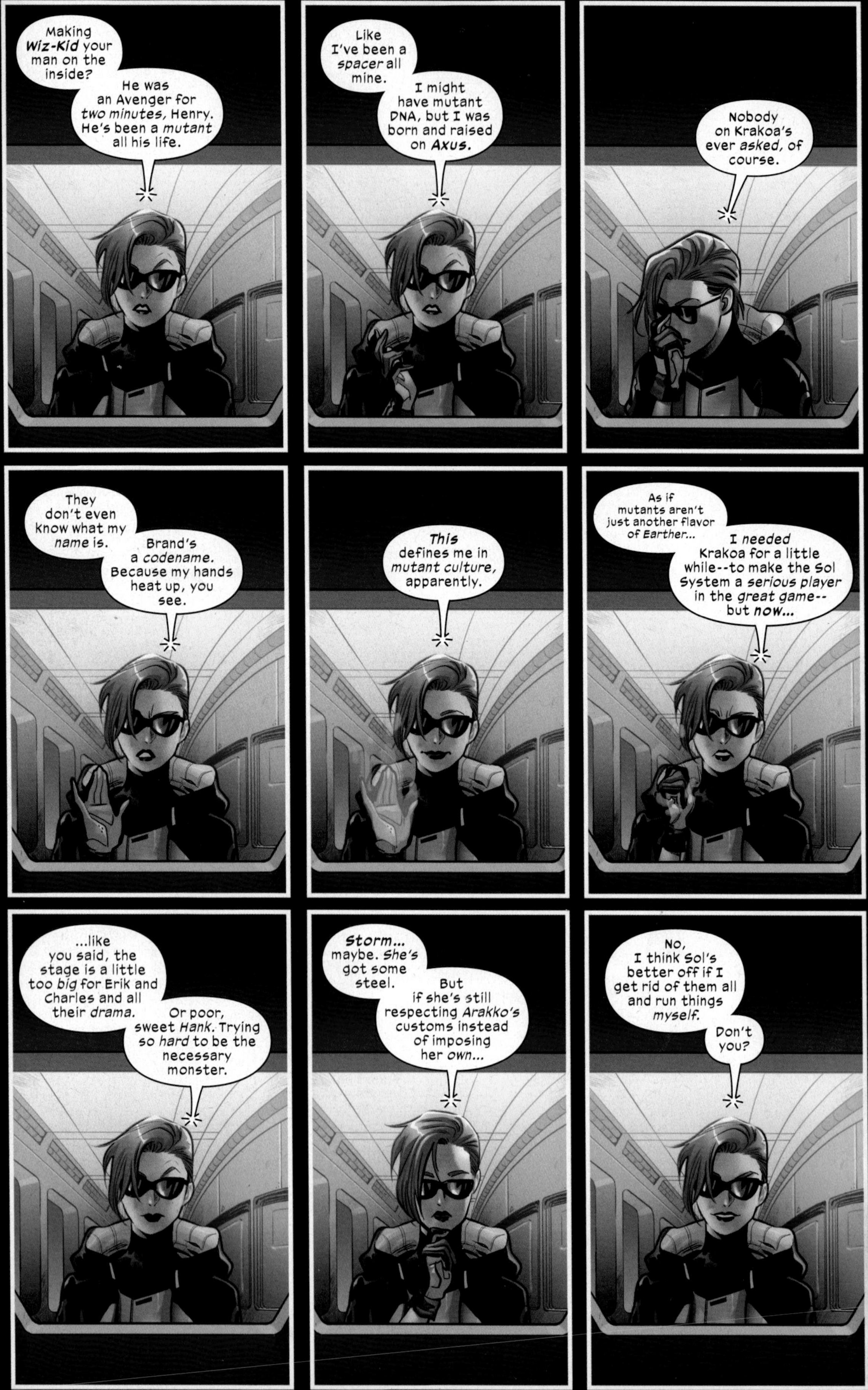
Making *Wiz-Kid* your man on the inside?
He was an Avenger for *two minutes,* Henry. He's been a *mutant* all his life.
Like I've been a *spacer* all mine.
I might have mutant DNA, but I was born and raised on *Axus.*
Nobody on Krakoa's ever *asked,* of course.
They don't even know what my *name* is.
Brand's a *codename.* Because my hands heat up, you see.
*This* defines me in *mutant culture,* apparently.
As if mutants aren't just another flavor of Earther...
I *needed* Krakoa for a little while--to make the Sol System a *serious player* in the *great game*--but *now...*
...like you said, the stage is a little too *big* for Erik and Charles and all their *drama.*
Or poor, sweet *Hank.* Trying so *hard* to be the necessary monster.
*Storm...* maybe. *She's* got some steel.
But if she's still respecting *Arakko's* customs instead of imposing her *own...*
No, I think Sol's better off if I get rid of them all and run things *myself.*
Don't you?

Anyway.

Time for you to leave us.

DIT!

What? What do you...?

SHHFFF

No.

No, no, no. NO--

You can't! You can't do this!

The X-Men have laws--

"Kill no man." Don't remind me.

I don't play by rules I don't *respect*, Henry.

I've made it look like *you* pushed the button. Like you were *in control* at the end.

That's me being *kind*, so I hope you appreciate it.

Please! PLEASE!

OPEN OUTER AIR LOCK DOOR

OPEN INNER AIR LOCK DOOR

And don't worry about your spot in ORCHIS, Henry.

It's in the best possible hands.

DIT!

OPEN INNER AIR LOCK DOOR

OPEN OUTER AIR LOCK DOOR

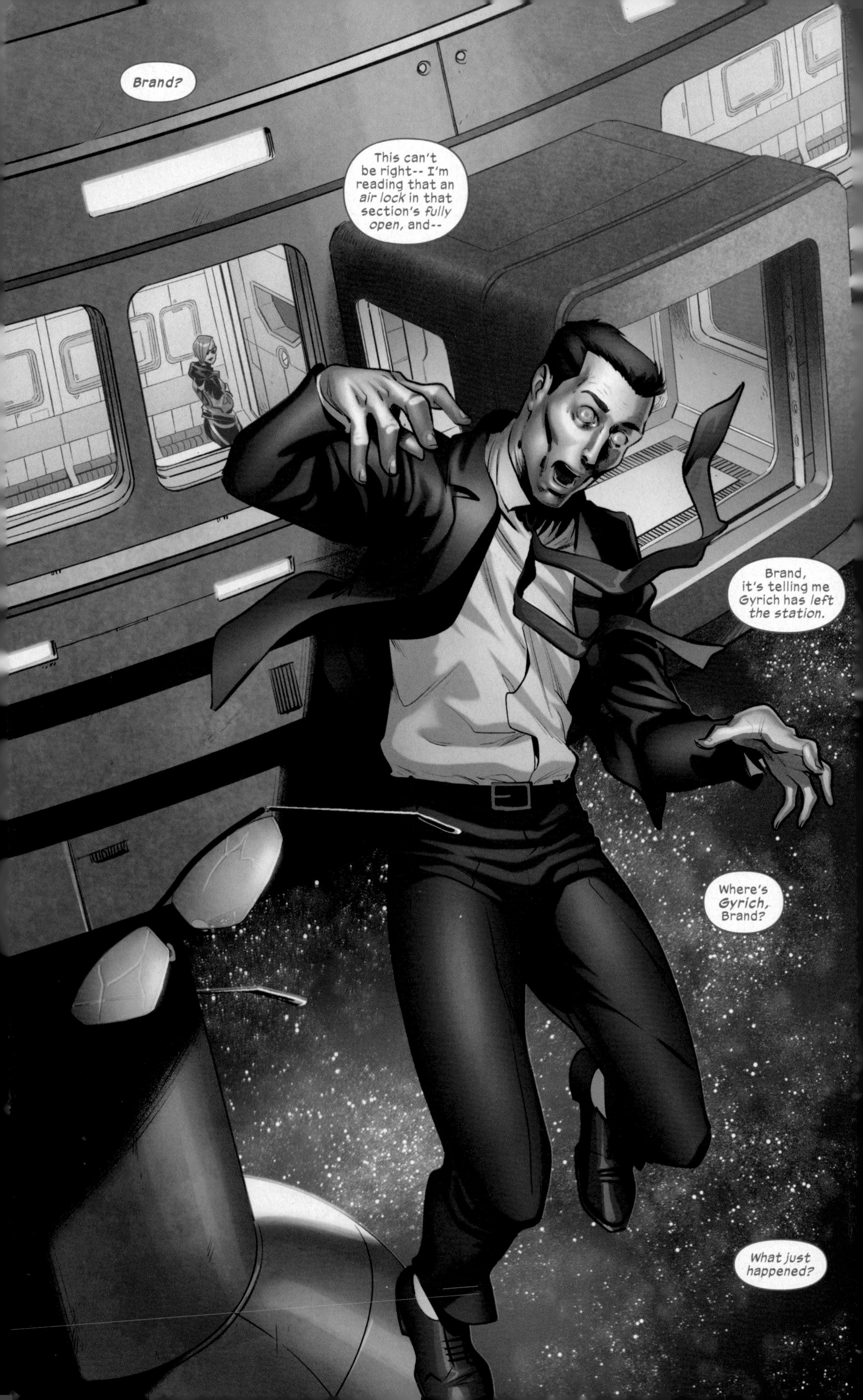
Brand?
This can't be right-- I'm reading that an *air lock* in that section's *fully open*, and--
Brand, it's telling me Gyrich has *left the station.*
Where's *Gyrich*, Brand?
What just happened?

# BEYOND DEEP SECRET:: DNA/AETHERIC MATCH ONLY

E...[ep]__0X]
EC..[ret]_11]

Once again, I'm keeping this private record so that -- in case of a sudden resurrection in my near future -- I know exactly what I've done and what I haven't.

So. What *have* I done?

I blasted Henry Gyrich out of an air lock, that's what. And frankly, I don't feel a bit bad -- Henry's had something like that coming to him for a very, *very* long time. Of course, I faked being annoyed about it -- I don't think Taki would have bought "genuinely upset."

Obviously, it breaks mutant law -- that charming little fiction Krakoa pretends has weight -- and if anyone found out, it'd make things very awkward. Hank might let me off, but I can't see anyone else giving me the benefit of the doubt. Even Erik -- I think, strangely he'd take it worst of all. He really believes in Krakoa... Glorp help him.

Of course, the real danger of Krakoa turning on me before I'm ready would be the chance of bigger dominoes falling. Krakoa is nothing -- useful dupes in the larger scheme -- but if the Shi'ar learn that I knew exactly what Orbis Stellaris was planning? If they understood that Empress Xandra dying would be a win condition for us both? *Then* I'd be in trouble.

Speaking of win conditions -- the falling S.W.O.R.D. station worked exactly as I hoped. Cable's techno-organic viral load is just barely under his control now -- perfectly balanced between killing him, which would put things back at square one, and being too weak in his body to make use of. I could have lived with the station crashing into Australia, as well -- it'd accelerate the downfall of Krakoa, but that needs to happen anyway. Still, I'm glad it didn't come to that -- Taki's potentially dangerous, but he's a little too useful right now to go in the hole.

Who does that leave? James Hudson is in my pocket. If he ends up as head of Alpha Flight -- assuming Alpha Flight survives the interstellar scandal -- all the better. But I've learned not to try to predict such things. I don't think he's a big fan of ORCHIS anymore though.

Which is ironic... because ORCHIS are big fans of me. That's what Gyrich got wrong, in the end. Having a mole on the inside? Just a double cross waiting to happen.

But being your own mole on the inside...

...now *that's* got potential.

[D_[en]Y.....
[EVE_r[yth]IN

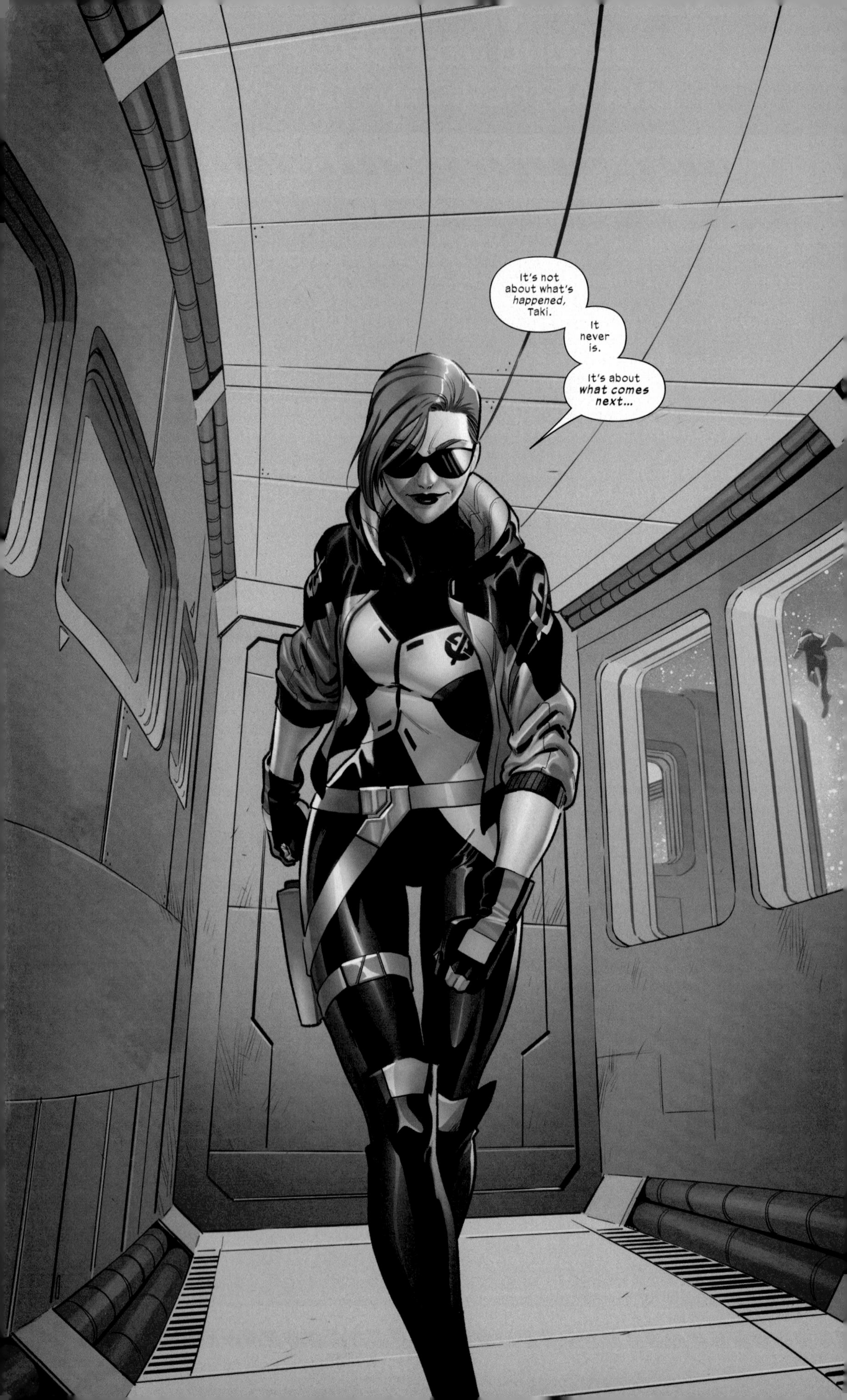
It's not about what's *happened*, Taki.
It never is.
It's about *what comes next...*

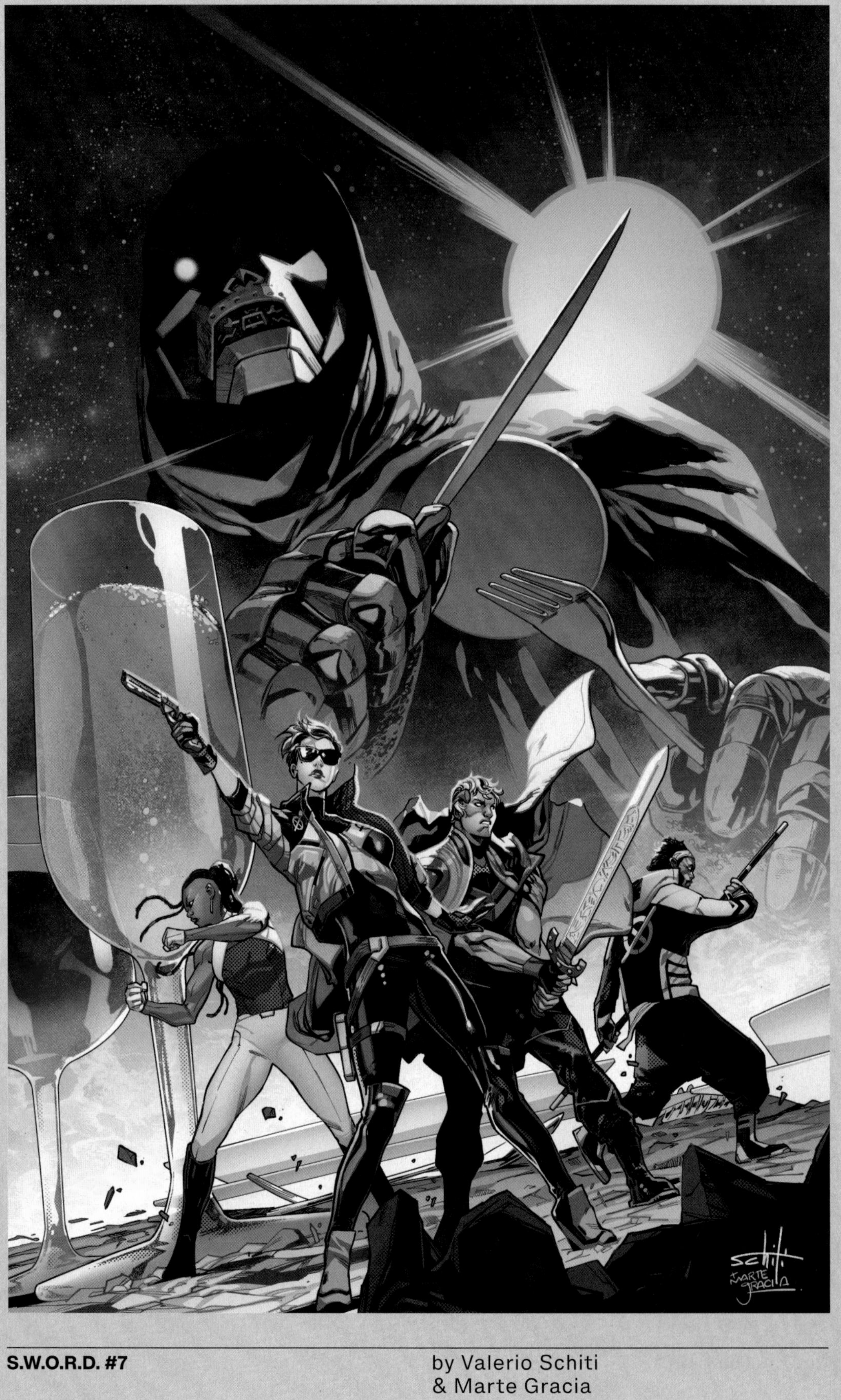

**S.W.O.R.D. #7**

by Valerio Schiti
& Marte Gracia

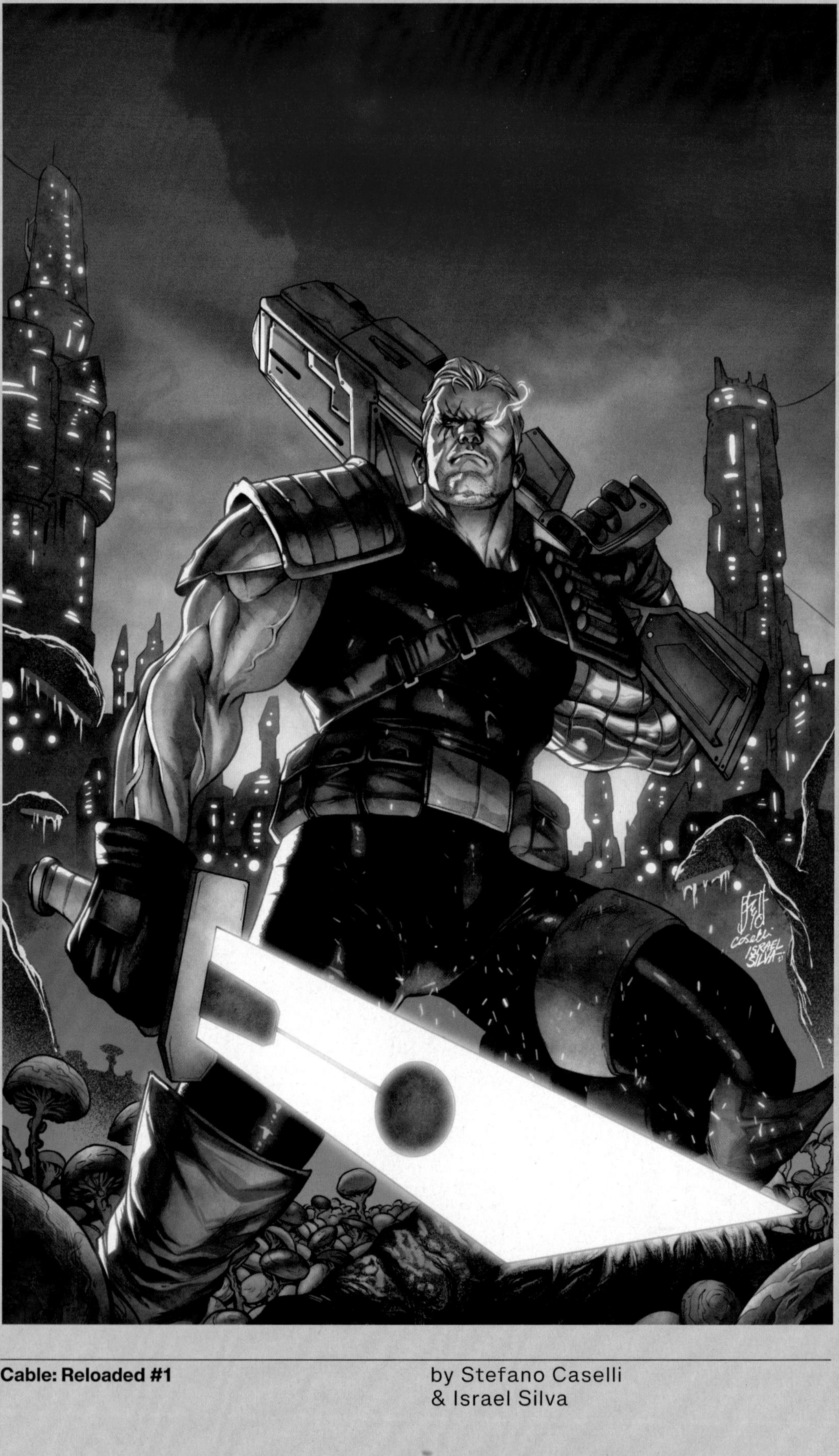
Caselli
ISRAEL
SILVA

**Cable: Reloaded #1**

by Stefano Caselli
& Israel Silva

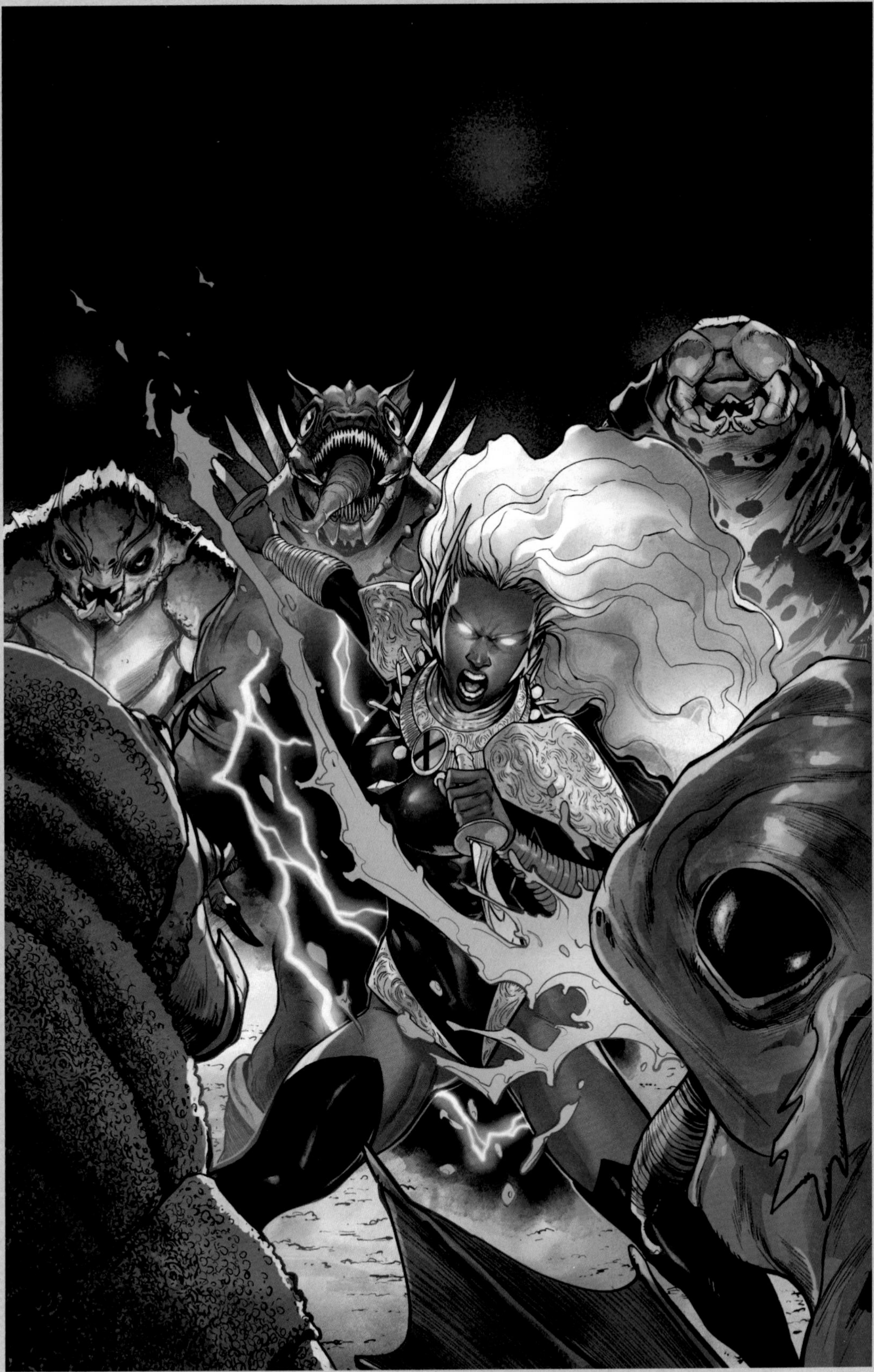

**S.W.O.R.D. #8**

by Valerio Schiti
& Marte Gracia

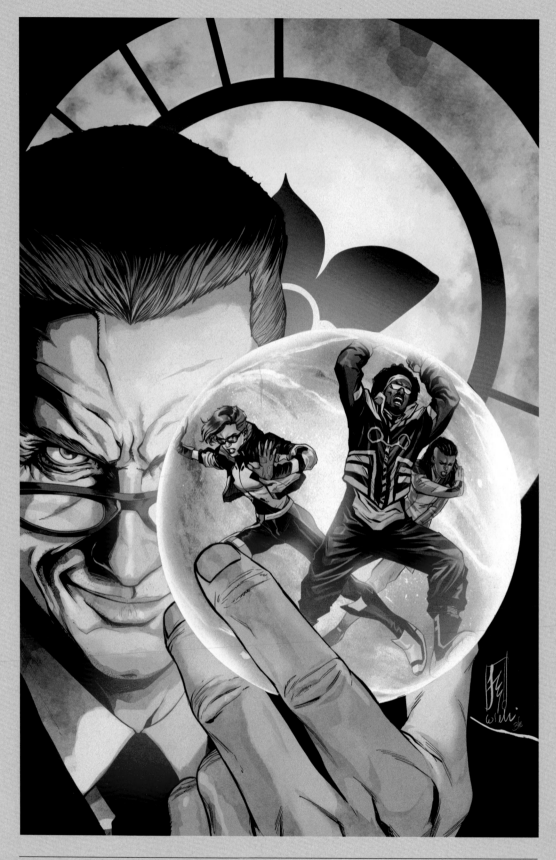

S.W.O.R.D. #9

by Stefano Caselli
& Federico Blee

**S.W.O.R.D. #11**

by Stefano Caselli
& Federico Blee

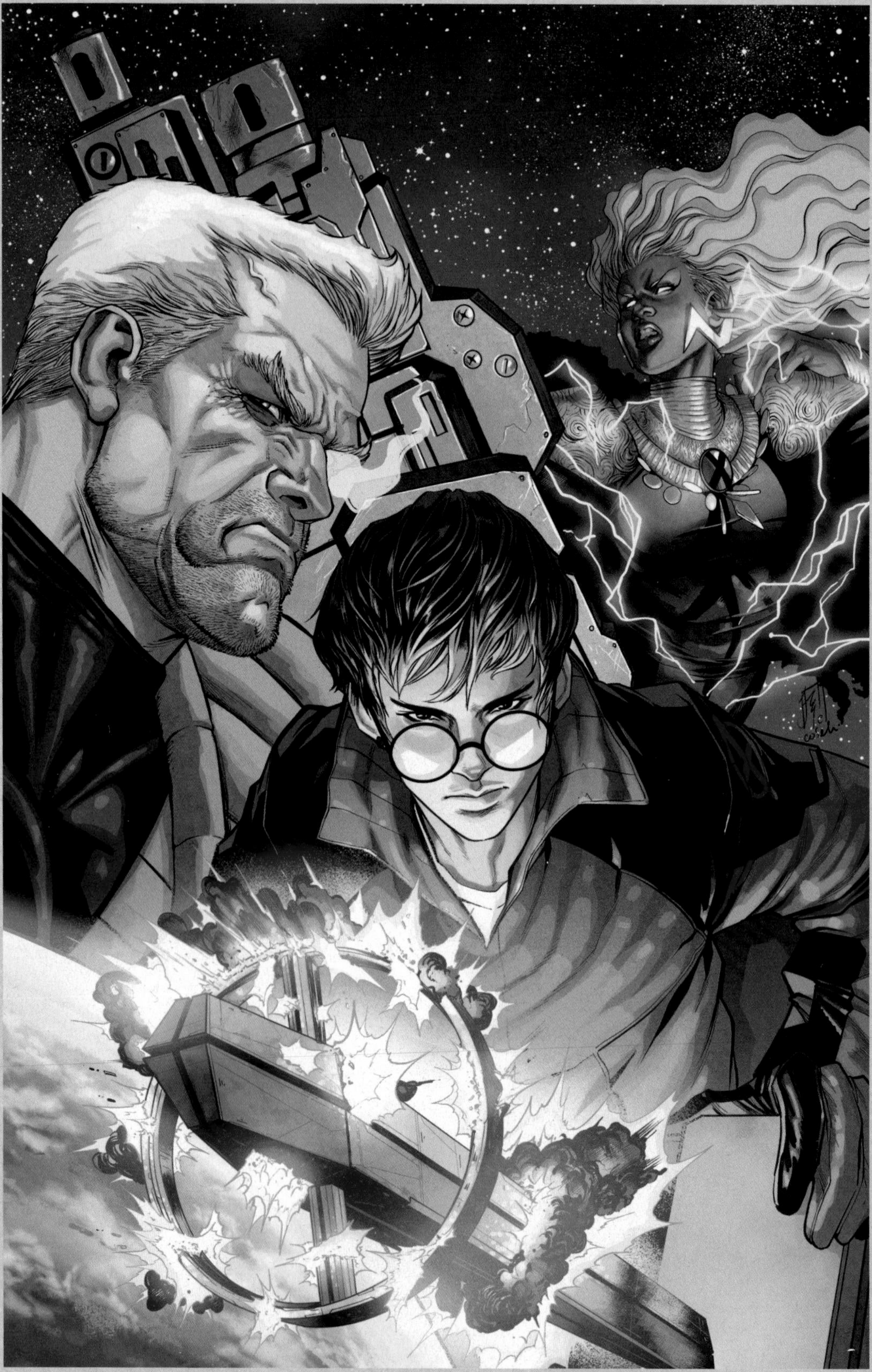

**S.W.O.R.D. #10**

by Stefano Caselli
& Java Tartaglia